NON-VIOLENCE AND THE
CHRISTIAN CONSCIENCE

Non-Violence and the Christian Conscience

P. RÉGAMEY O.P.

*With a Preface by Thomas Merton
and a Foreword by Stanley Windass*

HERDER AND HERDER

1966
HERDER AND HERDER NEW YORK
232 Madison Avenue, New York 10016

Original edition, *Non-Violence et Conscience Chrétienne*,
Paris, Les Editions du Cerf, 1958.

Nihil obstat: John M. T. Barton
                Censor Librorum
Imprimatur: George L. Craven
                Vicar General, Archdiocese of Westminster
                January 27, 1966

Library of Congress Catalog Card Number: 66–22610

CONTENTS

PREFACE

Shortly after the assassination of President John F. Kennedy, one of the most widely read American news magazines had this to say about the suspected assassin who had, himself, just been shot down. *"Oswald was a lone wolf whose background showed that he was inclined to non-violence up to a point where his mind apparently snapped."*

This little gem of double-think deserves our attention. Pages of exegesis would barely suffice to untangle the explicit and implicit mythology which it contains.

What especially recommends it to us here is its curious mythological conception of non-violence, a conception which is in fact diametrically opposed to reality and which, nevertheless, seems to be rather widely accepted. The most curious thing about this myth and its acceptance is that non-violence, which is the one political philosophy today which appeals directly to the gospel, should be regarded as unchristian, while reliance on force and cooperation with massive programmes of violence is sometimes seen as an obvious and elementary Christian duty.

The present book confronts these ambiguities. We can prepare ourselves for its message by meditating on the magazine writer's curious insistence on what he thought was Oswald's non-violence. After all, murder is hardly a non-violent act, and Oswald's past record showed him to be "inclined", if anything, to support a philosophy of violent revolution. How could the writer simply take it for granted that this statement, a pure self-contradiction as it stands, would be accepted without question and without comment as a perfect truism?

Bearing in mind the fact that this statement is typical of popular thinking on non-violence, let us examine its more obvious implications.

1. To begin with, this was an article which took it for granted, a few days after Oswald's death and before any serious investigation was possible, that Oswald's guilt was so obvious as to require no further proof. All the writer thought he needed was an

"explanation" which would give his readers the satisfaction of knowing all about what had happened, once for all. It is understood that the purpose of such magazines is to provide the reader with omniscience and endow him with the capacity to judge everything finally and for ever, without the need to resort to any further effort, once he has mastered the concatenation of clichés which pass for news in those lively columns.

2. The explanation, delivered with lordly and absolute finality, amounts to this: Oswald was a non-conformist. A non-conformist is capable of anything. Because Oswald the non-conformist was capable of anything, he killed the president. In order to drive home the point that Oswald was capable of anything, the writer deemed it sufficient to state that the man was "inclined to non-violence". What more could you want? Non-violence is so irrational and so dangerous that anyone "inclined" to it would obviously be capable of any atrocity.

3. Non-violence is here impressionistically represented as a kind of addiction, to which one may be "inclined", as for example to alcoholism or drugs. It is enough to suggest that he was *inclined*. To be *inclined* is to be predetermined. The reader provides the details for himself. Before the mind's eye rises the fateful image of one who is led in a hypnotic trance to mysterious evils. He is in reality a drug addict looking for a fix. A drug addict will do anything in order to get a fix. A man "inclined to non-violence" is in no way different from a drug addict. He will do anything, because he is "inclined". Such is the logic of suggestion.

4. It is taken for granted that addiction to non-violence follows the same (mythical) pattern of all other addictions. One's mind eventually "snaps". Hence, though people who believe in non-violence and practise it may not yet have reached the point where, with briskly snapping minds, they have shot a president or two, they are already virtually insane. This, in fact, brings us back to the basic principle on which the whole thing rests. Not to conform to the standards of reasonable men (in this case the readers of the magazine in question) is to be insane, capable of anything.

Here a great deal can be implied because it is all given and understood in the basic, vague, general presupposition of *all* the thinking in the magazine – everything in such a magazine, and in the mass media generally, assumed a particular mode of self-understanding which would be too complex to analyse here. Suffice it to say that this mode of self-understanding is a myth rather than a philosophy, a global secular faith which is assumed without question to be the only right view of life and of political and social actuality. It is a positivist, pragmatic, fundamentally amoral view of things, completely confident of its own logic, its own superiority (proved by power and affluence), its own mission to judge and direct the rest of the world, and to do so by the cheerful assertion of unlimited power. If necessary this world view appeals to a few semi-Christian slogans, as if to point out, in a modest, offhand way, that the possession of this superiority, this power and this manifest destiny is a warrant of divine and messianic vocation. Any other way of self-understanding is dismissed as heretical. Non-violence is based on radically different principles which bring it into head on collision with this mode of self-understanding. It is therefore heretical and in fact insane.

Conclusion : if a crime is committed, and if a person suspected of an inclination to non-violence was in a position where it was physically possible for him to commit the act, then he must have committed it. No further proof needed. You have your man. Or, as a practical corollary: if a crime has been committed, and if one wants to make sure that a suspect is convicted, one can help the cause along by discovering that at one time or other he showed an "inclination to non-violence".

Now in fact, there is nothing to indicate that Oswald was ever seriously interested in non-violence. On the contrary, the same argument, in the same breath, would insist that he was also a communist. Communists, as the same source repeatedly asserts, are intent upon the *violent* overthrow of peaceful and democratic society. Pushing the logic to its conclusion, in order to discover the nature of non-violence according to this source, we come up with the answer: non-violence is violence. *Quod erat demonstrandum.*

What is the purpose of our semantic meditation? Simply this. It shows how average Americans, not excluding average American Catholics, tend to understand the exotic and disturbing phenomenon of non-violence. Their understanding is no understanding at all. They have heard a great deal about it. They have their minds filled with confused and confusing images associated with it. They have never been seriously and accurately informed of its true nature, and it ferments in their minds as one of the more inscrutable myths of a world in crisis.

Those who have read a little on the subject may perhaps associate the origins of non-violence with Tolstoy, Thoreau, the Quakers. All this is, to a Catholic, religiously odd. As for those who have never heard of Tolstoy, etc., they know non-violence as something invented by Negroes (Gandhi was, of course, a "Negro"). They include it in the category of underworld activities which whites get into when they associate too intimately with Negroes. From there on, the shape the myth takes depends on your own regional outlook. If you are from the North, non-violence rates as something merely odd and irrational. If you are from the South, it is classed in the same sociological hell as all the other suspect activities in which Negroes and whites intermingle socially (exception made, of course, for lynching which is perfectly respectable, and in no way tainted with non-violence).

Here we come to the heart of the myth. While non-violence is regarded as somehow sinister, vicious and evil, violence has manifold acceptable forms in which it is not only tolerated but approved. Let us turn now from Oswald, who was obviously not non-violent, to some who obviously were: for example the Civil Rights workers murdered in Mississippi in the summer of 1964. Quite apart from the question of who murdered them, it is obvious that in the society where they met their death there was a fairly unanimous acceptance of their murder and of the inhuman brutality and cruelty with which one of them in particular was destroyed. If, in the practice of non-violent civil disobedience, civil rights workers should violate some trifling ordinance placed on the books to obstruct and harass a section of the population which is deprived of its rights, they are regarded with horror, treated as the most sinister and maniacal emissaries of hell. If on the other hand someone should proceed to commit murder or any other violent or unjust act, in defence of the prevailing myths, this may be on occasion publicly deplored in suitable terms, but in fact it is accepted as normal, sane, healthy, reasonable and indeed as fully consonant not only with democratic but even Christian ideals

Hence, whatever may be said about the supposed murderers of the civil rights workers (the supposition is known to everybody) no one has ever suggested that they were inclined to non-violence or that their minds snapped. As for the civil rights workers themselves, not only were they inclined to non-violence, but they had succumbed, they had gone all the way, they were poisoning the pure air of the South by its open practice.

We can now say it seriously, without irony and without exaggeration: *there exists in the American mind today an image of non-violence which is largely negative and completely inadequate.*

Non-violence is represented at best as an unhealthy kind of idealism, which implicitly becomes subversion and treason by virtue of its effects. At worst, it is purely and simply a tool of communist deceit, another gambit in the game of violent revolution.

This myth is systematically kept in existence by the mass media because, as was said above, non-violence is based on principles which call into question the popular self-understanding of the society in which we live. Even though in fact the number of people who are interested enough in non-violence to dedicate their lives to it is infinitesimally small, they are regarded as a serious and mysterious potential threat in so far as they bear witness to a radically different way of looking at life.

Now we know that from the first this has been the mode of action of God's word and of the Gospel in the world: it calls into question the routine self-understanding of man and of his society. It fractures the idols, it unmasks dead works, and it opens the way to new life. All history is full of examples to teach us that this mode of action is unacceptable. Those who decide in favour of the routines which are profitable and pleasant to themselves can always manage to do so in the name of truth and of God, and their appeal to truth and God can often be convincingly backed by social authority. But we also know that this tenacity in clinging to routine notions of good and evil always leads to the ossification of living moral organisms. It is by their resistance to the challenge of an unpalatable new truth that these organisms make themselves incapable of living self-renewal.

The real question that is raised by non-violent action is not at all whether the democratic ideal ought to be replaced by something else: it is on the contrary an accusation of those who, while mouthing democratic slogans, have in fact clearly betrayed the democratic ideal and emptied it of meaning. This explains the virulence of the counter-attack against the kind of thinking which non-violence supposes.

Non-violence does not attack the ideals on which democratic society is built, still less the ideals of Christianity. It claims on the contrary to be a genuine fulfilment and implementation of those ideals. And in so claiming, it rejects the counter-claim of that popular self-understanding which is in fact a secular myth and a betrayal of democracy and of Christianity.

The real question which non-violent action poses is this: whether it may not in fact be necessary to practise non-violent methods if democracy is to be kept alive and preserved against the sclerosis which is gradually hardening it into a new form of Totalism.

If, instead of fabricating for ourselves a mythical and inadequate self-understanding made up of the postures and antics of TV westerns, we return to a deeper awareness of our professed ideals, we may find that non-violence is very relevant to them. After all, the basic principle of non-violence is respect for the personal conscience of the opponent. Non-violent action is a way of insisting on one's just rights without violating the rights of anyone else. In many instances, non-violence offers the only possible way in which this can be effected. The whole strength of non-violence depends on this absolute respect for the rights even of an otherwise unjust oppressor: his legal rights and his moral rights as a person. If non-violence is allied with civil disobedience, and it certainly is, this disobedience is however strictly limited. It is confined to *disobeying an unjust law*, for only this disobedience can be carried out without violation of rights.

Where an unjust law is disobeyed, non-violent resistance nevertheless supposes *implicit acceptance of the penalty* which is imposed for violation of the law. The purpose of this disobedience and the prompt acceptance of punishment for it is, according to Gandhian principles, to make abundantly clear the injustice of the law, in such a way that even the unjust oppressor will come to admit the fact, and will himself be willing to help change the situation.

In this way non-violence claims to work not only for the good of the one who is unjustly oppressed, but also for the good of the oppressor. Ideally speaking, non-violent action is supposed to be conducted in such a way that both sides come to see the injustice as a disadvantage and a dishonour to both, and they then agree to work together to remedy things. In this way non-violence aims not at the disruption and disintegration of society, but at a more real and living collaboration, based on truth and love.

So much for the ideal.

It must certainly be admitted that not all those who claim to be practising non-violence have kept themselves strictly within the limits so prescribed. On the contrary, many have in fact a very imperfect understanding of these principles and have made their non-violence simply another form of violence. But on the other hand those who have taken non-violence seriously enough to dedicate their lives to it, have undergone the necessary training, and have carried out their tasks with the required discipline, have not only achieved great success but have demonstrated the truth of their principles. In spite of all attempts at misrepresentation and denigration, these achievements have been evident and impressive. The witness of genuine non-violence has been incontestable.

It is unfortunate that, along with dedicated and disciplined non-violence there has been much irresponsible and even immoral and anti-social protest which the general public has not easily distinguished from the real thing.

The mass media have been content to keep this distinction blurred and the whole concept of non-violence remains, as far as most Americans are concerned, on the level of fearsome and repugnant myth.

We badly need a clear, sound, fundamental treatment of the principles of Non-Violent Action. In particular, Christians need a theological exposition of these principles. Fr Régamey, himself a theologian, has been active in the French Gandhian non-violent movement and therefore knows his subject both theologically and existentially. His treatment is particularly valuable, not only as clarification but as witness. Above all, at a time when so many American Catholics have come to the point where they seem to think that to question the justice of the use of force is to betray the nation and to deny the faith, we need this perfectly sound, reasonable and exact argument in favour of Christian non-violence.

The chief value of such an exposition is that it clearly shows the difference between *non-violence* and *non-resistance*. Not only does non-violence resist evil but, if it is properly practised, it resists evil more effectively than violence ever could. Indeed, the chief argument in favour of non-violent resistance is that it is, *per se* and ideally, *the only really effective resistance to injustice and evil*.

This does not mean that in practice the solution to grave international and civil problems can be had merely by good will and pious gestures of appeasement. The non-violent ideal does not contain in itself all the answers to all our questions. These will have to be met and worked out amid the risks and anguish of day to day politics. But they can never be worked out if non-violence is never taken seriously.

Whoever reads this book carefully and objectively should put it down, if not convinced that non-violent resistance is the Christian way *par excellence* to resist evil, at least persuaded that it is a form of positive resistance which deserves respectful consideration. In any event, the reader may rest assured that if, on putting down the book, he feels himself "inclined to non-violence", he does not have to fear that his mind will presently snap and that he will go berserk. At least one thing should be clear, after one has studied these pages. Far from being a fanatical manifestation of misguided idealism, non-violence demands a lucid reason, a profound religious faith and, above all, an uncompromising and courageous spirit of self-sacrifice.

Abbey of Gethsemani,   THOMAS MERTON
Kentucky, July, 1965

FOREWORD

1. The time of the crusades marked a cataclysmic change in Christian attitudes to the problem of violence.

The early Church had thrived on the blood of its martyrs, and had followed closely, at least in its aspiration, the example of Christ, who chose to offer his own life in sacrifice rather than to destroy his enemies. It tried to remain scrupulously loyal to the teaching of the Sermon on the Mount, that a Christian's distinctive duty was to show love even for his enemies, and his specific task the building of a supra-national spiritual community transcending local boundaries and antagonisms.

It was not long however before the early protest gave way to practical compromise, and this particularly in the matter of military service and loyalty to the Roman state. As Christianity permeated society, as Christians became part of the establishment and members of the establishment became Christians, it became increasingly difficult to maintain the rigour of early attitudes, which implied abstention from military service and from all public office. St Augustine, as the theologian of the Church now officially "established" and reconciled with the secular state, was in the unhappy position of having to frame in logical terms the compromise which had been reached already in practice. He taught, though with an agonizing sense of difficulty, that there was indeed such an activity as a "just war"; he taught, against the express words of the early Church Orders, that it was possible to serve in the army and in spite of this to please God.

St Augustine's compromise remained at a lofty doctrinal level the official teaching of the Church for the next five hundred years. War was at least a *permissible* activity. Nevertheless, the spirituality of the early Church remained a strong and vigorous tradition, and was enshrined in the sacramental practice and the institutions of the Christian body. It was still necessary to do penance if you killed anyone in a war, no matter how "just". The ideal of the Christian was still that of non-violence and the loving response to enmity, however shadowy its realization. Monastic orders and clerics maintained the tradition of abstention from military service, and abhorrence of all human bloodshed. If soldiers were canonized, it was never for their professional activities.

At the close of the first millennium, however, Christendom as a self-conscious political entity gradually became aware of a rival civilization, that of Islam, on the opposite shores of the Mediterranean, and responded to this challenge, under the leadership of the papacy, with the hostility that is normal for human groups in such circumstances. The crusading movement established new patterns of sanctity. The Holy Lance, which for the early Christians had been a symbol of the sacrificial love of Christ, was now carried point foremost into the holy city of Jerusalem and became a symbol of the New Jerusalem which was to be built by the sword. The warrior's life became a way of holiness, equal to that of the monastic orders, the shedding of heathen blood became an act of piety, and death on the battlefield a sure passport to the eternal joys of heaven.

The impact of the crusades on the group consciousness of Christendom was far more profound and long-lasting than that of any logical formulation of the duties of sovereigns. Much of our popular mythology still goes back to this source. The legendary patron saint of England was born out of a cloudy dream of warriors on the battlefield, thirsty for the blood of the enemy. Scratch the skin of a gentleman, and you will still find a knight – a knight in armour, with weapons ready for use. Traditions of non-violence were submerged, and their theological and psychological implications were not elaborated or explored.

"Just War" teaching, which reached its final exuberance in the Spanish neo-scholastics, did little to stem the tide. It was well-intentioned, and stemmed usually from a serious concern of idealists to limit the savagery of international conflict. It taught, indeed, that a war must not be fought unless the cause were just; that the intention must remain just throughout the course of hostilities; that war should not be declared until other avenues had been explored; that the means used to fight should not be unlawful in themselves; that advantages to be gained from the war should outweigh the evils which it would involve, and that victory should be certain – or at least very likely. All these were, and are, sensible ways of thinking, sensible calculations to make; but they were

slender threads to hold in check the international violence which
became the normal mode of behaviour of the sovereign states
which emerged with their brightly burning nationalism from the
explosion and disintegration of Christendom. The whole doctrine,
as a pretending pattern of international justice, was of course
vitiated by a radical weakness, a stone missing from its very
foundations; it neglected the fundamental premiss of effective
justice, that no man can be a judge in his own cause. The result of
this was that the doctrine fell into disrepute among those who were
seriously concerned with the original Christian tradition of non-
violence. For Erasmus, the whole just war tradition was the result
of the Church's "swallowing a gobbet of the civil laws" – which
were not at all the same as the laws of Christ. Wars that were
declared "just" immediately became "glorious"; and what, he
asked, was the basis of this justice: "In practice it is the will of
the prince, be he child or idiot; and even a sane man is not likely
to judge that his own cause is unjust."

In a sense this criticism is unfair. There was no international
authority, the sovereign states were in fact judges in their own
causes, and there was no other realistic possibility to build on; in
the circumstances, it was better that someone should tell them
only to wage war justly than that they should be told, as they were
later by the positivist tradition of law, that they could wage war
whenever they felt like it (even though this did amount to the same
thing). There was however an unfortunate by-product of the theologians' concern with the theory of war. However much they tried
to limit the occasions of violence, they inevitably expounded a
theory of the *justice of war* in certain circumstances – a theological
doctrine which stated categorically that in some cases war was
absolutely the right thing to do.

What then of the scriptures, what of the tradition of the early
Church? The scriptures must be reinterpreted, the early fathers
could not have meant what they appeared to mean. The scriptural
teaching which seems to stand in the way of war must apply to
inward dispositions, not necessarily to outward acts – perhaps not
at all to outward acts; we must ask, not what is *commanded* by the
Sermon on the Mount, but what is *forbidden* by it; we must
remember the distinction between *precepts*, which we must obey,
and *counsels*, which we need not. Above all, we must bear in mind

the vital difference between *private* acts of vengeance and war, which are always to be deprecated, and *public* acts, which are of a completely different nature, and which are regulated by the tradition of natural law rather than by that of scriptural exegesis.

Taken as a whole, this kind of interpretation resulted in a doctrinal submergence of the non-violence of the scriptures as effective as its emotional submergence in the crusades.

The Church seemed to have become the prostitute of worldly powers, and condemned as heretics those who followed too closely the example of Christ.

2. Our history and traditions are therefore a considerable handicap if we wish to re-present Christianity, the official faith of western civilization, as a religion of non-violence. The reaction of those who know Christianity mainly through the corporate works of western culture is likely to be one of marked cynicism. Yet the world is crying out for such a re-presentation; and Father Régamey's book represents a remarkable theological departure in this direction.

The principal inspiration for the book comes, not from any representative of western culture, but from a Hindu, Mahatma Gandhi. It is a sobering thought that we had to wait for someone brought up in a culture utterly foreign from our own to take the teaching of the New Testament seriously as a guide for political action. The achievement of Gandhi was such that no one will be able to think of non-violence in the same way after his martyrdom; whatever attitude we take, he is a figure to be reckoned with – he has altered the composition of the "noosphere". Brought up in a tradition which has always regarded violence as a prime obstacle to spiritual progress, Gandhi found in the Sermon on the Mount and in the life of Christ an inspiration and a call to action. Convinced that love for one's enemies is fully compatible with the most vigorous of political conflicts, he succeeded in prising the English out of India with a gentleness which left neither conqueror nor vanquished, but only an increase of nobility on either side and a heightened awareness of a common human destiny. The later peaceful dissolution of the remainder of the British Empire owes more than we realize to the saintly hero of its first act.

Through Gandhi, Régamey taps the rich source of Hindu moral

philosophy, and links it with submerged themes of the Christian tradition. Old vices appear in a new light. The seven deadly sins find a new place, not as species of pride, or of *coveitize* and the pride of life, but as sources of violence, obstacles to *ahimsâ*. *Retaining for oneself what the world needs* is a kind of violence, and a source of further violence. Fear and hate are linked in a way that reminds us of the scriptural opposition, "Hate casteth out Fear". Along with attitudes of mind we recognize as "sinful" are other obstacles to *ahimsâ* which we do not classify in this way, such as *haste*, which is a kind of violence in the dimension of time.

Faith and non-violence, in the thought of Gandhi, are inseparably linked. It is only when the practitioner of non-violence accepts to the depths his own weakness, that the power of God becomes manifest through him. Humility, gentleness, faith and power are the hall-marks of the truly non-violent. This faith, though not what we should recognize as faith in a transcendent God, is a faith in the reality of a spiritual principle within men, a faith which demands of its adherents a readiness to sacrifice one's own life in testimony to it. Gandhi's "experiences of truth", every one of them tested by his own public life, form a bridge between Christian dogmatic theology and the living traditions of Hindu spirituality.

Régamey also learns to look with new eyes at the principal dogmas of Christianity, which acquire new meaning in the context of his non-violent exploration. He sees the whole story of the incarnation as the entry of the non-violent God into the life of man – the supreme act of respect for the sanctity of the human person. For it is a constant theme of this philosophy that non-violence is the only authentic relationship between human *persons*, between human *freedoms*. A violent action is essentially an action contrary to the nature of its object, and the supreme contradiction of the human person is to treat him as a thing without choice, without spirit, without the right of self-determination. The Son of Man who is to redeem mankind slips into the world and into our consciousness as the child born in Bethlehem, born not to force the wills of men, but to bear the burden of their suffering and of their sin. This child was born to be a king – a king of a nation in a situation of bitter racial conflict, of an oppressed people thirsting for liberation and vengeance; yet he chose not to fight, but to suffer –

to be led, like a lamb, to the slaughter. Christ's steadfast refusal of violence and retaliation is an integral part of the meaning of Calvary.

Finally, the love of enemies is explored by Fr Régamey, not just as a fine ideal, but as a serious possibility of behaviour highly relevant to our times, and requiring serious thought. How do we actually set about "loving our enemies"? Certainly not just by deciding that we like them as we like our friends, because that would be false. What we can do, however, is to seek out the justice of our enemy's position, and to embrace that justice with even greater enthusiasm, if possible, then he does himself. Our task must be to acquire the "taste of the enemy"; above all, to avoid the natural impulse to adopt the "anti" position, and thereby justify our enemy's attack on us. Is not this the meaning of the commandment to "resist not evil"?

The relevance of this to the political problems of today, to relations between East and West, between Catholic and non-Catholic, is at last being realized. Increasing signs of adjustment in communist thought to the possibility of living with Christianity are the direct result of Pope John's *aggiornamento*, and of a more serious consideration by Christians of the forces of justice embodied in the Marxist tradition. The quest for unity and fellowship has fortunately submerged the quest for heresy. Yet it would be a profound mistake to think that humanity is going to emerge suddenly from the primal mists of conflict into the millennium of peace.

3. It is only too easy to accept the gospels and forget about the reality of the world and the pressures which operate within it – just as it is easy to become immersed in political "realism", and leave the gospels aside as a beautiful but irrelevant gloss.

Régamey's book falls into neither of these dangers. If his "open" approach to the New Testament teaching concerning non-violence enables him to explore in a new way certain dimensions of moral theology, it also enables him to take the fullest account of violence in the world. Non-violence is indeed an absolute; but it is not the kind of absolute which gives a rule of thumb to operate in all situations – it is rather a signpost, telling us to go as far as possible in this direction on every occasion and in every aspect of our lives, for it is the direction of spiritual growth. The counsels are not rules for occasional application by exceptional people; they are always relevant, but in a multitude of different ways according to the complexity of the human situation, and may sometimes be temporarily overridden by the violence of necessary circumstance.

Such an approach, if it is indeed the right one, calls for a serious and exhaustive study of violence, its sources, functions, and disguises, in the human individual, in interpersonal relationships, and in inter-group relationships; for to make progress in the direction indicated by the gospels, we must first of all know exactly where we are, where we start from. The rule of thumb method would bypass such a study, for if we have a clear rule by which to judge all situations, from "outside", then there is no need to worry about all this complexity; we already know "where we are", spiritually, and if "they", "the others", are not in the same place, we need only shout at them to join us.

So we move from taking the gospel seriously to taking the world seriously; and the more we consider the many faces of violence in human life, the more baffling seems to be the task of the reformer.

Psychology reveals to us a dimension we little suspected. Daily, Freud tells us, in our subconscious minds we consign our enemies to perdition; the superficial smoothness of social life conceals antagonisms which would horrify us, if they were brought to light without heavy disguise. Study of social behaviour suggests that aggression is the normal human response to frustration, and that the thwarting of such aggression makes it more rather than less violent – the suppression of superficial manifestations of aggression has little to do with changing the spiritual force which animates it.

The study of primate social behaviour, of baboons and monkeys, provides further food for thought. Baboons live in closely integrated groups. Conflict with foreign primate species is rare; an elephant can wander through a group of feeding baboons without any vestige of hostility. Conflict between different groups of the same species, however, is normal, as is conflict within the groups, though the conflict is formalized in patterns of threat and submission, and bloodshed is rare. The biologist's professional concern is to understand the function of these behaviour patterns; and, in general terms, the answer seems clear. Conflict between groups is a means of territorial spacing; conflict within the group is a means of determining the hierarchy and providing a stable social structure; it is especially important in the process of selecting the dominant male warrior, whose function is to protect the group against hostile groups and hostile carnivores. An element of violent conflict, and the threat-behaviour which symbolizes and announces it, is thus built into the structure of primate society, and even into the physical structure of the body. The hairiness of the male head increases its apparent size, and when the hair bristles outwards in anger it adds greatly to the effectiveness of the threat behaviour.

Sociology suggests that violence or potential violence remains more important than we realize in our own social structures. Reinhold Niebuhr maintains, with good evidence to support him, that justice is born out of violent conflict, out of the assertion of force against force. We pride ourselves on the equity of our labour relations, on the equality of the sexes before the law, on the emancipation of the slaves, on respect for human rights. But we forget, if we are pacifists, that all these advances which seem to have brought in some sectors of our lives the peace which is the fruit of justice, have been victories won as the fruit of conflict and violent self-assertion of subordinate against dominant groups.

What, then, becomes of our non-violence? The dogmatic pacifist has a ready-made answer. If non-violence is our "good" and violence our "evil" then we simply choose the former and reject the latter; and to reject a certain type of behaviour means to call it "sin", to regard those who practise it as "sinners", to exorcise it perhaps by the mysterious process of guilt and confession.

But to do this is to avoid reality, not to face it; it is in fact an illusion to imagine that we can throw away constituent parts of our own personalities; if we try to do so, then we only cover them over with a disguise, or thrust them into a darkness where they become more unmanageable than they were before. It may well be that the early Christians fell to some extent into this kind of error. Was their non-violent "conquest" of the Mediterranean world completely innocent of a kind of spiritual violence, the consequences of which may still be with us? Is the spirit of peace as we understand it compatible with the violent denunciation of heretics, which is also a hall-mark of the early Church?

The early Christians may have made mistakes which we are not entitled to make. They were in a position that we are not in, we know what they did not know. It is no longer possible for us with a sweeping gesture to confine all the violent aspects of our beings to the outer darkness, for we know only too well that the outer darkness thus constituted is still part of ourselves, all the more dangerous because consciously discarded. The kind of group hostility which can play a part in war should be understood as having a certain positive function, whether for territorial spacing, or for ideological spacing, or for some other purpose not yet understood; only by this approach can such attitudes be tamed, and their meanings modified. The personal antagonism involved in the struggle for status, especially among males, should not just be thrust aside and covered with a cloak of shame, but recognized for the integral part of human nature which it is, not to be bypassed even in the most secluded of monasteries, where it will only appear in new disguises if condemned in old. The violence done to human nature by refusing to accept it in its most vital manifestations is perhaps more than anything a source of neurosis and of violent and disordered personalities among those with the loftiest moral aspirations. Perhaps the ancient liturgical traditions are a surer guide here than many pious disquisitions. Nowhere can we find the passionate desire for victory in battle, nowhere the yearning for the reward of "pre-eminence among peers", more tellingly expressed than in the Psalms, which form the bedrock of our liturgy.

Unless we are open to such disquieting thoughts, our presentation of the non-violence of Christ is in danger of degenerating into a new Pharisaism worse than the old, and equally without creative power in the moment of crisis.

4. Yet we retain our faith in a revelation which teaches us the ultimate reality of love, the unity of mankind, which calls upon us to love our enemies, and to overcome violence by gentleness. The signposts are clear, and we should not lose sight of them in our preoccupation with the jungle reality.

Since men are capable of thought and speech, their lives have meaning in a sense that the lives of other animals do not; and since they have free will, they have the unique power of transforming the meaning of their lives. It is precisely with such a transformation of meaning that the New Testament is concerned, and it is this which we are called on to achieve with regard to the violence we have now become aware of in ourselves, in our society, in our international relations.

Responsibility for changing the meaning of our situation implies the fullest loyalty both to the world and to the gospels. The world is our raw material, it is our potter's clay; and, like true artists, we must know and respect our material, use its qualities, enter into a dialogue with it, and by no means seek to impose upon it a pattern from outside. But neither must we just try to read "natural laws", like codes of instruction written into the materials; for this would be again to fall under the slavery of the law, from which the new life of the spirit has liberated us. The material awaits the shaping of our freedom to give it form and beauty, to liberate its hidden potentialities; and our inspiration in this work must be the revealed word of God.

Part of this material is violence and aggression, the meaning of which we are only beginning to understand. It is an integral part of us and of our society – a part of us "gone wrong", we may think, but still part of us, not readily to be exorcised by confession or disarmament, and the forces which produced its present manifestations are still with us.

The first step towards a more integrated understanding is to accept to the full the ambiguity of human situations, for it is by virtue of this ambiguity that they can be modified. The violence of aggression, even in its most destructive form, can be a manifestation of that same spirit which has led man to "conquer" disease and famine, to "destroy" ignorance and superstition, to "master" his environment. The very instinct of destruction can be a necessary contribution to the upward creative drive of humanity, which implies the breaking of the old to make way for the new. The evil of conquest and imperialism is a move towards human unity, the evil of war a means of peace.

Must we then condone this evil? By no means, for the task of the Christian is to bring good out of evil. Yet the commandment *not to judge* has a deeper meaning than we have yet fully realized. It is a

commandment not to *reject*, not to say "Thou fool"; for to reject
in this way is to reject part of the texture of reality, to reject part
of ourselves and of our own situation – "Judge not that you be not
judged" – and such a rejection destroys the ambiguity which is
creative of new meaning, producing instead the "absolute evil"
which is its own natural counterpart.

Not to condemn, not to accept, but to transform – this must be
the specifically Christian, the specifically human task; and it is
such a transformation which was supremely realized in the
crucifixion, accomplished under the sign of ambiguity – "Jesus of
Nazareth, King of the Jews".

The task presented to us is not that of finding gaps for non-
violence in a world dominated increasingly by brute force; it is
rather that of seeing the larger meaning of contemporary history
as embodying a challenge to mankind to assume in a new way
responsibility for his own destiny, and to take a dramatic step
forward in the direction of human fellowship.

For the nuclear stalemate which confronts us is, like all human
situations, profoundly ambiguous. It can, quite legitimately, be
regarded as the culmination of aggression and counter-aggression,
the result of a diabolical cooperation between primitive human
instincts and the terrifying advances of science, resulting now in a
situation of frozen opposing hatreds, threats and counter-threats
of mutual annihilation, from which neither side can budge without
bringing about a final catastrophe. From such a situation, it might
be argued, a Christian can only recoil in horror, for it is a radical
denial of human fellowship, and of the love which the gospel
preaches; it is a situation which threatens to involve the majority
of mankind in the guilt of murder, and the just retribution of
sudden death.

On the other hand, it could equally be said that this is not the
whole meaning of the nuclear stalemate. It is also the culmination
of a "balance of power" system, which is one of humanity's most
ancient forms of peace-keeping between large antagonistic units.
It has a different meaning for the opponents considered jointly
from the meaning it sometimes appears to have to each individu-
ally; whereas each side tends to view its armoury as a means of
defence against the utter evil of the aggressor, for the two considered together it begins to have the appearance of a structure

of order which increasingly reduces the scope of war as a means of resolving disputes. It is not unusual for human actions to evolve meanings for the community which are not entirely "possessed" or controlled by any individuals; indeed the whole development of human language and of all meaningful behaviour is of this kind. In this case, however, the joint meaning of the nuclear balance is one which is being increasingly assumed by the leadership of both major opposing blocs.

Through this structure of opposing forces, a certain minimum of "justice" is secured. Just as the balance of power between organized labour and management ensures a degree of justice between them, and a balance of power between husband and wife provides a firm foundation for true equality, so the balance of opposing systems has prevented a world empire of one or the other which would undoubtedly have been to the detriment of the human race. An imposed unity would surely have been a less secure and less healthy environment than a world in which opposing systems had discovered for themselves the necessity of coexistence.

Of course, the situation is highly dangerous. The balance is never really stable, the danger of war by accident is substantial, and above all the prospect of nuclear proliferation is grim, threatening to destroy whatever positive meaning there might have been in the temporary stalemate. Problems of non-proliferation and arms control are becoming increasingly urgent, and their resolution demands great technical skill. But the Christian cannot for this reason simply leave it to the experts; for what is at stake beneath all the technical problems is the whole meaning of international violence; the disarmament negotiations are merely the focus of a submerged debate about the nature of war itself and of the human community – and every reiteration of the more primitive values of war, whether in Vietnam or Kashmir or elsewhere, makes more difficult the task of elucidating and consolidating new meanings.

The situation is critical, and heavy with ambiguity. For this very reason the task of Christian prophecy is now more urgent than ever before.

5. The Christian's peculiar responsibility is to take the gospels and the world equally seriously as referring both to the same spiritual realities; he must learn to read the meaning

of this moment of history in depth, in order to devote all his energies to enable the child of peace to be born from the womb of darkness.

The Christian will have nothing relevant to say until he has studied the problems of international life in the language of the historian or the political scientist. But given this competence, his role can be a prophetic one, and the world is ready to listen to him as it has never been ready before.

It is difficult to define in advance what would be a "Christian" approach to this or that problem; but there is a certain "style" which one would expect of anyone who took seriously, as Fr Régamey does, the full implications of Christ's teaching and example.

One aspect of this "style" would be a strong attachment to the words of Christ in the Garden of Gethsemane: "He who takes the sword shall perish by the sword." Violence always tends to breed counter-violence, and in the struggle which ensues justice is often submerged and hatred triumphant. We have no right to say that violence is always forbidden – there is no such easy formula to cut through the texture of reality; but we equally have no right to neglect our prophetic role.

Sometimes the temptation to concede the justice of violence is very strong. In South Africa the leaders of the disenfranchised majority have shown extraordinary patience in pursuing their just aims for many years by non-violent means, taking their inspiration both from Christianity and from Gandhi. One after another the means of non-violent protest were closed to them by a frightened "nationalist" government; their political parties were banned, meetings were banned, strikes were banned, and the position of the dominant group was maintained by all the machinery of a powerful modern state and by military forces stronger in proportion to the population than those of any other state in the world. Violence seems inevitable, and justifiable. There are those who call for terrorism within South Africa, and those who call for international action with the deliberate aim of provoking an internal explosion within the Union. The problem must be studied in all its complexity; but the Christian, for all his sympathy with the suffering and the oppressed, must, if he is worth his salt, sound the same note of warning: "He who takes the sword shall perish by the sword." What sort of legacy of bitterness and hatred would be left by a slaughter of whites in South Africa – or by the slaughter of blacks, which would surely accompany it? What sort of justice could be achieved by the unconditional "victory" of either side against the other? There is a powerful myth about violence which the Christian must destroy. It is instinctive to regard violence as the "final solution", as a means that is always there, ready to be used, and guaranteed to be effective, "in the last resort"; violence in international and interracial disputes is less and less "available", nor does it carry any such guarantee.

Another aspect of the Christian "style" must be directly related to the commandment, "Judge not, that you be not judged". Such an attitude runs directly counter to the tradition of "just war" thinking. It is an easy and a comforting moral activity to allocate praise and blame, to condemn one side in a dispute and to sanctify another, and such an activity might appear to be "moral". In reality, "judgement" of this kind is little more than a participation in violent conflict from a distance; it is a spiritual dimension of violence, and as such it falls under the same suspicion as more overt acts of physical destruction. To condemn is to reject, to reject is to wish to destroy. He who judges will be judged; he who takes the sword shall perish by the sword.

One of the worst dangers of judging is that it creates a complete block to understanding; and it is only on understanding that peace can be built. By a pseudo-magical rejection of one particular human group, whether they are communists in general, the white men in South Africa, the Americans in Vietnam, or the Vietcong, we close the door to dialogue, we consecrate a situation of violence, we take a step towards the "crusade"; and it is not the Vietcong who will destroy the world, nor the Americans, nor the Chinese, but the virus of the "Holy War" which still rages in our "Christian" bosoms.

Like other forms of violence, judgement reproduces itself in an escalating pattern. The man who attacks us, perhaps with good reason, we condemn as simply "evil", to be rejected and destroyed. From his point of view we appear then, with good reason, to be simply "evil", and our enemy "judges" us; and we, now with good reason, "judge" him, for he is simply out for our defeat or destruction. Thus we have the traditional pattern of the crusade, the "just" war on both sides.

It is precisely because judgement of this kind tends to be self-verifying that it becomes extraordinarily difficult to avoid, especially in international affairs. Passions are aroused, justice is embattled against injustice, and one is tempted to indulge in the luxury of moral condemnation, of enlisting vicariously with the soldiers of light to destroy the soldiers of darkness. As the interminable war in Vietnam begins to look increasingly like a war of national liberation and democratic revolution against American neo-imperialism, it is easy and tempting for the enthusiasts to cry, "my heart is with the Vietcong, I am with them in their fight"; it is particularly tempting to those who are sick at heart with anti-communism, and perhaps with those who harbour a hidden grudge against the over-dominant leader of the western camp. But the Christian will be aware of dangers of judgement involved in such a stand; he will be too sensitive to the ambiguity of meaning on both sides, to the strange mixture of thirst for justice with violence and self-assertion which typifies all human action, to reject out of hand one side or the other in this tragic conflict – for in so doing he would but reject part of mankind, part of himself.

Must the Christian "style" then involve perpetual fence-sitting? Is not this a depressing and lifeless doctrine to offer to those who hunger and thirst for justice?

It is not the fence-sitters who are the children of God, but the peace-makers. Abstention from judgement is not a negative act for the Christian; it springs from a profound faith in human fellowship – in what the Quakers would call the "spark of God in every man", and in our community in a shared situation. Consequently, we can never stop short at not judging; an urgent search for the construction of order and justice, for the materials with which to build the temple of peace, must follow from the same faith which forbids condemnation.

This will be a third aspect of the Christian "style" in approaching international conflict. Conflict is not just an ignoble, selfish squabble, but is also an assertion on both sides of the nobility of man. In order that the dispute should have a positive resolution, each side must clarify its aims publicly in terms of justice recognizable to the other, must make every effort to recognize and promote whatever is just in the attitude of its opponents. The Christian doctrine that we must love our enemies is by no means absurd as a formula of conflict resolution.

What does this mean in concrete terms? In Vietnam, for example, the Americans are committed, as a submerged aspect of their policy, to the principle of self-determination. They are convinced, or so they maintain, that their presence in the South has as its sole purpose the prevention of a take-over in the South by a government which the people do not want. But the communists also talk in terms of self-determination and are inspired by the ideal of national liberation. Here is an area of positive thinking in which the opposing sides overlap, and it is here that the dialogue must begin. The United States must make it abundantly clear that they really do believe in self-determination – and this will not be clear until they make it a central and declared purpose of their policy to promote free elections, to welcome whatever government emerges from such elections, *whether communist or not*, to leave it free to negotiate its own future relationship with the North, and with other powers. The Vietcong must for their part accept – as they already do – that a free expression of the will of the people is the only valid basis of rule, and that self-determination does not mean extermination by the majority of any minority group, but may well entail provisions for the safeguarding of minority rights within a majority system.

We can begin to discern here the outline of an approach to conflict which is distinctively Christian, and at the same time highly relevant to the present situation. It is a style suggested directly by studies, such as Régamey's, of the authentic tradition of non-violence. One can hope, too, that Christians may once more become in their everyday lives more aware of the imperatives of the Sermon on the Mount, more aware of the practical significance and profound psychological relevance of Christian "gentleness".

At the same time, if the Christian contribution is to be anything more than marginal, it must be based not on an utter rejection of violence but on a recognition of its positive role and ambiguous meaning. For if the world is ready to listen to talk of the peaceful resolution of conflicts it is because of the increasing futility of armed combat as a means of resolving any issue of justice; and this futility is itself in part the result of a massive stalemate of opposing antagonisms, which seems to be the logical conclusion of the history of total war. This antagonism has only been able to assume a positive meaning because from the beginning it was ambiguous in its meaning – an assertion not just of hatred, but an assertion of justice, of opposing rights. Similarly, if the world is increasingly recognizing that nations have a right to self-determination, this is partly because the opposing pressures of antagonistic empires can now only be reduced by the joint recognition of the rights of smaller nations to decide for themselves about their own destinies. If it is sensible to seek for the resolution of a conflict, such as that in Vietnam, or in South Africa, it is only because one is capable of recognizing within the violent assertion of each side a positive element of justice, which must be assumed and asserted in a new form. Rights do not grow without being asserted, and whatever justice we enjoy is the outcome of a forcible assertion inspired by an ideal. The interweaving of force and justice is part of the very texture of our individual and collective lives, and to ignore this is to abdicate intelligence and responsibility.

The realities must be accepted, the meaning transformed. The transformation is possible, because the world is redeemable. Violence and war are part of our natures, themselves to be redeemed, by the inscrutable providence of God, and the faith and cooperation of man.

August, 1965   STANLEY G. WINDASS

INTRODUCTION

In a world of violence and hatred . . .

Non-violence, as it was taught and practised by Gandhi,[1] stands as a challenge which the Christian conscience cannot ignore. In this cruel world of violence and hatred, a way of love has been opened up. It has been tried; we have seen an immense people liberated without violence, and we Christians can recognize in the victorious appeals of Gandhi the purest strains of the gospels – strains of such purity that one hardly dared believe in their efficacity. Crushed by the weight of systematic oppression, the weak are in danger of giving up the struggle at the very moment when their constantly frustrated hopes are being awakened. There are many people who would agree with the words of Dr Corman:[2] "The fate of humanity is being worked out within the souls of each one of us. We have to choose between violence, which will destroy us all, and non-violence which, with God's help, will save the world."

What should our attitude be towards non-violence? One thing is quite certain: the hope to which the teachings and achievements of Gandhi seem to supply an answer is indeed the hope for those who despair, for those who, among the countless victims of injustice, ask themselves with anguish how they are to live without becoming unjust in their turn. How are they to avoid becoming bitter, or prevent outbreaks of murderous violence as a result of the frustration of their passionate urge to live? It is the hope of those who wish to remain poor in spirit, gentle in spite of violence and bitterness, without resentment in their affliction, without hatred in their hunger for justice, merciful, pure and peace loving.[3]

The poor and the oppressed of today feel, alas, that they cannot find this hope in Christ. It seems to them that the gospel only throws a faint glow upon the darkness of our present world, and that it has not the power to protect us against the destructive forces

---

[1] See Part III, Chaps. 9 and 10
[2] L. Corman, *La Nonviolence* (Stock, 1949) p. 2
[3] Mt 5: 3–11 (the beatitudes)

that have been unleashed – besides, how do the poor and the oppressed know Christ except through Christians? And they have too often failed them!

It is not for us to judge. It is for God to decide whether the organization of the faithful in "Christendom", such as existed in the early centuries, then under the feudal system and finally in modern states, has done more good than harm. We could argue endlessly on this point, but we are not going to try to solve problems of history from the standpoint of present prejudices. What is quite certain is that this organization involved frequent wars and every type of coercion; and the evils were too inextricably bound up with these systems for evangelical gentleness to be able to assert itself in the face of violence.[4]

---

[4] It would be presumptuous and superficial to condemn Christendom out of hand because of its abuses. It is doubly difficult for us to determine where these abuses started, firstly because of the difficulty of getting an accurate picture of all the facts, and secondly because the interaction of spiritual values and human institutions and behaviour is always puzzling. Yet, on the other hand, it is scandalous to canonize manifest abuses because they happened in Christendom. There are many, alas, who do just this. In taking this line, they naturally oppose any contemporary progress in moral awareness and become all the more reactionary about what they ought to condemn in the past. For instance, an influential Catholic periodical, which shall be nameless for the sake of keeping the peace, published an article which asserted that only opportunism had made the Church drop its teaching that rulers should "exterminate heretics". Fr A. M. Dubarle, on the other hand, reminded us in *La Vie Intellectuelle* (Jan. 1952) that the word "exterminate" meant only confiscation of goods and banishment. But even in this reduced form, this sanction is in no way an obligation imposed by the Church, and mere prudence should see that it is no longer applied today. The Fourth Lateran Council in 1215 did prescribe such a sanction, but disciplinary measures decreed by councils, even ecumenical ones, cannot in any way be compared with infallible dogmatic decisions. They are part and parcel of the social and mental outlook of a particular period. Thus Thomas Aquinas thought that an obligation to put incorrigible sinners to death could be found in the divine law itself (IIa IIae qu.25, art.6, ad.2); this was due to the fact that his mind was not equipped with the necessary means to distinguish what belongs to historical conditions even in the inspired writers. (Cf. Pius XII, *Divino afflante*.)

Pius XII himself said that institutions evolved for the defence of the faith may have assumed "over the centuries, forms and methods, not required by the nature of things, but which are to be explained in the light of particular historical circumstances"[5]. He recognized that "in ages gone by, even the saner part of mankind had set out on its mission without sufficient seriousness and purpose and it is now a question of being firmly resolved to fulfil it", that is, to put an end to war.[6]

"If ever," exclaimed Pius XII, "a generation has cried out from the very depth of its soul: war against war, it is certainly the present one."[7] And he stated explicitly: "The theory of war as a method of settling international conflicts is now superseded."[8] Many other teachings of Pius XII unite in encouraging christians to enter into the warfare of this world with weapons of the Spirit.

We are therefore invited to have a fresh look at the gospels. Many christians have become used to associating the fate of Christianity with human systems which they did not recognize as being in the service of Mammon or Moloch. Many today are still down this blind alley, even to the extent of looking to the bomb for their salvation. We may well contrast such a betrayal with the hopeful appeals to charity on the part of the Vicar of Christ. We are now at a turning point in history and the Christian conscience is calling in question certain attitudes which were hitherto taken for granted. In antiquity and during the middle ages slavery, for instance, was not considered to be shameful, because it was at the basis of the whole social structure. Neither was it explicitly condemned by Christ and the apostles. They relied on the growth of Christendom, knowing that when it had arrived at a certain stage of development, it would have changed the very soil in which it was rooted. Today, we can no longer close our eyes to the scandal of violence, for which Jesus has explicitly commanded us to substitute his gentleness.[9]

---

[5] Allocution of 6 October, 1946

[6] Message of Christmas, 1944

[7] ibid.

[8] ibid. Cf the dictum of 1 January, 1951: "Less now than ever is war the right way to eliminate conflicts and re-establish justice".

[9] We shall use the word "gentleness" to translate *douceur* throughout this work, rather than "meekness", which has an archaic flavour – (Tr.).

But what are the precise implications of the teaching of the gospels? What does Jesus expect of us – he who is so patient with the world – what is he prepared to tolerate? We have reason to fear that there is no universally valid answer to this question. We see the "very gentle Christ on earth" as St Catherine used to call the Pope, being so reticent on this question in spite of the torment of the world . . . The situations are so diverse and each one is so complex that one cannot in honesty give a definite theoretical answer. An elucidation of principles is therefore all the more urgent, so that men who are faced with these varying situations may courageously decide one way or another as Christians.

Since it is Gandhi who has awakened us, it would seem natural to start by recalling his pre-eminently non-violent action and doctrine, and then to reflect as Christians on their value. But all this work of information and interpretation can only be preparatory to the formation of our own consciences. It seemed more profitable to get the reader to face the heart of the problem from the very beginning, after a few introductory remarks on the nature of violence. Any reader can, if he wishes, verify this preparation or go over it again with the help of footnotes or quotations he will find in the text.

The author has himself devoted three years to the task of gathering information, to exegesis, reflexion and discussion. In assimilating the thought of Gandhi he has had the invaluable contribution of the constant advice of Mme Camille Drevet, who knew the Mahatma more intimately than anyone in France.[10] Furthermore, for the exegesis that underlies his meditation of the Scriptures, he has not only consulted the works of many specialists, but he has benefited from the advice and fraternal criticism of a most competent and subtle exegete, Fr A. M. Dubarle. A further blessing: the second version of this book – this is the fourth – was riddled by the criticisms of censors, who at least did the author the good turn of making him more aware of the resistances of readers who would be equally difficult to convince. It is doubtless not superfluous to warn readers that the foundations have been painfully built and severely tested, for it can be most disconcerting when the Christian conscience is fully awakened. It requires an unusual and difficult change of outlook, for to be seen properly in focus from a

---

[10] Author of *Pour connaître la pensée de Gandhi* (Bordas, 1954).

Christian point of view, as when we adjust a telescope for a given distance, the teachings of Christ should cease to appear as a set of fixed ideas, or warnings and precepts which we consider from the outside as a rigid doctrinal system. We must rediscover something of the original impulse which they had when they were fashioned in the Heart of Christ himself. You are protesting, I hope! I hope you feel at once how intolerable such a claim is in danger of becoming. Does it not deserve the withering rebuke which God gave to Job: "Where wast thou when I laid the foundations of the earth?"[11] . . . Even when God unites himself to the stuff of our mortality,[12] his thoughts are not our thoughts: nor his ways, our ways. For as the heavens are exalted above the earth, so are God's ways exalted above our ways, and his thoughts above our thoughts.[13] Even if our many shortcomings did not distort our view of Christ, we would still not be sufficiently "conformed to the Lord" during this life, because we do not yet see him "as he is".[14]

Certainly; but it would be presumptuous to claim to think and feel perfectly like Christ. Imperfectly, we not only can but must strive to share the movements of his heart, from which his teaching springs. It is precisely there that his teachings invite us to look, otherwise we can never have anything more than a superficial understanding of them; we lose ourselves in all sorts of problems which his words conjure up. But these are solved when we listen to those words in the same spirit as Jesus uttered them; he has told us the secrets of his Heart,[15] which are incomprehensible to the wise and clever of this world, but luminous to those who become like little children.[16]

It is the same water which you see one moment as a block of hard ice and later becoming a cloud of steam. Let us not despise the waters of life of God's words when they appear to us cold and hard because of the state of our minds. Neither must we be surprised if they have no effect upon the world in this state. They will only recover their power if they are drawn warm and living

---

[11] Job 38 (the whole wonderful chapter)
[12] *Communicantes* of the Mass of the Epiphany
[13] Cf. Is 55: 8–9
[14] I Jn 3: 2
[15] Jn 15: 15
[16] Mt 11: 25

from the fountains of the Saviour.[17] "Now we have not received the spirit of this world, but the Spirit that is of God."[18]

It is a matter of constant surprise to us that the faithful are so rarely encouraged to rediscover for themselves, from what they already know of Jesus, the situations in which his teachings originated, particularly in the case of those things they find disconcerting. There is no risk in this, as long as submission to the Church, which is the cornerstone of faith, preserves one from dangerous deviations from the truth. We have often noticed how many difficulties vanish away, how many divine sayings can be assimilated, and what new strength they acquire the moment they are seen in the light of their origins. "It seems to us then," as St Ambrose puts it, "that the Word ascends the heights of dogma as he did the highest mountains, that he appears to us as he did upon the hills, and that he enlightens our spirits."[19] We then experience faith as truly a participation in the knowledge that God has of himself and of all things within himself.[20] When we dare to

---

[17] *Haurietis aquas in gaudio de fontibus Salvatoris* (Is 13: 3). We have "the spirit of the living God" (II Cor 3: 3) which "quickens us" (Rom 8: 11), cf. Gal 4: 4, 7. "That Christ may dwell in our hearts by faith" (Eph 3: 17); "We have the mind of Christ" (I Cor 2: 16), "Know you not . . . that Christ Jesus is in you?" (II Cor 13: 5). We, the children of God "he predestined to be made conformable to the image of his Son" (Rom 8: 29), "But we all, beholding the glory of the Lord with open face, are transformed into the same image from glory to glory, as by the Spirit of the Lord." (II Cor 3: 18). If we are to reflect this light in such a way that it gives us a deep understanding of the divine words, we must throughout our lives keep this thought in our hearts; we must inform each separate word of Christ's with the knowledge of the fullness of his Mystery. We are entrusted with the "wisdom of God" which is "in a mystery . . . which none of the princes of this world knew", but which God "ordained before the world unto our glory". So that we can truly say something about what the "eye hath not seen nor ear heard, neither hath it entered into the hearts of men what things God hath prepared for them that love Him" (see the whole passage), I Cor 2: 6–16.

[18] I Cor 2: 12

[19] In Ps 118, Serm. VI, 8, quoted by Denys Gorce in *Le laïc théologien*, p. 349.

[20] *Sum. Theol., Ia Pars.*, Qu. 1, art. 3, ad. 2

give faith its integral place, then we have the *mind of God, the mind of Christ*; it ceases to be a vague aspiration of our being towards God and towards Christ, and becomes from that moment a redirection of our lives in which redemptive love comes down upon us from God through Christ. He leads us outside ourselves and turns us towards the world so that we may become a means of salvation to it. Naturally, such an undertaking requires both scientific thoroughness and humility in our study of the word of God. But the word of the scriptures will not yield its meaning to us until we see God's saving action and the truths of his revelation as springing from the very Heart of God.

When we have reached this plenitude of Christian consciousness, the reordering of our thoughts which it involves will appear in quite a different light from that suggested at first sight by the title of this book. After a few observations about this world of violence seen from a human angle, we shall then look at this same world from Christ's point of view. It is not sufficient to participate in the knowledge of the one who knows "what is in man",[21] we must do our best to enter into that movement of love, which can be called either gentle or violent – a love which meets violence face to face and infuses into the world a power which can overcome it. Then, in Part II we shall consider what takes place in the human heart when it is caught up in this movement of redemptive love. We shall then consider what directions our action itself will have to take, and the third part in particular we shall follow the teachings of Gandhi, because it is he who has attempted the boldest and most integrated "experiments with truth", of a truth which consists entirely of love. We shall come across his teachings in the second part too, since he so frequently had a most pure and profound understanding of the meaning of the gospel.[22]

---

[21] Jn 2: 25

[22] Christians are in general badly prepared for this kind of study. Some examples of this lack of interest even on the part of experts can be cited: there is no article on "Enemy" in the *Dictionnaire de la Bible*, neither is there in the Supplement; it simply gives a cross-reference to the article on "War", where an enumeration of the peoples who (according to the bible) were enemies of Israel is given. No less significant is the insufficiency of entries on "enemies" in the *Dictionnaire de*

But are we qualified to turn our attention to and reflect upon such things, when in ourselves we feel so manifestly unfit for action on such a scale? This question has never been out of our minds. The author has often put his pen down, and it is with some sense of shame that he offers this work. He is unfortunately not a man of action, and he is not an expert in any "area of human misery". Only men who have such qualifications, and particularly those whom Fr Lebret calls *"les experts des ensembles"* (sociological experts), and whose rarity he regrets, are qualified to visualize what evangelical gentleness might mean in our present world and prove its possibilities. A book such as this should not be written in ink but with one's blood. We go so far as to ask ourselves whether anyone can truly participate in the Truth of salvation as an existential mystery, who is not able to translate this Truth into practical action, owing to lack of realism and effectiveness in dealing with human situations. If we are incapable of showing, in this world of violence and hatred, that love can produce results, have we any right to talk about it? But each has his own vocation according to the measure of his gifts; we are all being led. The author is the first to be surprised at finding himself dealing with a subject he has not chosen. This book will only be able to present the most modest and pathetically inadequate conclusion, and it will leave us with agonizing perplexities. It will be for others to complete its task. To realists of integrity, that is to those who have realism of the spirit as well as of human affairs, this book will seem both pathetic and decisive: pathetic in comparison with what they will be able to achieve in the world, and decisive if it is this book

---

Théologie Catholique, the *Dictionnaire des connaissances religieuses*, and even in the more recent dictionary *Catholicisme*. There is nothing in *Initiation Théologique*, nor is there an article on "Violence" in the *Dictionnaire de Théologie*.

The love of enemies and Christian gentleness, "non resistance to the wicked", are not normally treated in sermons throughout the year, since these themes are not suggested in the Sunday gospels and epistles, except for the Third Sunday after Epiphany (Rom 12), also Mt 5: 43–8, and the following verses concerned with almsgiving for the Friday after Ash Wednesday. The Beatitudes occur on All Saints, but it is not surprising that they should not be considered specifically from this angle.

that has provoked them to action. They will be the heroes, the wise men, the prophets and the saints. They will give the lie to our fears.

Although lacking the essential and unique fruits of personal experience, the following pages are at least honest in only claiming to examine the deep spiritual truths which must govern any action if it is to be in conformity with evangelical gentleness. We can also inform readers of certain experiments which have been tested, but with which the West has lost touch, though they are the very things that are needed by men of goodwill in implementing the Beatitudes. It may be, therefore, that this book will provide some guidance in making important decisions. This fills us with fear, for if it is to be used in this way, there are men whose whole future will be affected by reading these pages. They are written as a very humble prayer addressed to Him who, unseen, is about our ways and leads us "whither we would not go".[23]

---

[23] Jn 21: 18

CHAPTER ONE

First Thoughts on Violence

IT IS WITH MISGIVINGS THAT WE USE THE term "non-violence". It has the defect of being negative and the added defect of resembling "non-resistance", whereas, as we shall see, Gandhi has conceived and practised non-violence as a most resolute, efficacious form of resistance to evil.[1] The reality we are dealing with will be virtuous only if it is positive. It will only be so to the extent that it is violence, that is negation. Gandhi coined the word "*satyagraha*"; we shall speak later of its richness of meaning. We have the word "gentleness" ("meekness" in the bible) also a rich word, with a long Christian ancestry. But one writes to be understood and the word conveys little today. However, even if we did have positive terms, we would still have to define our subject matter in relation to violence.

Indeed, one has to see why *satyagraha* involves essentially a rejection of violence; why Christian gentleness tends to reabsorb it and substitute itself for it. This is an essential prelude to our main thesis. Is violence an evil in itself? Certain forms of violence seem not only inevitable but intrinsically good; for instance, the Kingdom of Heaven "suffereth violence and the violent bear it

---

[1] In his book *Mahatma Gandhi*, Romain Rolland, oddly enough, speaks of "non-resistance".

away".[2] This should be made clear even before we begin to listen to Jesus' words. The supernatural message presupposes the acquisition of some degree of human wisdom.

VIOLENCE AND THE PERSON

Ancient thinkers used a simple illustration: if a stone is thrown downwards faster than it would travel by its own impetus, or if thrown upwards into the air, it is subject to violence. Violence is thus directly opposed to what is in the *nature* of things.

But let me be more precise. If it is not *natural* for a stone to fly in the air by its own impetus, it is *natural* for a human being to throw it in the air. What is contrary to this particular nature, taking into account simply that limitations of the weight of the stone, fits into a more general and superior order of natural elements. If the stone were aware of this higher order, it might agree to be subjected to this sort of violence. In as much as it is a stone, it would recognize this to be violence, but seeing itself as part of a greater whole, it would accept this as something just and normal. It might even find satisfaction in being caught up in something that transcends its own limited capacities. As a general principle, it can be seen that the harmony of the whole cannot achieve its complexity and richness without a multiplicity of inter-actions which compel things of a lesser nature to be caught up in violent subjection to the higher and more perfect operations of superior beings.

Let us now consider the human order. The natural tendency of man, his urge to become, to accomplish, or surpass himself, we call his *will*.[3] He *suffers violence* in as much as he suffers something

---

[2] Mt 11: 12; Lk 16: 16

[3] This is what the word "will" should mean to us; this is how it was used in the past. It is unfortunate that the word in its present sense usually means the will in its reflective and deliberative aspect. This causes confusion in dealing with any problem of love, and hence all spiritual problems. For instance, we continue to speak of the part of the "will" in the act of faith, but it leads to misunderstandings and resent-ment; why this *diktat* of the will, this having to believe? The whole thing is seen in a quite different light if the will is understood as a spiritual dynamic force; faith is thus demanded by a vital need for self-fulfilment and transcendence.

which is contrary to his will. What he suffers thus is precisely the sort of evil which theologians since St Augustine have called the evil of "pain", in contrast to the evil which is done voluntarily, called "fault" or "sin". But there are such depths in the human will, and it has so many ramifications. It is so full of contradictions, and subject to so many changes and misapprehensions. Given for the same person what is "violence" in certain respects, in others is not.

We become immediately aware then of the bewildering complexity of these things. It is bewildering from the point of view of the person suffering it, but also from that of the established order or disorder inflicting it on that person. One would have to be unbelievably naïve to claim to practise *absolute* non-violence. Where does one fix a limit to blameworthy *violence*?

Independently of any bad intention, violence is inevitable. It is, as we have seen, inescapably bound up in the very nature of things. Any imposition of order involves constraint and sacrifices.[4] Now this imposition is good; it is necessary to all living things. Their ecological environment is proportionate in its complexity and perfection to their own development. It is their participation in the total good of an ordered whole, which ensures their perfection. But the more complex and perfect they become, the more their ordered wholes multiply and intensify these constraints and the more sacrifices they demand. More and more is asked of man. The societies of which he is part: family, country, trade, are constantly exerting "violence" upon him. More or less automatically, any established order penalizes failure to adapt and that means violence. The established orders, at least those of human origin, are in fact always largely "established disorders": forms of violence which it is impossible to escape, prevent or resolve. In most case we suffer under them without knowing where we have failed, what is the flaw in the established order, and above all how it could be reformed without causing even greater evils.

Sometimes the systematized urge for non-violence appears to us

---

[4] We recommend on this subject some fine words in Sertillanges, *Le problème du mal*, vol. 2, p. 44. The work was unfinished at his death but the essential had been done. The entire second volume is undoubtedly the finest thought on this problem which disturbs so many people.

not only as naïve. In certain cases we have grounds to ask ourselves whether it does not imply a more or less conscious resentment against the very things in the order that are good. A friend reading over my shoulder remarks: "Fundamentally, a world from which one would wish to exclude all violence, would be a world without order, incapable of defending itself. It would be a world without laws, without stable reality, without true goodness." If absolute non-violence may involve some unacknowledged revolt against order, it is also our sense of order which spontaneously protests against it. The supporters of non-violence should be clearly aware of this. To lack this sense of order is to compromise the requirements of that very gentleness they are striving to serve.

Disapproval of established order is usually most strongly felt with regard to the punishment of faults. But as Pseudo–Denys remarked "the evil is not in being punished but in deserving punishment".[5] When the punishment inflicted is just, this evil of pain, in the strict sense,[6] is purely and simply a good thing, it is restorative.[7] It achieves "the amendment of the sinner, or at least

---

[5] *De Divinis Nominibus*, Ch. 4, quoted by Aquinas *De Malo*, Qu. 1, art. 5; Ia Pars. qu. 48, art 6.

[6] Pain in the strict sense is *contrary to the will* – afflictive – imposed because of a fault: Ia, IIae, Qu. 46, art. 6, ad. 2. If we extend the term "pain" (*poena*, *peine*) to any evil which is not sin, it is because though this particular pain is not the punishment of a particular sin we have committed personally, it is nevertheless from a Christian point of view a wound resulting from our personal participation in humanity's fallen condition.

[7] The order injured by sin is threefold, hence a threefold sanction: the order of reason which prescribes virtuous actions, to which corresponds remorse of conscience; the social order, hence human punishment; the eternal law, hence punishment coming from God: Ia, IIae, Qu. 87, art. 1 – "The modern mind would want us to believe that the sanction having been applied, the evil of pain (i.e. punishment) is added to the evil of the fault, which involves a double evil. The truth is that good springs from the synthesis of these interrelated evils, namely the good of right order. It is as if to say that gangrene is an evil and the amputation of a limb is an evil; therefore the amputation of a gangrened limb is a double evil. We should not confuse the number of evils with their integration, which changes their kind. . . . The relative evil of punishment appears as a remedy, not precisely of sin, which has no

his repression, public order, the maintenance of justice, the honour of God and of the Church".[8] Thus an unlimited series of observations, reflexions and problems open up before us. True order will often only be re-established by forcing persons or groups of persons by violence, into a right relationship with it. It therefore becomes apparent to us at one and the same time that the distinction between good and bad violence is quite clear in theory, but that its application is extremely baffling. Bad violence appears to us an external act of unjust aggression against a person, even though it is done in the name of law and order. Good violence appears as the means used as a last resort in order to achieve the true good of a person. It can immediately be seen that this question is intimately bound up with the whole philosophy of the human person (and communities of persons).

We can never be absolute on the subject of violence. The greater the difficulty in deciding where the true good of man lies and how it can be obtained without violence, the greater the chance for violence to step in and avert it. The reduction of violence to the *bare minimum* should certainly be a major concern of men who are mindful of the dignity of the human person.

The deep reason for this is that man as a person can only benefit by what he *assimilates* freely. Why is this life given to us? In order that we should build ourselves up from within. What we can only endure without assimilation in accordance with the essential laws of our being, is more than a burden that hinders us, it is an assault upon our integrity, frequently affecting those basic vital impulses which are required for our self-realization.[9]

The faint hope of anyone who feels himself compelled to use violence, because he can see no other way of ensuring some higher

---

remedy outside penance, but of the disorder which would follow from sin, if the retribution of the moral order did not restrain the sinful will", A. G. Sertillanges (*La Philosophie morale de Saint Thomas d'Aquin*, p. 572; *Saint Thomas Aquinas and his Work*, Aquin, 1961).

---

[8] This is how Aquinas justifies the punishment of sin: IIa, IIae, qu. 108, art. 1, ad. 4.

[9] The distinction being made here is between an immanent action which benefits the doer, and a transitive action which terminates in some external operation – violence is of the second type.

good, is that he may elicit a generous and positive reaction from the one who is subjected to its severity and constraint. How likely is this to happen? There is always a great risk of eliciting a wrong reaction.

It is disturbing to see how lightheartedly the majority of people accept and practise violence as something quite "natural", showing no concern at the fact that it is contrary to the nature of those who are at the receiving end. Quite a few priests add their weight in backing this lighthearted attitude with their well-worn dogmatic distinction that violence is not a sin but a pain (punishment). They do not seem to notice that they only aggravate the moral problem instead of solving it, for every pain inflicted here below should be truly "medicinal".[10] There can easily be faults on the part of those who inflict it. A poison can be used as a medicine; it does not thereby cease to be a poison. If it is administered in larger doses than is required for a person's health, that is murder. The evil that punishments can cause if they are applied injudiciously, and the great dignity of the human person which they can harm, are the measure of the extreme care we must take to avoid any excess in this matter.

Fundamentally – and subsequent reflexion will confirm and add precision to this view – the unbelievable levity with which one opts for violence arises from the fact that human beings are not thought of as persons. In extreme cases the view of Hitler is adopted: "I cannot see why man should not be as cruel as nature." But it is precisely man's task to bring nature to perfection by loving care, and to heal the damage that his malice has caused in it.[11]

Is human violence "natural"? Only to the extent that it is

---

[10] A fundamental principle of Church legislation. Still more important in Moral Theology, in countless texts in St Thomas. Thus IIa, IIae, qu. 68, art. 1: remedies for the guilty and others; qu. 108, art. 4: with regard to past sin, or to prevent further sin. In canon law, there is the general principle, which must govern the inflicting of all sentences and their interpretation: *Odiosa sunt restringenda*; see Canons 1124, para. 2, and 2219.

[11] This does not mean that we are partisans of the untenable position of Alexander of Hales, which some of our contemporaries have strangely adopted, attributing the violence of brute creation to man's fall. We

inevitable, and often when this is so it is because man's nature is corrupted and bears the wounds of sin – basic malice, weakness, concupiscence, and want of intelligence[12] – all these make him unable to establish order without using force against people. Human orders and their disorders cannot be purely and simply

---

are simply thinking of the disorders man has caused in the human sphere and in the cosmos.

Far more profound than Alexander's sentimental explanation is the concept of the *innocence* of evil in the physical world, which can not appear scandalous to those who suffer it. This is but an ill-considered anthropomorphic view of things by which we project our way of suffering on to the animal world. Fr Sertillanges considered this question in the book quoted above. This passage from Rilke is illuminating: "Man should once and for all give up appealing to the cruelty of nature in order to excuse his own cruelty. He forgets how far that which is dreadful in nature happens with infinite innocence: (nature) cannot be a spectator of what happens because it cannot stand outside itself – it is completely inside these dreadful happenings as is its generosity and fruitfulness. One might truly say that its dreadfulness is nothing else but the expression of its fruitfulness. At the level of nature, consciousness consists in plenitude, for it contains everything, including what is excessive. But man by definition will never be in a position to embrace everything; he is never certain when he is choosing something terrible – for instance, murder – that he is also including the contrary of this debasement. Thus his choice condemns him instantaneously, making him into an exception, an isolated being, a part sundered from the whole. At the other end of the human scale there is the good man, the man of integrity, who knows how not to separate good from evil, suffering from joy . . . or, if he happens to, is plunged into distress (Claire Lucques, *Le Choix de Rilke*).

---

[12] It is a pity that the traditional teaching on the four wounds is no longer taught in catechetical instruction. The cheapening of words and their distortion are doubtless in part due to this. The deepest "wound" is caused to the will, it is "malice", but the word is not taken seriously enough. We must try to find more suitable words in different contexts to describe its effect: the rooted pride and selfishness of a being who sets himself up and his self-sufficient cause and end, centring everything upon himself, instead of finding his true place in his relationship to the Creator, and to the rest of reality – (*Natura recurva in seipsa* – nature bent back on itself).

treated as necessary combinations of quite innocent "natural" factors. Free wills are involved. Ours too must be brought to bear. This is the work of love. These institutions are so deeply distorted by every kind of disorder, that our love needs to become outstandingly strong and ingenious. Our estimate of the relative rights and obligations of the two elements involved – a just social order and the human person – vary inevitably according to time and place, which again complicates everything. The social order at the time of St Paul included slavery, as we mentioned before; every christian seemed to accept it; but Leo XIII called it: "this ancient shame of pagan nations".[13] In St Thomas's time it was thought quite normal that a son should be punished for the sins of his parents, or a servant for those of his master.[14] Ecclesiastical justice itself, like many other kinds of justice, for a long time made use of torture; today it arouses the indignation of the virtuous, both in theory and practice. Let us not boast too soon about our progress. There certainly has been progress in the theoretical recognition of the rights of the individual. Has there been a corresponding progress in our understanding of the highest personal values, and of the meticulous care that is required in their service? Argue as you will, but we shall no doubt get many surprises on this score at the last judgement.

However this may be, an action is *violent* to the extent that it fails to recognize persons, to the extent that force treats people as

---

([12] contd.) "Concupiscence" still conveys something today, but it is a word that provokes an indulgent smile, or among well-read people, it recalls the learned disputes of theologians, which have had some influence on contemporary literature. "Infirmity", this is clearer, as long as one translates it by "weakness"; *difficultas ad bonum* is clearer still, but how can one express the "wound of ignorance"? One has to describe all the defects in knowing, the blunting (*hebetudo*) of spiritual perception, which can go as far as complete blindness in spiritual matters, and all the disorders which gradually ravage the memory and imagination . . . In fact, this doctrine on the "wounds" is the most lucid and articulated synthesis for an understanding of man's pathetic state. This is possibly why it is so frequently ignored.

---

[13] Encyclical *Libertas Praestantissimum*, June 20, 1888 (Bonne Presse, vol. 2, p. 185).

[14] Ia, IIae, qu. 81, art. 1; qu. 87, art. 8

things; whereas an action impinging on other people is only truly human in as much as it is applied to them as *beings* with a spiritual life.[15] Unfortunately there is a mysterious correspondence between our blind spots and stupidities and those of others. The greater the area of our being that is insensitive to the things of the spirit, the more we will harden others in their insensitiveness. Their violence has the effect of hardening us. Of itself it never corrects us, it only makes things worse; if finally we accept it and derive some benefit from it, it will only be because it has fortunately acted as a spur to our love.

In truth violence in its worst forms is within our heart. If it thrives among men, it is because these unhappy people are at war with themselves.

LET US NOT BE NAÏVE

"Violence, usually in a cruel form, is the mainspring of history," says Paul Ricœur.[16]

To face this truth squarely is a necessary prerequisite of any effective non-violent action. Up till now, this is true: it seems that apart from the early expansion of Christianity and the liberation of India, nothing has had a notable effect upon the course of history without the coercion of violence.

Let us not take refuge in a false eschatological outlook by refusing to face the lessons of history. It is by changing its course according to God's intention that we shall work out our own salvation and that of others.

"By failing to look at the vast scale of violence in history," writes Ricœur,[17] "pacifism comes to be looked upon as easy, it

---

[15] Cf. the admirable lines of Jacques Maritain on the mystery of subjectivity in his *Court traité de l'existence et de l'existant*, where he shows what it is "to love one's neighbour *as oneself*". We do not love ourselves as *things* placed before us but as the subjects from which our love flows out. To love our neighbour is to apprehend him from within, as it were, so that he becomes an *"alter ego"*.

[16] *Esprit*, Feb., 1949
[17] ibid.

becomes facile. It is considered as belonging in the world, as springing from man's natural goodness, and as being simply obscured and prevented by a few wicked men. It is not seen as something difficult, something that has the whole weight of history against it, that can only come from somewhere else, that calls on history to show what is not normally read as history."

Eric Weil sees violence, passion and evil as identical. He does not recognize any motive of action apart from self-interest.[18] In order "to make the individual see beyond himself and his own desires by a negation of his own interests" he can see no other means than war.[19] A will for peace can only arise out of war and fighting.[20] "On the plane of reality and achievement, good has no power, all power is on the side of evil. If good has to be achieved, it can only be achieved by means of evil."[21]

This extremist view seems to proceed from an implicit manicheism. But perhaps Weil is only claiming to observe what happens *most frequently* in history. That we may not give way to despair it is enough to note that even passion is not in itself evil, that love can also be a spur to action, which thank God is evident. Mercy, justice and the other virtues do sometimes lead the individual to look beyond his own interests, and these can even inspire whole nations for the tasks of peace. Starting points are therefore available for actions devoid of cruel violence. "In history, it is not only violence that gives rise to rational behaviour."[22] But within what terrible darkness a ray of divine light has to penetrate . . .

Is it not true then that any profound insight into our human condition gives us grounds for despair in the very things that should give us hope? But inversely, can we not find hope in the very things that overwhelm us? Reread the admirable ending of the *Twelfth Provinciale*:

The war that violence wages against truth is a strange and long one. All the efforts of violence cannot weaken the truth; they

[18] *Philosophie Politique*, (Vrin, 1956) p. 45
[19] ibid., pp. 231 and 232
[20] ibid., p. 233
[21] ibid., p. 45
[22] Phrase used by Jean Lacroix in reviewing Eric Weil's book, *Le Monde*, Nov. 13, 1956.

only help to bring it into relief. All the power of truth can do nothing to prevent violence, it only aggravates it. . . . Violence and truth are powerless against one another. Does this mean that, here below, war against unjust violence cannot be victorious? Such a war in this world would be fatal to truth, for if the forces of the spirit can do nothing against the forces of brutality, these latter have their revenge against the bodies in which the spirit of truth is enshrined. In fact, disaster is possible, and we can only be certain of an invisible victory. But at least we are assured of the outcome of our history. It is even now fulfilled in the person of the glorified Christ. Now it is here below that the battle is decided, it is for us to enter the lists, so that some light from the victory of Christ may reward us. It is because of this victory that the last words of Pascal are not just empty rhetoric: "Violence has only a limited span in the plan of God, for He directs its results to the glory of the truth it assails, since truth subsists eternally and triumphs over its enemies, because it is as mighty and eternal as God himself."

The temptation to use violence is too great. The meek themselves hardly dare to believe that they are in the right against the evidence of history. The "realists", big and small Machiavellis, run the world, and all of us under their leadership, overwhelmed by our own conflicting ideas, unable to match up to our destinies, and urged on by our growing needs, add to the ruins; we build upon ruins what will in its turn fall down in ruins. We must act quickly, and hasty work means violence. Few men manage to gain a foothold on firm ground and build solidly: it requires so much more time. It will be lucky if we do not bury them also under our ruins. But if they do manage to build, it will stand firm; it will last indefinitely. Provided that the superficial, hasty and proud men who come after them do not claim to carry on their work with our methods.

Time is running out. One must overcome these difficulties at once, otherwise . . . Subsequent difficulties will assuredly be greater, but there will be time to deal with them . . . An even more violent blow will get rid of them. Then, the ground being completely swept clean, we shall surely no longer need to have recourse to violence? No, this is not the way. If we take this line, we shall go on generating violence or regretfully condoning it.

In the tragic history of mankind it seems that the energy used in destruction never disappears. If you put violence into anything that you do, an equal or greater amount of violence will be found in its outcome.[23] Sooner or later by various devious ways it will attack whatever has been erected with its help. It really does seem as if violence emits evil influences into the world which the winds shift here and there without dissipating them, like radioactive particles which continue to do their deadly work, or like pro-liferating viruses . . . Only the gentle do work that has no evil outcome. But violence and hatred have such a hold on the world, that those who have the gospel at heart will have to make unwonted efforts of mind and heart in order to overcome them. Neither the naïve optimist, who is unaware of the virulence of violent instincts, nor the pessimist, who ignores the capacity of man to reach beyond himself, are capable of thinking or behaving in a manner which is worthy of man.

It is said that violence works. True, but what does it achieve? Where does it lead you? What, in your opinion, is the destiny of man? If you are not a materialist, can you resign yourself to a

---

[23] "They sow the wind and reap the whirlwind" (Hos 8: 7). "Sow for yourselves righteousness, reap the fruit of steadfast love" (Hos 10: 12). "You have ploughed iniquity, you have reaped injustice, you have eaten the fruit of lies. Because you have trusted in your chariots, in the multitude of your warriors, therefore the tumult of war shall arise among your people and all your fortresses shall be destroyed" (Hos 10: 13–14). "Peoples labour only for fire and nations weary themselves for nought" (Hab 2: 13; cf. Jer 51: 58). "As I have seen, those who plough iniquity and sow trouble reap the same" (Job 4: 8). (It is true that these are the words of Eliphaz who has an over-simplified conception of immanent justice and reward for good and evil here below; as against him Job is right. But he is right in saying that experience here speaks through him, and St Paul later takes over his words (I Cor 3: 19, which parallels Job 5: 12–13). "Do not be deceived; God is not mocked, for whatever a man sows, that he will also reap. For he who sows to his own flesh will from the flesh reap corruption; but he who sows to the Spirit will from the Spirit reap eternal life. And let us not grow weary in welldoing for in due season we shall reap if we do not lose heart" (Cf. Prov. 12: 14; 22: 28; Gal 6: 7–9).

solution of despair: that men simply cancel out one another by erecting and knocking down each other's works, that they behave like the "elements of this world",[24] at the risk of losing their souls? Are men but the playthings of the elements? At best, their intentions and efforts (paradoxically) attribute the virtue of the Beatitudes to what is essentially evil. Let us rather strive to insert into this fatal pattern as many purely good works as possible, not done under the promptings of the devil. A lot of smoke for very little fire and for a fire smouldering under a pile of corruption. You are looking for results? Violence effectively smothers and stifles, and leads nowhere.

WHEN PERSONS ARE SEEN AS THINGS

We have shown precisely where we must look in order to see the evil of violence and its consequences in true perspective; it is just there, too, that love and the power of truth must be made effective. Violence gets hold of people against their own inclination; it often forces them to act in a way they would not freely choose and *to this extent it destroys them as persons*. It treats them as things; it mocks at love, which belongs to persons and is due to them. If it destroys the other as a person, it is because it proceeds from the "death wish", to which we shall refer later. This is frequently evident in the callous utterances of the violent who show that to them the other person is something in his way.

Anyone whose dignity as a person has been injured is faced with two alternatives, either to accept the indignity or to revolt against it. His sense of exasperation incites him to an even greater violence, indeed to boundless violence. For see what this means: human personality has a capacity for the infinite; since he is beyond value, if he is belittled or scorned the outrage is felt to be beyond measure. This, no doubt, is why reprisals go beyond all bounds. One is caught up in an ever-widening vicious circle.

It is rare for an injured person not to fall back on the law of retaliation. In the Mosaic law a limit is set to it; we do not even live up to this. Primitive man, who exists within each one of us, is ready to burst out into Lamech's savage song: "I have slain a man

---

[24] Col 2: 20

to the wounding of myself and a stripling to my own bruising."[25]
Violence is no remedy for real evils. All it may achieve is a state
of affairs in which it is possible to start applying remedies and
improvements, but these will only be humane if they are applied in
conditions of personal freedom. A reckless child who darts out
into a busy thoroughfare has to be snatched back on to the pave-
ment. He is picked up like a parcel. *Everything still needs to be
done* in order to teach him to be reasonable. Therein lies the whole
difference between training and education. For the necessary
violence to which he was subjected on this occasion and many
others threatens to make him more difficult to deal with; every
educator should be aware of this risk. Violence can make inroads
into a child's character, cause traumatic wounds, and put him
obstinately on the defensive. War or revolution never lead to
peace in itself, but to a state in which it may be possible to work for
peace, and to achieve this only peaceful means are of any use.
These are often likely to be compromised by the injustices of a
so-called "peace", so that the settlement of a violent conflict is
in fact nothing more than established violence.[26]

Violence, because it often aggravates the very evil against which
it is directed, produces resentments which work havoc in personality. These may perhaps be so dangerous that the violence may
even be a lesser evil. Who knows?[27] Since it is contradictory in its
own nature, violence can only lead to contradictions.

It degrades anyone who uses it, for it is indeed a degradation
to injure the dignity of the person attacked. In treating him as a
thing, one finally forgets he is a man. Evidence is not lacking on
this score. To what depths of insensitiveness and hardness it can

---

[25] Gen 4: 23

[26] Pius XII said in his first Encyclical, *Summi Pontificatus*, 1939,
"the provisional condition created as a result of war has no right to be
called peace. . . . Peace cannot come by the sword".

[27] *Who knows?* For it is wrong to imagine that an outburst of violence
is simply a "letting-off of steam" and that this is beneficial. The
conception of "accumulated charges in the subconscious" is valuable
in some ways but we must not be misled by it. We are apt to think
that once the "charge" has been "exploded", the air is cleared and all
is well. But it is an oversimplification to reduce the life of the spirit to
the behaviour of accumulations of matter.

reduce even the best people. They allow themselves to slip into the very ways they condemn in their own enemies and are imperceptibly won over to the very mentality they are out to fight against.

"There are not two races of people," wrote Lanza del Vasto, "the good and the bad. A man is good or bad according to what he does. If I oppose the wicked by doing what he does, I become like him, and the counter-evil I so smugly carry out is a redoubling of that evil and it is thereby an even greater evil."[28]

To these "chain reactions"[29] of violence leading to more violence along the same lines can be added compensatory reactions in other directions; and these are regressive. For instance, the tyranny of modern state control generates a lack of civic responsibility; the excesses of scientific abstractions and technique[30] provoke outbreaks of brute force and sensuality; the arbitrary nature of international organizations which overlook national characteristics exacerbate nationalistic feelings. Assuredly one can, one must, say that these distressing effects are not absolutely inevitable. Of course, since violence, as we must always remember, is not in itself a moral evil, it can even be good. One can at least in principle take care that the violent rejoinder does not go further than the attack. Even the hardening of the aggressor is not fatal. It is not necessarily impossible that a victory obtained through violence can be so used that peace worthy of the name may be worked out. . . . This is obvious. But can we at this stage alter the normal course of events? The present trend is such that the very suggestion of a favourable outcome may seem ironical. These "chain reactions" are such that we cannot hope to have the slightest effect on their trend and evil consequences, but only by a radical alteration of their root causes.

For the "realist" what is "natural" cannot be overcome, for he treats as fixed, limits that in fact the nature of man should constantly be trying to extend – a point made by Aldous Huxley, with characteristic humour:

---

[28] *Vinôbâ*, p. 78
[29] Cardinal Feltin, *Congrès de Pax Christi* (1955) p. 75
[30] See page references to "abstraction" and "technique" in the Index for clarification of what may seem obscure about these words.

To murder one's unfaithful wife, or the lover of one's sister or mother, was something that used to be "done". Being socially correct, it was regarded as inevitable, a manifestation of unchanging "human nature". Such murders are no longer fashionable among the best people, therefore no longer seem to us "natural". The malleability of human nature is such that there is no reason why, if we so desire and set to work in the right way, we should not rid ourselves of war as we have freed ourselves from the weary necessity of committing a *crime passionnel* every time a wife, mistress or female relative gets herself seduced.[31]

A soldier who has fought and killed may be tormented by the thought: "Perhaps he had a wife and children. He was a man like me." He drives away these thoughts. His duty would be intolerable if he had to live with them; to do his job he must dismiss them as unreal. "War is only possible," said Berdyaev, "in as much as men become things."[32]

Men have been made into instruments of fate. This is something which is conveniently forgotten by logic-chopping thinkers, who go on reiterating the commandment "Thou shalt not kill" to bemused soldiers. Even a misguided conscience commands, and we must realize what this implies where it is subject to a régime of violence systematized in institutions stronger than man's nature. Men simply become their instruments. The men one fights then appear no longer as men but as deadly forces bent on destroying all we love and all who love us. This is how the combatants look at things; it is their moral outlook and is so compulsive that one cannot really accuse them of murder. One has therefore to be careful not to trifle with their consciences, because the duty of defending what is being attacked is so great.

But in fact those terrible agents of destruction against which one wants to defend oneself by obliterating them, are simply men, and basically nothing could be more odious and shameful than to reduce men to this state. The obligation to reform the general moral outlook by enlightening men's consciences so that wars can no longer break out is surely far more urgent than the obligation of

---

[31] *Ends and Means*, pp. 93–4 (Chatto & Windus, 1957)
[32] *Freedom of the Spirit*, London, 1935

defence, urgent as that, unfortunately, may often seem to be. At present defence must have the first call on our resources.[33] The main obligation should however always be present and active, and not become a mere dead letter. It forbids the use of means which the common consent of mankind considers to be inhuman; but it needs to go much further than this, to inspire men to give themselves totally to the ideal of working effectively for peace. This cause also needs its heroes and martyrs.

"One must dare to face dreadful truths." This was a favourite saying of Fr M. A. Couturier.[34] There are however two types of people who had better not follow this general rule: the faint-hearted, and certain generous souls. The faint-hearted can only live by cherishing their hopes, but sometimes the only hopes are cruel ones for they will prove deceptive. How many of us would find it difficult to go on living without them! There are, on the other hand, certain generous natures of great simplicity, for whom the consideration of the dark side of reality is without profit; it only discourages them and reduces them to impotence. We therefore hesitate to invite our readers to consider truths far more disturbing today than they have ever been in the past.

Yet do it we must. There will not be lacking facile optimists to bolster up the hopes of the weak with promises of changes for the better, and to persuade them that the clear-sighted are not seeing straight. The cry of "Peace, peace" is all the more welcome when peace is non-existent.[35] As for the generous souls who need to concentrate their whole energies in single-minded pursuit, they will not be disturbed for long, and will soon regain their equanimity. Only the truth can make us free.[36] Really earnest minds find a deep satisfaction in facing disturbing truths; they do not want to be told that it is easy to be a Christian, or to be truly human. This is the real inspiration that lies behind this book.

Why should we waste our time listening to the groans of our

---

[33] In all his teaching on the subject of peace, Pius XII reminded us of the right of legitimate defence.

[34] M. A. Couturier – a well-known French Dominican, who did much for the cause of religious art in France – (*Tr.*).

[35] Jer 6: 14; 8: 11

[36] Jn 8: 32

contemporaries who keep sighing "It is difficult"? By this they mean: it is too difficult, therefore I am not going to try. For "it is difficult" should be an invitation to clearer and more serious thought. The problems of the world are so great that in the last resort we can but fall back on the words of William the Silent: "It is not necessary to hope in order to act, or to succeed in order to persevere." Meanwhile let us at least face up to the hard facts of man's present condition.

It is difficult to be simply "a man". The nature of man requires that he should transcend himself, for as a spiritual being no limit is set to what he can become. "With the help of grace he can become god-like."[37] However, his nature is also less than itself; it is wounded. It will only become completely whole in heaven, but it is not sufficient to say this in general terms; one has to put one's finger upon the wounds and sort out the inner conflicts that tear man asunder. In order to discuss the deep causes of violence it is necessary to uncover a fundamental flaw in man's nature. We shall indicate three of its characteristics: the first is psychological, the second is intellectual and the third is related to love.

AGGRESSION CORRUPTED INTO A DEATH WISH

Our psychic energy needs to overcome what is hard.[38] It belongs to man's rational nature to recognize its character and to give it a moral value, in other words to turn it into *a virtue*.[39] Man's high

---

[37] This is a well-known expression of the Fathers of the Orthodox Church, signifying the transformation of human nature and its elevation to supernatural life through grace. It is sanctioned by II Pet 1: 4, *consortes divinae naturae.*

[38] There would seem to be some similarity between the teaching of Aristotle and Aquinas on irascibility and psychological theories on aggression. The approach is different but the reality the same. Cf. A. Plé, "St Thomas d'Aquin et la Psychologie des Profondeurs", *Supp. de la Vie Spirituelle*, No. 19, p. 415. Philippe de la Trinité, *Amour et Violence*, Etudes Carmélitaines, pp. 84–9 (where we find this felicitous definition, "aggression is the conquering aspect of love").

[39] *Virtus* means "strength" in Latin

and difficult destiny requires that he should have great strength (virtue). But now it has more or less taken the form of a "death wish" – sad, but it is a fact. Nothing could give clearer proof of the fallen state of our nature.

Reread the famous texts in which Freud puts forward his disturbing discovery. Even if the inspired philosopher exaggerates a bit – carried away, it would seem, by a kind of perverse joy, which is aroused in him by the very evil he denounces – the reality he perceived is now beyond doubt. "In our unconscious we daily and hourly suppress all who stand in our way, all who have offended or injured us."[40]

Let us insist on the word "unconscious", which is going to crop up again. The persons concerned would be very genuinely surprised if they were told that they "willed the death" of their adversaries, or simply of those who stood in their way. As far as their conscious will is concerned, they may very generously want to do them good. The unconscious wish is at odds with their deliberate will. The whole of their consciously developed personality is revolted by such desires and will not even admit their existence. Freud continues: "The expression 'Devil take him', which so frequently comes to our lips in joking anger, and which really means 'Death take him' is, in our unconscious, an earnest, deliberate death-wish." A striking resemblance to the warning of St John, "He who hates his brother is a murderer".[41]

Our unconscious – Freud writes – will murder even for trifles; like the ancient Athenian law of Draco, it knows no other punishment for crime than death; and this has a certain consistency, for every injury to our almighty and autocratic Ego is at bottom a crime of *lèse-majesté*. And so if we are judged by the wishes in our unconscious, we are, like primitive man, simply a gang of murderers. It is well that all these wishes do not possess the potency which was attributed to them by primitive men; in the cross-fire of mutual maledictions mankind would long since have perished.

---

[40] Freud, *Collected Papers*, vol. IV, p. 314 (Hogarth Press, 1925)
[41] I Jn 3: 15; and Paul: "To set the mind on the flesh is death" (Rom 8: 6) translated by C. Spicq as "the flesh is set on death".

We hope there is no one left in this second half of the twentieth century to object: "What does it matter? Even if things are as you say, they are but involuntary manifestations for which we are not responsible, and which are therefore without moral or spiritual significance." No one can ignore these upsurges from the hidden springs of their being. The disguising and covering up of these death-wishes, which are frequently accompanied by real heroism so that we deck them with mantles of glory, only renders them more vicious. You, Paul, my friend, who set yourself up as a righter of wrong, I warn you that your unconscious desire is simply to harm the unjust (or those you believe so); watch yourself. Unless you take care not to do anything, say anything, or even think anything which is not inspired by a real love of the one you are setting out to correct, we may well have misgivings about the integrity of your fine passion for justice. And you, Andrew, watch your self-righteous indignation; does not its very violence give grounds for suspicion? And as for you, dear sir (or Reverend Mother or Reverend Father), the satisfaction you derive in inflicting humiliations for the amendment of those who are in your care . . .[42] The world offers us the spectacle of a colossal expenditure of energy, where men excel when they are called upon to kill or destroy, but for constructive work they hang back and drag their feet in apathy . . .

Bad violence is not only connected with what is worst in man, but with what is best. One has to have the courage to face this fact. This is a "dreadful truth". One sometimes wonders whether in order to attain some degree of virtue, the best of men do not need to have recourse to partly or even wholly impure forms of violence. In order to build worthily for life, is it not necessary to pay this ransom to death, to accept the sinister law of violence? Is this not an inescapable law of our fallen nature? A dreadful truth indeed, if it is true. But the connection – though indubitable – is perhaps not so close that it is impossible to be both pure and heroic.

---

[42] "Humiliation," says André Gide, "causes a wound which is very difficult to heal. Humility opens the gates of heaven, humiliation those of hell." Certain humiliations can of course be salutary, but what single-mindedness, what psychological awareness, and what true love are required on the part of those who inflict them!

To what extent is death at the heart of life? *Media vita in morte sumus.*[43] There is no simple answer to this tormenting question. We can neither close our eyes to the value of the human actions which give rise to it, nor accept a state of affairs whose disorders we have, with the grace of God, a responsibility to put right. The negative side of this fine human task is to help us to escape from these fatalities, to do our utmost to overcome as far as possible our "disgraceful" situation. This is precisely where the difficulty lies: our instincts to fight, to overcome, have to be vitally spontaneous in order to spur us on to surpass ourselves; but in their spontaneous state they are always more or less contaminated with cruelty. The perfect integration of a St Francis or a Gandhi is a very rare thing indeed. Gentleness does not come easily, that is true gentleness which permeates the whole of our vital strength in such a way that it purifies it of all malice without diminishing any of its intensity. In fact the plenitude of this gentleness was only found in its *perfect* form in Christ and his immaculate mother. It will be necessary for us to rid ourselves of the old leaven by the grace of the risen Christ.[44] How real and active this potent leaven is that it may permeate our being! Grace cannot substitute itself for our nature: it will work, and use the good elements, "the antibodies" so to speak, it finds within us. It does not act without our cooperation in this process. Such a purification requires the discipline favourable to its development.

We are now considering how urgently this purification is required, and what depths it has to reach. It should be a commonplace to us, as it was to Aquinas (and earlier to Aristotle) that *we judge things according to what we are*. It is easier for us to flatter ourselves that we have a sound judgement because we have right principles and reason correctly. But we can make the most sound judgements about right or wrong in theory, either with regard to human justice, or in the light of divine law, and apply these in a most wrong-headed way to particular cases. To appreciate these cases in all their surprising complexity and uniqueness requires

---

[43] From the Lenten liturgy. This made Thomas Aquinas weep "In the midst of life we are in death". Superficially it means that from maturity on, man feels himself approaching death: that it is already near him. But the deeper significance of the text is as we have indicated.

[44] Cf. I Cor 5: 7–8

our perfect conformity with what is good, the correction of all those tendencies which might prejudice us.

To add to our perplexities, we must remember that our corrupt aggression can turn against ourselves rather than against others, so that we have the illusion of overcoming it because we give way to them. The victims of this evil – which is so apparent today, and takes so many forms – lower themselves and work their own downfall. Many who believe themselves to be gentle, pacific, "non-violent", may in fact simply be instinctive abdicators.

It is not only what is thought and felt which is significant, but still more how it is felt and thought. There are too many pacifists who are virulent in their aggression for the cause of peace.

We cannot be too attentive to the warnings of psychologists who are suspicious of systematically "non-violent" behaviour, because they know of the serious damage done by repressed aggression;[45] aggression must be used. Repressed in one direction, it explodes in another, or takes refuge in hypocrisy. The ideal solution, what is well known as "sublimation", cannot just be obtained at will. It is an unconscious process which we must not confuse with noble intentions which never really get to grips with the depths of our being. Dr Eck goes so far as to say: "Only the strong can afford to be non-violent."[46] Taken out of its context, it can be misleading. It seems to suggest that the weak are condemned to be violent. In fact they must be warned not to mistake for gentleness what *might* in fact be the residue of aggression inhibited by long-standing suppression. When it is pushed back and blocked, aggression takes hold of a person; he is enslaved by bitterness, and unacknowledged resentments and by a fear, which more than any other vice, disqualifies him from truly non-violent action. This action presupposes "a reserve of instinctive vitality which gives a person moral ascendancy" (Dr Eck). It does not follow that gentleness is impossible for the weak. What is denied to them is any really ambitious task: whatever form it may take,

[45] See for instance Freud's *Why War?* in *Correspondence of the Institute of Intellectual Co-operation*, No. 3, 1934 and Dr Eck in *Conférences de Pax Christi* (1953).

[46] Op. cit., pp. 90–91

it will have to be on a small scale, in so far as it depends upon them. That is what psychologists warn us about.

Whether the psychological potential is great or small, it is a question of working towards excellent objectives, which will provoke a vital interest. In this kind of activity our power of loving is aroused, while our aggression is also implicated. One of the secrets of mental health, inner harmony and effective action is that our love should be directed towards the same object as our aggression. It then penetrates into and purifies it of its "death-wish". The love of God and our neighbour has to play a decisive part in this reformation. But for this it has to become so vitally sincere that it is conformable to the supernatural life of grace. It is imperative that the highest form of charity and our psychological eros should be fused into one love.[47]

It must of course be understood that what we have just said cannot be achieved by a mere act of will, either as an end, or as a means. It is an ultimate effect, a state of completion, the deepest result of sanctity. We shall be tending towards it if we strive to put the best of ourselves in our actions and to open our hearts continually to a fullness of love, to take the gospels as our constant guide. To use an expression of a contemporary spiritual writer: there is a virtue of "assumption" which gathers all the divergent currents of our poor nature into its own stream.[48]

We must seek for nothing less than this, to reabsorb the "death-wish" which is almost natural to us; this is what the healing power of love must strive to achieve in our inner life. Nothing will make us see more clearly the depths of man's enmity for man, and the

---

[47] We can only touch on one of the points where depth psychology in its own way agrees in a striking fashion with true Christian thought. The Lutheran theologian Nygren understood the Agape of the New Testament as completely detached from desire, from even spiritual concupiscence, from any kind of Eros. The tremendous interest aroused by his thesis brought about a more vivid awareness of the essential incorporation of Eros in Agape according to both the New Testament and Catholic tradition. (We refer here only to indications in Mouroux, *La Vie Intellectuelle*, vol. 14, 1946, pp. 28–38 and J. Daniélou, *Platonisme et Théologie mystique*, pp. 212 ff.)

[48] *La Vie Spirituelle* (Feb. 1956), pp. 146–7

corresponding need for an equally powerful love which combines
gentleness with a sanctified violence.

WARPED ATTITUDES

Our failings affect our powers of knowledge. It is almost impossible
for us not to do violence to reality in the act of knowing it. The
action which results from our distorted judgements does violence
to all living things. "The divine mind," writes Mgr V. Ghika,[49] "is
the only one which does not take away anything from objects in
order to know them." Hence when the knowledge of created minds
is correct they do damage neither to things nor to themselves. All
they have to do is humbly recognize the limits within which they
can reach the truth. However, it is difficult for the mind, made in
the image of God, not to play at being God. We must not be surprised at the downfall of so many innocent spirits.

The infirmity of the mind bound to a body should induce in it
a more circumspect modesty than that of the angels. Our act of
knowing cannot be, as with the angels, a perfectly simple matter
in which we are totally involved. We have to elaborate the concepts
which we abstract from sense perceptions. There is no harm in
this either, as long as we realize how easy it is for us to distort
reality in our act of knowledge.[50] We think correctly as long as we
keep alive in us, as we judge and reason, a sense of the living and
rich reality out of which we are constructing our own conceptual
patterns.[51] We are alas constantly in danger of reducing reality to
the ideas we have about it, and we then proceed to falsify the ideas

---

[49] Quoted by Jean Daujat in *Monseigneur Ghika*, p. 23

[50] Somewhere a psychiatrist or psychoanalyst says that "reason is
essentially sadistic". Surely he is wrong if he is referring to rational
thought. We ought to do our utmost to raise it in the estimation of our
contemporaries who tend to mistrust it (see the Encyclical *Humani
Generis*). But the higher we esteem the genuine working of intelligence
the more we recognize its rarity and how fatal its misuse is. The view
we have quoted above seems to indicate very definitely an *abuse* of it.
Of course the end of the paragraph must be understood as referring to
pseudo thought.

[51] To do this we must constantly refer back to our sense-impressions
("conversio ad phantasmata") Ia Pars, qu. 84, art. 7.

themselves. We are constantly careless in giving serious thought to what we say; our reflexion is constantly defective. We seek escape in words which run away with us. How rarely one comes across real thinking, one in which intelligence is truly present. And how often we lose the meaning of what we once saw clearly. So we patch up, we build systems, "a theory out of bits of ignorance", as Stendhal put it. If we look closely, what often passes for thought is most frequently a gap covered up by a lot of pretences.

Now it is generally the emotions that suggest these pretences. The dulling of perception and the loss of control of the mind over itself leaves a vacuum which is filled up by instinctual urges. As one has no longer any serious grasp of what one is talking about, one accommodates the truth and gives the emotions free rein in conversation. They then take control of behaviour.

This evil is made worse by the appalling increase of modern images and superficial slogans. Everything around us conspires to dissipate our minds in half-truths. Not so long ago, the majority of men knew very few things, but they were all *real*, objectively as well as subjectively; men had an immediate and comprehensive experience of what they knew; their knowledge had come at first hand; they assimilated it and quite naturally adapted their behaviour to it. Thus they were wise in their knowledge; it had a spiritual quality. They "kept things in their hearts". Moral awareness went hand in hand with knowledge. Our mind, by contrast, is just like a sheet of paper that only retains the news of the last fortnight, to use an image of Charles Péguy. A flood of information which has not been assimilated by personal thinking does violence to the mind, by stupefying and blinding it. It has no longer any certainty to speak of, it makes an arbitrary choice among various opinions. A Marxist naturally says: "When one has accepted the primacy of economic development, psychological and spiritual explanations of the world just fade away." This acceptance produces results but it ruthlessly cuts out a whole area of life.

Let us be watchful, or everything will fall into the mould of "organization man" who is so typical of the modern world. Everything, even religion, is reduced to dry formulae, to what can be explained and docketed. Everything suffers violence and does violence to the real, often beginning with any true spirit who cherishes "non-violence". Anyone who is in the slightest degree acquainted with pacifist literature will have read passages like this one: "We recognize no human authority. We only accept one king and ruler (God, conscience or what have you). We love every country as much as our own. A nation has no right to defend itself against its enemies." Abstractions like this do great harm to essential and vital realities.

Meanwhile qualified specialists, technicians, technocrats, using rigorous methods, arrive at conclusions which are perfectly objective within their own frameworks; but they reduce reality to the measurable. There can of course be no objection to measuring the measurable. Needless to say man, being subject to time and space, to the "elements of this world" and all they involve, is the subject-matter of the statistician, chemist, physicist and economist . . . Their work is of course necessary. Equally, of course, economic, social and political techniques are going to benefit greatly from it. But then, as one thing leads to another, with astonishing speed and on a huge scale, the combination of these technical means turns into an autonomous universe, developing along its own lines, and substituting itself for nature and man.

The primitive techniques were simply "intermediaries between man and his environment",[52] through which man could exercise some mastery over that environment. In this way he worked for particular ends, and only used such means as were required for life and to adorn it.[53] Today he has lost his mastery over his techniques, they no longer provide him with any goal or purpose, he can no longer tell why he strives for progress along all the lines of possible development. It has become a combination of factors which of themselves bring forth further results. Discoveries and inventions thus indefinitely give rise to one another. Man has become the slave of a process which unfolds itself as a deterministic system governed by sheer efficiency, but with no end in view.[54] Within this metaphysical misuse lies a radical and essential violence which results ineluctably in indefinite chains of violence. When one

---

[52] J. Ellul, *La technique, ou l'enjeu du siècle* (A. Colin, 1954), p. 58
[53] ibid., pp. 60 ff.
[54] ibid., pp. 90-91. All technical progress has an end, but it is simply an immediate one with no ultimate end in view such as is worthy of man.

examines the processes which led up to the dropping of the first atomic bomb on Hiroshima, one sees men being led step by step, so that one cannot decide the precise moment when one of those responsible for it made a decisive act, or even who was responsible. Men have been caught out at their own game and have alienated themselves. "They are all being driven by external forces to an external end: the object to be attained, the movement towards it."[55] Where does it lead to? When must one make a stand? How can one withdraw? This is the crux; the setting in motion of certain causes inevitably begetting others sometimes leads so clearly to such excesses that modern man must prepare himself at some point to make this stand, just as the martyrs of the early centuries had to be prepared for martyrdom. There must be downright refusals, no more talk. One has to oppose evil, even if one cannot prevent it; the time will come when one will have to choose to be a victim rather than an accomplice. This preparation entails taking care that our consciences do not, meanwhile, become blunted. We cannot hope to build an ark which will sail through the waters of perdition. There is more than a mere atmosphere that needs rejection in our technical world. But let us not take refuge in a foolish optimism which can only be a form of voluntary blindness. We need to be constantly on our guard against the seductive illusion that a distinction can be made between our techniques and the use we make of them; indulging in such daydreams as "that man will direct his discoveries in the service of good and not of evil . . . that he will produce health-giving drugs and not lethal gases, atomic energy and no more atomic bombs, commercial airliners instead of fighter planes", etc.[56]

There is not much that man can now direct. What we must face boldly is this *almost indivisible* combination of the features of modern technology which powerfully limits the possibility of re-orientation, and which Ellul describes as "automation of technical choice, auto-accretion, indivisibility", this latter term signifying that one cannot accept certain techniques and reject others for moral reasons for instance: they are all necessary to each other, "a linking up of techniques, a universalism". Let us face

[55] ibid., p. 389
[56] op. cit., pp. 89–90; (with some reservations however)

it: it means the progressive extension of this process over the whole world so that it includes all human activities, even those of the mind – in short "autonomy" covering economics and politics, social conditions and morality.[57]

"Only a technical power can stand up to another technical power: the rest has been thrown overboard."[58] They oppose one another in the same manner as the blind forces of nature. As Malraux puts it, we are faced with "a reawakening of blind fate". The "thinking reed" has always been the plaything of storms. But it is he himself who has unleashed these. He recognizes in them, on a vastly magnified scale, the results of his own pretensions at spiritual mastery, while so much of his spiritual potentiality escapes him. The worst thing about it is that these blind forces are not merely content with enslaving and crushing him in their mad destructive progress, they require his collaboration; they exert their influence even upon the conditions of his inner freedom (through psychological techniques), and the time may come when he will no longer be able to see his way to exercise any free activity within it.

THE INJURY TO LOVE

The deepest flaw in us is one that turns aside love.

The tarnishing of all our loving by selfishness is the most radical form of violence, from which all others follow. We are made for God, in communion with our brothers. Our movement towards him and them should be as natural to us as the force of gravity. The state of *sin* properly so called is, in its actual culpability, a perversion of nature. The true and lawful love of self which should find its completion in overflowing into the love of God and others turns back upon itself in that "self-love carried to the point of contempt for God", which St Augustine sees at work in building the city of the devil on earth: "I and there is none beside me", the cry of the great city of Assyria according to the prophet Zephaniah.[59] When sin is forgiven and divine grace is restored to the soul,

---

[57] ibid., pp. 75 to 134
[58] ibid., p. 79
[59] Zeph 2: 15

it nevertheless leaves its wounds. Christian conscience has always realized that the wound left by malice, consisting in a fatal propensity to consider self as the beginning and end of everything, is at the root of all evils that spring up in man's knowing and loving. The urge towards God and a right harmony with his other children are so much the law of our very being that their rupture or diversion has sinister repercussions on all our powers.

Antagonism towards our brothers in God is an aspect of evil that must particularly claim our attention. Why is it that when our love goes out to someone this nearly always involves some sort of dislike of others and frequently their total rejection and hatred? This is not of the nature of true and legitimate love. Because Peter backs one side, he hates the others. Because John loves his country, he sees other countries as the enemy. These are but extensions of selfishness even into the love of others, in which the inner conflicts resulting from self-centredness are projected into outward behaviour. The love which we have for one of our brethren ought to overflow towards others, make us open to them, for it is through him that we have become aware of the value of all. But in order that this may happen we must love him for his own sake rather than love ourselves in him.

The evil which we deplore has been expressed in its stark nakedness by Hegel, in his well-known dialectic of the master and the slave.[60] This philosopher of Idealism can only conceive as a starting point a perfectly autonomous and absolute consciousness of self. When it meets another conscious self, it must make itself accepted by the other. The ghastly thing about Hegel's position from a Christian point of view, is that what consciousness has to force upon the other's recognition is his own exclusive absoluteness. The other is bound by no less a necessity; whence a fight to death. There is no need for us to pursue this theory. These indications, however brief they may be, are sufficiently provocative to make us see more clearly three essential points with which we must be concerned.

---

[60] Hegel, *Phénoménologie de l'Esprit* with notes by Jean Hyppolite (Aubier), vol. I, pp. 155–61. The commentary by Jean Hyppolite, *Genèse de la Phénoménologie de l'Esprit*, pp. 159–71. Kojève, *Introduction à la lecture de Hegel*, pp. 17–18.

Firstly, the need to be recognized. Hegel is quite right in giving it the first place. It is greatly to be deplored that this factor is frequently overlooked in treating of fraternal love.[61] There can be no love without mutual recognition. Everyone suffers from being ignored. Certainly the friendship of God ought to be sufficient for us; and our marvellous serenity and the source of our boundless joy should flow from the fact that "we are known by him".[62] But since our earthly relationships should be vehicles of the love God bears towards us, they should be under the sway of a loving understanding which reflects and gives constant witness to God's love. They ought to reverse Hegel's claim: instead of aiming at recognition by others, let us strive to have that "imagination of the heart" which enables us to visualize what is going on in the hearts of our neighbours. The flaw which disfigures love, and often brings it to nought, manifests itself cruelly in the hardening of hearts embittered by lack of understanding and treacherous love, which then take their revenge – consciously or unconsciously – in violence towards others. A true revenge and liberation would rather be found in understanding and loving others.

Secondly, Hegel accentuates the true cause of violence and boundless cruelty: pride, the self-sufficiency of the one who makes himself into an absolute. This "absolute" man kills the other, for he cannot tolerate sharing, or if he does not kill him, he reduces the other to the condition of a slave despised because he chose servitude rather than death. But finally this being the "master" will itself come to be seen as deadly . . . a happy ending indeed! On the contrary, as creatures and children of God, we are happy to consider ourselves as nothing, except through God's grace. "What hast thou which thou hast not received?"[63] Gentleness resides in this fundamental attitude. It is only manifestly sincere and efficacious by virtue of a love which overcomes the propensity

---

[61] There are two notable exceptions: Salman in his contribution to the symposium on *La Vie Commune* in the collection "La religieuse d'aujourd'hui" (Cerf) and Louis Lavelle, *Conduite à l'égard d'autrui*, pp. 46–8, 84–6.

[62] This is the great theme of the New Testament – Mt 25: 12; Jn 10: 14 and 27; I Cor 8: 2, 3; 13: 12; II Cor 6: 9; Gal 4: 9; II Tim 2: 19.

[63] I Cor 4: 7

to pride. Hatred is only overcome by the conquest of jealousy, and the latter will threaten to flare up as long as delight in the good of others does not replace our thirst for our own exaltation.

In fact there would be plenty of food for fruitful reflexion in this fight to the death through which man finds himself and gains self-mastery. In the first confrontation, as Kojève says, "one only sees the other as a hostile and dangerous animal which needs to be destroyed and not as a self-conscious being, having an autonomous value". This is violence in perfection. In order that it may be overcome it is required that men should see that they have complementary and harmonizing callings. Discord then gives way to harmony; the fight to the death becomes a communication of life. We grow and develop what is best in ourselves to the extent that our own growth helps to reveal and encourage growth in others along their own proper lines.

Let us pause a moment. We must, we should . . . As we have been considering the extent of the deep flaw that reaches all man's faculties and gives rise to violence in all its various manifestations, we have at one and the same time seen what is required for man to overcome his inhumanity. Ricœur said we should "recognize the vast scale of violence". We become aware of its depth and so we realize the need to renew ourselves in depth. It is an issue of spiritual life or death. But we fail to discover its time dimensions along the two, as it were, horizontal directions where it is a question of *doing*, without which the claim to *being* is a farce. I mean that today violence forms such a monolithic whole, that it is not possible to measure its extent from the technical angle, or in terms of the resentments and ambitions it arouses. As for the resentments and ambitions of rulers, nations and social classes, it might be argued that they were no less brutal in the past than they are today; but even if the world were as big in the past as it is today, nevertheless the reserves of power that could then be called up were derisory in comparison with those which ambition and hatred can summon up in present conditions. Manifestly when a huge empire crushed a small nation, or when a big brute oppressed a single peaceful man, it was even then a manifestation of the abuse of power. But it was power in the form of a natural force which drove the empire or brute in the urge for self-assertion, the more so since neither the prince nor the commoner used it deliberately or controlled it. As long as the world has been in existence any emperor or ordinary man who gives way to his blind instinct for power, has as much consciousness of the evil he perpetrates as a typhoon or a thunderstorm. Blind cosmic urges have always risen up from the depths of fallen nature – hell is familiar with these depths. But today there is no longer any limit to a power which spreads so relentlessly.[64] We can see certain connections between these three factors: the depth of man's wounds, the extent of man's will to power, and the means to power. Since great nations today, embittered by centuries of humiliation, have access to power, is there not a grave danger that this newly found power will spark off the accumulated bitterness into a conflagration involving the whole of mankind? We cannot hope that various forms of violence will cancel out one another. Their inherent opposition is not productive of peace but of further violence. I write these lines in sight of the sea. A great tide is running in from the north in huge waves, while a violent south-west wind is raging. The floods of water flow on irresistibly, but instead of advancing with calm, they tower up in breaking foam, piled high against the sinister darkness of the open sea, in four or five ranks of tumultuous, tragic, tormented cascades. Men of peace, who have a deep vision of the signs of the time, can you perceive some favourable breach in the apparently impenetrable front of brute force, where the powers of the spirit can infiltrate and assert themselves? Where can the gospel make its impact on this world? Has the world become so unpropitious to it that the faithful are now faced only with martyrdom?

Can the Sermon on the Mount still be heard in such a world? In the tumult of these tormented waves not a single human cry could be heard.

---

[64] See the fears expressed by Romano Guardini in his excellent short book *La Puissance* (Seuil, 1956).

In St Matthew, Chapter V (verses 20–24, 38–48), we read:

For I tell you, that unless your justice abound more than that of the scribes and Pharisees, you shall not enter into the kingdom of heaven.

You have heard that it was said to them of old: Thou shalt not kill. And whosoever shall kill shall be in danger of the judgment. But I say to you that whosoever is angry with his brother shall be in danger of the judgment. . . . If therefore thou offer thy gift at the altar, and there thou remember that thy brother hath anything against thee; leave there thy offering before the altar and go first to be reconciled to thy brother . . .

You have heard that it hath been said: An eye for an eye and a tooth for a tooth. But I say to you not to resist evil . . . But if one strike thee on thy right cheek, turn to him also the other. And if a man will contend with thee in judgment and take away thy coat, let go thy cloak also unto him. And whosoever will force thee one mile, go with him the other two. Give to him that asketh of thee; and from him that would borrow of thee turn not away.

You have heard that it hath been said: Thou shalt love thy neighbour and hate thy enemy. But I say to you: Love your enemies; do good to them that hate you; and pray for them that persecute and calumniate you; that you may be the children of your Father who is in heaven, who maketh his sun to rise upon the good and bad and raineth upon the just and the unjust. For if you love them that love you, what reward shall you have? Do not even the publicans this? And if you salute your brethren only, what do you more? Do not also the heathen this? Be you therefore perfect, as also your heavenly Father is perfect.

PART I

The Violent Gentleness
of Christ

CHAPTER
TWO

Violence and Gentleness of his "Humiliation"

THAT GOD SHOULD HAVE ASSUMED OUR HUMAN condition implies both violence and gentleness. "The goodness and loving-kindness of our God."[1] How does he manifest himself, "he who is *in the Father and the Father in him*"?[2] As a little child. He slips unseen into our humanity. Defenceless he puts himself into our hands. He is divested of all might. It is the coming of infinite love. How could God better show us what such love is – all embracing, caring love, than in coming to share our lot? This is how he shows his faithfulness.[3] "*I will come as the dew.*"[4]

But this gentleness has the infinite intensity of divine love. A terrible love, *a consuming fire*.[5] We must constantly remind ourselves of the implications of the intensity of this divine love as

---

[1] *Humanitas* is used in the liturgy and is the expression used by the Vulgate for "the love of men", Tit 3: 4.

[2] Jn 14: 11

[3] *Faithfulness* of God, a fundamental theme in the bible

[4] Hos 14: 5

[5] Deut 4: 24; Heb 12: 29. See note 15, p. 97; Lev 9: 24; Num 21: 28, etc.

we dwell upon the acts and the words of Christ. Everything that he is and does is thereby endowed with a dimension, a power, a meaning, a depth which are beyond our comprehension and which are, in the true sense of the word, formidable. We catch a glimpse of them when this divine love is repaid by ingratitude: in his *jealousy*,[6] his *anger*.[7] It will become even more apparent in his *rage* in his "treading of the wine press",[8] in his passion and upon the cross, for if this rage and jealousy are always the other side of frustrated divine glory and love, the *Man of Sorrows*[9] in his fury, will not crush any enemy under foot, as was predicted by the prophet: it is he himself who will be placed in the wine press,[10] his garments will be stained in his own blood. In "reconciling all things in his blood"[11] the divine jealousy, the divine wrath will reach the utmost extremity without men having to suffer from it: on the contrary it will bring their salvation. "He killed the enmities in himself" as St Paul puts it.[12]

But his gentleness is still violent in the precise sense in which we defined it, namely as contrary to nature. See how deep it goes. This gentleness is a characteristic of that love which enters our human condition without doing *violence* to it in any way. Now the condition of our nature is violent. Hence a fundamental paradox which will assume countless forms. This incarnate Love is both torn and tearing asunder. Christ is necessarily "a sign of contradiction"[13] and a source of endless conflicts. "Peaceful among those who hate peace",[14] their reaction will be to "draw a sword".[15]

He is the love that comes to awaken love. Therefore he will not force it; the result would not be love. He seeks the gift of free

---

[6] Ex 20: 5, 34: 14; Deut 5: 9, 32: 16–21; Is 59: 17; Nah 1: 2; Prov 27: 41; II Cor 11: 2.

[7] Ex 4: 14; II Cor 11: 2; Num 11: 10, 12: 9, 25: 3; Is 51: 17; Jer 10: 10; Nah 1: 6.

[8] Is 63: 31

[9] Is 53

[10] The mediaeval image of the cross as a wine press

[11] Col 1: 20, 22

[12] Eph 2: 16

[13] Lk 2: 34

[14] Ps 120

[15] Mt 26: 52

wills. His gentleness consists in a most exquisite respect for the human heart; he will never try to bribe it with favours. He will therefore never do violence to our human condition, neither by some magic or miracle, which would exempt from its rigours those who are to be saved; nor will he restore all men in a paradisal state by some spectacular intervention. In short, his gentleness is an expression of the respect which God has for man's dignity. He will offer man his grace as mysteriously as he slipped into the world as a small child under cover of darkness.

First and foremost, he gathers and sums up all our Christian destinies within himself, so that in taking on our human misery and getting to grips with it, his way leads inevitably to the cross.[16] Love can only take the form of sacrifice and suffering in identifying itself with a human nature ravaged by sin and its consequent evils. As perfect man – the Son of Man – he submits to this law in its fullest and bitterest form. This is why the eternal decree of the Father and Christ's perfect acceptance,[17] his "Behold I come",[18] when he entered this world, are *violent*. They are like this through the strength of gentleness.

Since the Incarnation takes place in suffering, to the point of utter crushing and abjection, it is like an annihilation, a process in which God seems to empty himself out, to use the daring expression of St Paul in the well-known hymn from his epistle to the Philippians. Not assuredly that the Son of Man empties himself of his divinity in becoming man, but he divests himself of his glory:

> Who being in the form of God, thought it not robbery to be
>   equal with God
> But he emptied himself, taking the form of a servant, being
>   made in the likeness of men, and in habit found as a man.
> He humbled himself, becoming obedient unto death, even to
>   the death of the Cross.[19]

---

[16] See P. Régamey, *La Croix du Christ et celle du chrétien* (Cerf, 1945).
[17] II Cor 1: 19
[18] Heb 10: 7
[19] Phil 2: 6–8

He therefore chose to come into a most violent situation and wished to live in a country under the yoke of cruel invaders. The atmosphere of the gospels is in no way idyllic. St Luke gives us a hint of how things were when he tells us of the Galileans whose blood "Pilate had mingled with their sacrifices".[20] We have even clearer indications of its sinister nature. For instance, when Jesus was a child, the Romans cruelly crushed a revolt by destroying the capital of Galilee, quite close to Nazareth, reducing its inhabitants to slavery and crucifying twenty thousand men.[21] Palestine twenty centuries ago was a centre of hostilities.

"Resentment and bitterness were in the very blood of the people (of the Near East) where villages and tribes were like bodies made up of several members; anyone who lived outside its boundaries was regarded as an enemy and had no claim to be considered or cared for."[22]

The greatest hatred was of course directed towards the oppressors. The resentment of an often hard religious outlook exacerbated the bitterness of national humiliation. The chosen people instructed, as they thought, by God waited for a Messiah, "to rule the gentiles with a rod of iron and to break them in pieces like a potter's vessel".[23] But the Messiah chose to be himself *broken* by the hatred of men.[24] He resisted the temptation to assume earthly power.[25] He hid himself from the enthusiasts who wished to make him their king here on earth.[26] He even habitually concealed his messianic character because his contemporaries thought of the Messiah as a violent leader.[27] Humanly speaking his drama consisted in having to deceive them in their hopes that he would put himself at the head of these "zealots", fanatical nationalists whose trust in God's promises interpreted by their chauvinistic outlook

---

[20] Lk 13: 1

[21] Lebreton, *Jésus et son peuple sous la domination romaine :* in *Construire* (4th series, 1941), pp. 79 ff.

[22] Willam, *Vie de Jésus* (8th Ed., 1947), p. 199

[23] Ps 2: 9

[24] Is 53: 5

[25] Mt 4: 8

[26] Jn 6: 15

[27] Mk 1: 34, 3: 12, 7: 30; Mt 10: 27

incited them to foment revolt. It was in fact their agitation which was to provoke the total destruction of their nation in the year A.D. 70. Against this background, it is understandable that Christ's miracles fanned their hopes that he would use his power to ensure the success of a violent uprising against the Romans.[28] He was rejected when it became manifest that he was not the man for this undertaking.

Three incidents in his Passion are particularly indicative of his absolute attitude of *non-violence*; one must certainly use this expression of him. St John tells us that the soldiers "went backward and fell to the ground",[29] when they tried to seize him: he thus made them see how terrible could have been the effect of his power, but he did not choose to use it. Then when the over-hasty disciple cut off the ear of the servant of the high priest, he performed his last miracle by healing the wound inflicted by this indiscreet use of violence, saying: "Put up again thy sword into its place, for all that take up the sword, shall perish by the sword. Thinkest thou that I cannot call my Father, and he will give me presently more than twelve legions of angels?"[30] Finally he made a similar declaration before Pilate: "If my Kingdom had been of this world, my servants would certainly strive that I should not be delivered to the Jews; but now my Kingdom is not from hence."[31]

His mission seemed to collapse in shame and death, because he refused to have recourse to violence. The disappointment of the frustrated mob then burst forth in the cries for the release of Barabbas and the angry rejection of Jesus; Mark adds that Barabbas had been "put into prison, with some seditious men, who in the sedition had committed murder".[32] The very name of Jesus

---

[28] Oscar Cullmann has shown clearly in his book *The State in the New Testament* (1962) the importance of the relationship between Jesus and the Zealots and how decisively his decision not to follow them affected his fate. But the author seems to exaggerate the significance of certain episodes and words – notably the Agony in Gethsemane and his words to the women of Jerusalem.

[29] Jn 18: 6
[30] Mt 26: 52–53
[31] Jn 18: 36
[32] Mk 15: 7

signifies salvation.[33] Yet far from saving his people in a manifest
way, the long awaited liberator sent by God was not even able to
save himself.[34]

"And I did not resist . . . I have given my body to the strikers,
and my cheeks to them that plucked them: I have not turned away
my face from them that rebuffed me and spat upon me".[35] "He
opened not his mouth. He shall be led as a sheep to the slaughter
and shall be dumb as a lamb before his shearer, and he shall not
open his mouth."[36]

He treated as a friend the one who betrayed him,[37] he invoked
the pardon of God for his torturers as they drove the nails into his
flesh.[38] To the inaccessible heights of the mysteries of his humanity
and divinity are added an enigma as to the value of his example in
refusing to use any form of violence. There is no doubt that each
of his actions has the value of an example, but this applies particularly to the general pattern of his life and to his passion and
death. They have an even greater value than this, as we said from
the very beginning of this book: his life continues in us. *If he came
into this world* it is that we *might live by Him*.[39] But how far must
our lives be conformed to his? What does his example demand of
us? With regard to violence and its rejection, does he call us to
absolute gentleness, which in our present spiritual condition and
situation would mean doing the most terrible violence to ourselves?
Does he require from us this complete break with our age? St
Peter seems to demand it. It is true that he was envisaging a
particular case, that of slaves who were subject to difficult masters.
He exhorts them to endure *unjust punishments and blows* and to
welcome them as a grace from God.[40] This teaching may make us
tremble (it is in fact the only one which can act as a tonic under
such excessive and inescapable testing). But he goes on to generalize

---

[33] The word "Jesus" means "God saves".
[34] Mt 27: 42
[35] Is 50: 5–6
[36] Is 53: 7
[37] Mt 26: 50
[38] Lk 23: 34
[39] I Jn 4: 9
[40] I Pet 2: 18–20

without qualification: "For unto this are you called: because Christ has suffered for us, leaving you an example that you should follow his steps. Who did not sin, neither was guile found in his mouth. Who when he was reviled, did not revile; when he suffered, he threatened not, but delivered himself to him that judged him unjustly. Who his own self bore our sins in his body on the tree: that we being dead to sin, should live to justice."[41]

This text, particularly if we see it in its context, can be interpreted as giving a general line of conduct; it need not be seen as laying down a hard and fast rule except under inescapable injustice and oppression. We do not possess the absolute integrity of Christ so that in him total abstention from violence was perfect gentleness; and above all we have not been given the task to redeem the world through death. When Jesus refused the help of the legions of angels, it was precisely to indicate the purpose of his task, and to explain its character: "How then should the Scriptures be fulfilled, that so it must be done?"[42]

Similarly when Peter struck off the ear of the servant: "Put up thy sword in the scabbard. The chalice which the Father has given me, shall I not drink it?"[43] And if his followers did not fight it was because his Kingdom was not of this world.[44]

There are grounds for us to maintain from these very teachings of Jesus that the use of certain human means involving violence are not forbidden to us. This seems plain to us, the guidance of the Church being one of the essential data upon which the Christian conscience is formed. The imitation of Christ and our conformity with him have to be adapted according to the demands of different vocations. The master in whose footsteps we have to follow certainly throws us into great perplexity when it comes to this adaptation and to the understanding of particular cases.[45]

---

[41] ibid., 21–24
[42] Mt 26: 54
[43] Jn 18: 11
[44] ibid.: 36
[45] "He that abideth in him ought himself also to walk even as he walked", I Jn 2: 6

CHAPTER THREE

"I am Meek"[1]

THE GENTLENESS OF CHRIST IS NOT JUST ONE
of his virtues. It is one of his essential characteristics. It appears
as such whether we dwell upon his divinity and more explicitly
as the second person of the Trinity, or as the man: Jesus of
Nazareth.

God is gentle – "taste and see for the Lord is sweet".[2] Let us
nevertheless not strive to explain what gentleness implies within
God. It would assuredly be necessary for us to know this in order
to have a full comprehension of God's plans and of the ways along
which he leads us. But it is senseless for us to wait for this comprehension before we start to follow him. God always seems to do
violence to us by placing us in conflicting situations. But we are
sure of him, sure that he is Love.[3] Love is gentle, while being as
strong as death.[4] Let us taste this ineffable gentleness in the depths
of our souls and remain silent about it.

There is something, however, which we can begin to understand

---

[1] When quoting from the bible we use the word "meek", but otherwise we use the word "gentle" wherever possible – (*Tr.*).

[2] Ps 34: 9, quoted in I Pet 2:3.

[3] I Jn 4: 16

[4] Song of S. 7: 6

and express here on earth; it is God's gentleness in his government
of the world. His gentleness resides in the discreet way in which he
acts.[5] He rules his creatures through the laws that he has instilled
in them. To such an extent that he seems absent from his creation.
He hides himself in the activity of created causes, so that they
can be truly and fully causes.[6] We could not claim an equal
gentleness in our dealings with others. We have neither the infinite
transcendence or immanence of the creator. But we shall only be
children of God to the extent that we strive for this respect for
others. It was to him that Christ was conformed in his work of
redemption as we saw in the previous chapter; our Father is
gentle in giving opportunities to all, "Who maketh his sun to rise
upon the good and the bad and raineth on the just and unjust."[7]
And God is gentle in his merciful patience: "O Lord, the Lord
God, merciful and gracious, patient and of much compassion, and
true, who keepest mercy unto thousands. . . ."[8] In return, gentleness shall spring in us as a result of our loving acceptance of the
ways of his divine providence. "Blessed is the man that hopeth in
him."[9] Within the Trinity, the Son is the perfect "image of the
substance" of the Father.[10] His whole being consists in his relation
to his Father. How could there be any violence of opposition, hardness or bitterness in him? But here too we have to limit our concepts and words by focusing our contemplation on the inexpressible
of which grace gives us a foretaste within our hearts.

These reflections were necessary, because the gentleness of
Jesus as man is the shining forth of his divine gentleness, so perfect
in his unity. As a person he is God. Nevertheless, using words in
their modern sense, he has a very definite psychological "personality": he has a mind of his own, a human will, a sensibility
coloured by the impressions received. His divine ascendancy, far
from diminishing his originality, brought it to that perfection

---

[5] Wisd 8: 1
[6] *Sum. Theol., Ia Pars Qu.* 103, *art.* 6
[7] Mt 5: 45
[8] Ex 34: 6
[9] Ps 2: 12, 34: 9
[10] Heb 1: 3

which is set before us as the ideal type of man. All human gentleness derives its laws from his; let us try to see what they are.

It is immediately apparent to us that Christ's gentleness is so perfect because he is completely at peace: in tune with the will of the Father, with himself and with all reality. We have already explained how his absolute non-violence in action followed from his complete submission to the will of his Father. It was a perfection of behaviour, better still of a way of life, which we must now consider in its principles. As he never relinquished the beatific vision through which "he was in the Father and the Father in Him",[11] his heart was immersed in an ocean of peace, and his action can be that of the "Prince of Peace".[12]

With regard to his inner peace, the divine action achieved it in him without difficulty, since it was not impeded by the slightest "wound" in his human nature.[13] The variations caused by the reflection of light in a broken piece of glass are pleasing to the eye; thus grace brings beauty, both on earth and in eternal glory, in and through the wounds of our nature. But it cannot be compared to the untroubled limpidity of light reflected in a crystal without blemish. Such are the hearts of Christ and Mary, and this is why their actions can be perfectly peaceful and appeasing. On the other hand, the peace and gentleness of Christ involves a wrench away from all that opposes men to God and to one another. We must maintain that already here on earth there coexisted in him a fundamental peace and gentleness, in the light of his work as Redeemer, which will shine forth in a new heaven and a new earth,[14] but also a profound anguish, indignation and unspeakable distress in the face of the obstinacy of the human will which refuses to be open to him.

It is most enlightening to notice the incidents in the gospels when he was troubled.[15] We shall restrict ourselves to those troubles

---

[11] Jn 14: 11

[12] Is 9: 6

[13] See preceding chapter

[14] Rev 21: 1

[15] Mt 9: 36, 14: 14, 15: 32; Lk 7: 13; Mk 7: 31; Jn 11: 33–35; Lk 7: 50; Jn 13: 21; Jn 12: 27; Mt 26: 38; Heb 5: 7; Mt 24: 6 ("Let not your hearts be troubled").

that affected his gentleness. On one occasion it is the "hardness of heart" which grieves him, as St Mark tells us,[16] so much so that he "looked round with anger" upon those who placed the formalities of religion above mercy. We find the same severity in the terrible denunciations of the Pharisees which Matthew recounts: "Whited sepulchres – You serpents, generation of vipers, how will you flee from the judgment of Hell?"[17] And on another occasion: "O generation of vipers, how can you speak good things whereas you are evil?"[18]

Pharisaism is Christ's foremost enemy, for it is essentially a satisfaction with one's own excellence which prevents access into the sphere of pure gratuitousness, the open door to God. Love is helpless against it, and in despair can only utter cries of warning which echo through the centuries against this most pernicious attitude – the worst error of all.[19] On two other occasions Christ inveighs against hardness of heart, manifesting itself in the form of unbelief: "A perverse and adulterous generation seeks a sign."[20] "O unbelieving and perverse generation how long shall I be with you. How long shall I suffer you?"[21] Otherwise we never see Christ departing from gentleness except when "consumed with zeal for his Father's house he made as it were a scourge of little cords, and drove them that sold oxen and sheep and doves, and the changers of money, out of the temple",[22] or when eaten up by zeal for the mission which his Father had entrusted to him he predicted his passion and Peter wished to prevent it: "get behind me Satan, thou

---

[16] Mk 3: 5

[17] Mt 23: 27, 33

[18] Mt 12: 34

[19] It is disturbing that in the vast *Dictionnaire de Théologie Catholique* there is no article on Pharisaism, which means that theologians have made no serious study of it. It is left to historians of the Jews and exegetists. Even more astonishing is the way the terrible 23rd Chapter of St Matthew has been played down. Surely this is a matter that now demands to be considered far more rigorously by the Christian conscience than hitherto?

[20] Mt 12: 39

[21] Mt 17: 16

[22] Jn 2: 15

art a scandal unto me, because thou savourest not the things that are of God, but the things that are of men".[23]

The remaining marks of an effaced circle enable us to retrace it and find its centre. The traces of violence in the gospel can be perfectly reconciled with traces of utter gentleness, and they appear as shining manifestations of God's merciful love within man's self-appointed order of things. The deep centre from which everything flows resides in a burning zeal which manifests itself habitually with complete gentleness, because it is a zeal for the glory of the Father and a gift of supernatural love for men. These two aims, the glory of the Father and "the more abundant life"[24] of regenerated men, were and are to all eternity most perfectly identified in the heart of Christ. It was so from the beginning, and it will always be from this burning centre of Christ's heart that the mystery of his work will shine forth with irresistible power. "In the days of his flesh"[25] and now in the highest heaven, Our Lord never ceases to be possessed by the vision of his Kingdom, fulfilled in its "plenitude" and "delivered to his Father"[26] in a "new heaven and a new earth".[27] In order to perceive as deeply as we can how truly he is the *Prince of Peace*[28] and what his gentleness implies, we have to raise our minds to the inner mystery of his redemptive love, in which he worked out among us to perfection those graces necessary for the fulfilment of the great mystery of his plenitude, "unto a knowledge of the Son of God, unto a perfect man, unto the measure of the age of the fulness of Christ".[29] It is he who is the Perfect Man in whom all human potentialities and their development must find their completion and their infinite transcendence. As *Prince of Peace* he is the active principle of our peace; and in order that he might truly become this, during his earthly pilgrimage he extended his prophetic knowledge and love, and as it were diversified them and made them more subtle, in such a way that

---

[23] Mt 16: 23
[24] Jn 10: 10
[25] Heb 5: 7
[26] I Cor 15: 24
[27] Rev 21: 1
[28] Is 9: 5
[29] Eph 4: 13

he might in advance reconcile within himself so many forces which are at war within us. It was these treasures of wisdom and knowledge which dwelt corporeally in him that he invited us to share.[30] In him the barriers that separate us are broken down, for "he reconciled our enmities in his flesh".[31]

Now that he is glorified, "he establishes all things under his dominion[32] and he perfects the saints for the edifying of his body[33] from among the people whom he acquired for the praise and glory of his Father".[34] By sending the Holy Spirit at Pentecost, and with every new sending of this same Spirit, he introduces himself into every human situation as truly as he did during his stay on earth, when he belonged to the Jewish people, to his family at Nazareth, to the things of his trade, to his friends – John, Lazarus and Mary Magdalen. He does this now with as much reality but in a more intimate way, from within, by virtue of his grace. He is French, Chinese, Russian, American, English. In his heart all that conflicts and divides is abolished;[35] not so as to fuse us in a vague uniformity, for he enhances our differences according to the harmonious diversity of our vocations, which go to "make up his Body".[36] But it is this same peace already acquired for us in his glory and the graces that flow from it, it is this same peace, creative of our own inner peace if we welcome it, which is torn asunder by our hatreds. He gives himself wholly to us, but we are divided. Thus his heart is wounded; Christ is divided.[37] How is it that all our deadly enmities are not swallowed up in his victory?[38]

When we contemplate the infinite depths of Christ's peace and consider our own lives, we may wonder that our dissensions do not provoke his wrath. But far from his being irritated by them, they are an occasion for manifesting his extreme gentleness. Thus when

---

[30] Col 2: 3–9
[31] Eph 2: 14
[32] Eph 1: 10
[33] Eph 4: 12
[34] Eph 1: 14
[35] Gal 3: 27, 28; Col 3: 11; I Cor 12: 13
[36] Rom 12: 4–7
[37] I Cor 1: 13
[38] I Cor 15: 54

a discussion arose among the disciples as to which among them was the greatest,[39] it was then that Jesus called a little child, and his words enable us to imagine how lovingly he gave them this child as an example. This should not surprise us; this action of Jesus contains a great truth. Only an increase of love can heal the desperate quarrels that divide men; to show forth this love requires infinite gentleness. The zeal from which it proceeds gives it violence, naturally, but without cruelty, so that it can surmount the temptation of taking the easy way out, remove the obstacles to the outpouring of this love, remind us of God's sovereign rights and help men of goodwill to react against the ever-present threat of hardness of heart. But the wound in our hearts caused by divisions among men must be sufficiently deep, as it was in Christ's heart, so that we may reach that secret sanctuary where love and everlasting peace are supreme. Irritation only aggravates existing disorders. "The peace of God which surpasseth all understanding"[40] must "rejoice in our hearts"[41] with such conviction that it overcomes all our troubles.

The final words of Christ's last discourse to his disciples were a prayer to his Father, "that the love wherewith thou hast loved me may be in them, and I in them".[42] He wishes "that we may be filled with his joy, and that we may be filled unto all the fulness of God".[43]

For our part, gentleness can never become systematized; it must remain spontaneous. If it is merely negative, it is useless and false. When it degenerates into sugariness and softness it is a caricature of the gentleness of Christ and is loathsome to any healthy minded person. It must flow in us from the powerful action of the Spirit of Christ.

It is the gentleness of Christ which shows that he holds sway over our life: "Learn of me," he told us, "for I am meek and humble of heart".[44] What does this imply? His gentleness guaran-

---

[39] Lk 9: 46
[40] Phil 4: 7
[41] Col 3: 15
[42] Jn 17: 26
[43] Eph 3: 19
[44] Mt 11: 29

tees that he will not bludgeon us with unassailable truths, but that he will humbly work with what is best and most positive in us; he will, to use an analogy from photography, "develop" us. "Our souls will find their rest in him."[45]

Is this not the kind of gentleness the world is blindly seeking? As soon as Jesus gives us a taste of his gentleness, we realize we are miserable without it. "Blessed are the meek for they shall possess the land."[46] The land of their own souls from which they were exiled through their violence; their participation in the violence of the world does violence to their souls, it alienates them, whereas they reconquer themselves to the extent that they are openhearted. This is the eternal home of all living souls of which Christ's gentleness gives us a foretaste. But what about this present land of conflicts? Can it truly be conquered by gentleness? Will it not rather annihilate us? How many really accept this joy which is the fruit of gentleness? It costs too much! It goes too far! Precisely, the fate of this gentleness, joy and peace seems to be without hope in the world, because the world is not prepared to pay the price for it. Jesus had no illusions as to the risk it involved: "I send you," he warned us, "as lambs among wolves."[47] We are therefore faced with these enigmatic questions: will the wolves devour the lambs, or will they be won by their gentleness? Or has the simplicity of the lambs the power of anticipating that paradisal state of peaceful coexistence in which "the lamb lies down with the wolf"?[48] The lives of the saints offer us these three possible alternatives without our being able to see which will prevail. They are all equally wonderful; all three are a victory of gentleness.

---

[45] Mt 2: 29
[46] Mt 5: 4
[47] Lk 10: 3
[48] Is 11:6, 65: 25

CHAPTER
FOUR

"I have come to cast Fire upon the Earth"

THE FUNCTIONAL LAW OF CHRISTIANITY

The whole Christian order is an expression of divine love. "God is love"[1] – this is the supreme revelation of the New Testament. It is at the heart of God's inner mystery, in which each person of the Trinity gives himself totally to the two others:[2] the Word and the Spirit exist only through the Father, who makes them a gift of all that he is, and they in return give themselves totally to the Father. This divine life overflows through a superabundance of love. It creates other beings so that they may share its truth, goodness and joy. They add nothing to it: how could anything be added to the Infinite? The glory of God

---

[1] Jn 4: 8

[2] The whole theology of the Trinity – that is, the reflective and explicit consciousness that intelligence with faith can have of this mystery – lies in the development of this statement: the three Persons being God have all the divine attributes. They cannot in any way differ among themselves except in the *relationships* they have to each other. And it is these relationships that *constitute them*.

consists in the fulfilment of his creatures.[3] A further excess of generosity: man fell through a misuse of his freedom, so God in human form comes to his rescue. "God so loved the world as to give his only begotten Son; that whosoever believeth in him may not perish, but may have life everlasting."[4]

This life consists in a participation in the great movement of the outgoing of divine love and a return to the Father, enhanced by the love he has inspired, "And as the rain and the snow come down from heaven, and return no more thither, but soak the earth and water it, and make it to spring and give seed to the sower and bread to the eater".[5]

Consider a living organism, a plant or an animal, the minutest details or the whole; you will find everywhere the same laws of integration, the same reactions at work. The Christian order of things also has its law in the same biological and functional sense. For man it takes the form of a commandment because the parts that make up the body of Christ are conscious and free. Because it is a law of love, essentially free and creative, God calls us to be inventive and original, he invites us to a voluntary acceptance of our vocations, to make real his Truth[6] and his Will, in other words to do his work in the world.[7] He has left us to our own counsels.[8] He has therefore instructed us in the laws of our fulfilment and of our transcendence. Now the law which sums up all the laws of the Christian order is constant in this organism, which by its operation becomes the society of partakers of the lot of the saints in light.[9]

---

[3] "The glory of God," says Ireneaus, "is living man." This "accidental glory" which creatures "give" to God is found in creatures and not in God, since nothing can be added to him; it is they who benefit. When we say that God creates for his glory, we must understand it rightly. It is usually interpreted in a narrow, anthropomorphic sense as the meanest kind of vainglory, as if God were showing off. We must restore the right outlook which sees that God simply creates for the happiness of his creatures.

[4] Jn 3: 16
[5] Is 55: 10, 11
[6] Jn 3: 21
[7] Mt 6: 10, 7: 21, 12: 50, etc.
[8] Ecclus 15: 14
[9] Col 1: 12

This law is indeed so essentially Christian that Christ has called it
the New Commandment, emphasizing it even further by calling
it "My Commandment".[10] From Christ and the Virgin Mary,
through the angels and the saints in heaven, to us who begin eternal
life on earth, the love of God is poured forth not so that it may
terminate in us but that it may flow through us to others. In truth,
this law sums up the whole newness of the gospel. It is not only
new by contrast with the Old Law, but seems likely to remain
increasingly and alarmingly new in relation to what is happening
in the world today. It stands out in singular contrast with the
accepted morality of men, and let us face it, with conventional
forms of Christianity. "Love one another", says Jesus, "as I have
loved you."

St John reminds us that law is both old and new.[11] In fact it is
identical with the old precept "Thou shalt love thy neighbour as
thyself",[12] if one fulfills that to the utmost that is to say in its
universality and in communion with Christ. But this law is new in
that it reveals its specifically "Christlike" character. It has therefore
a twofold newness: the imitation of the love Christ has for us, and
participation in this love. The two correlatives are required: if we
dare to imitate such a love, it is because of our certainty that he
will come to our aid; but, on the other hand, he will not enable us
to participate in it unless we try to emulate him. No trivial conception of the love of our neighbour is therefore possible. It impli-
cates us in terrifying demands.

Gentleness then becomes one of our most essential qualities,
as it was in Christ and according to what we have perceived in him.
It is hardly necessary to point out that one cannot be caught up in
such a process by a simple abstention from violence, and still less
if this abstention is considered to be the essential feature. Divine
love is creative. A sterile and negative attitude would be a betrayal
of the gospel of which one of the major themes is "to bear fruit";[13]
in fact, Christ chose as the last miracle of his earthly life the wither-

---

[10] Jn 13: 34, 15: 12
[11] I Jn 2: 7
[12] Deut 6: 5
[13] Jn 15: 2, 8, 16; Mt 3: 8, 10, 13: 8, 23, 21: 43, 25: 14–27; Lk 13:
6–8.

ing of the barren fig tree.[14] The supremacy of love, if taken seriously, will of course find expression in a reduction of external violence, in a sublimation of internal violence, and a continual increase in gentleness. And if we dwell on this latter, we shall see that such increase must in various ways become the object of a positive concern; it cannot be taken for granted that it will develop automatically; on the contrary, it will have to inspire practical originality in the implementation of this law of charity. Nevertheless, gentleness, though primary, is only one result of charity among others; it is charity itself which is essential. Unfortunately it often cannot achieve its aim without violence. Will it therefore surrender? No, it must overcome this. One has to be acutely aware of the paradoxical and perilous nature of such a course of action: the danger of failing and of total loss. Nevertheless the risk must be taken, it is the ransom to be paid for man's fallen nature. It is in this extremity that the primacy of charity must continue to assert itself in a way as authentic as it is paradoxical.

Infinite love breaks into our lives and breaks up their commonplace pattern. It sets no limit to its inspiration and what it expects us to undertake. "The Lord has cast a fire upon the earth."[15] The

---

[14] Insufficient attention has been paid to the fact that the cursing of the barren fig tree was the last miracle of Christ's teaching life. (Although on the eve of the Passion he did heal the ear of the High Priest's servant, cut off by Peter and this is important from the point of view of non-violence.) The miracle is a parable made the more arresting since it was "not the season of figs" and the lesson he draws from it is the need to pray. The fruitfulness God requires of all of us, which will give glory to the Father (Jn 15: 18), is grace and that can be obtained only through prayer in faith. Note the symmetry with his first miracle at Cana when he gave abundance and excellence. "Bearing fruit" is one of the major themes of the gospels. The obligation to grow is symbolized by increase, as in the parable of the talents, together with the well-known saying that "To him that has shall be given, but from him that has not shall be taken away even that which he has". This appears in different contexts six times in the gospels, which underlines its outstanding importance.

[15] Lk 12: 49. In the Old Testament divine fire is simply terrifying (Ex 19: 18). It is the glory of God manifesting itself; the symbol of God's "jealousy" (Deut 4: 24), of his wrath (Jer 15: 14). But it is also

fire never says "It is enough."[16] He "casts a seed",[17] a seed which is incorruptible and "must be born again";[18] it is destined to become "a tree so that the birds of the air can find shelter in its branches".[19] He wishes us to be light, salt and leaven in the world: "a light which reaches all who are in the house,[20] salt which gives savour to all food",[21] leaven which will penetrate the whole.[22] He assures us that boundless power is hidden in our faith: "If you have faith like a grain of mustard seed."[23]

We are called to do something extraordinary.[24] It is precisely when he is talking of the love of our enemies that he makes this clear. If we are satisfied with loving those who love us, we have not entered upon his ways. His love seeks to be creative to the point of overcoming enmities. We draw back. But supernatural love is extraordinary; so is the divine world we must enter. Ordinary human behaviour is a closed circle even when good. Jesus requires us to break out of this circle. He sets before us no other limit than the perfection of his Father who is in heaven.[25]

THE OBLIGATION OF THE EVANGELICAL LAW

It is in these perspectives and – we insist on this – in this trend that we have to understand the words of the Sermon on the Mount, in contrast with our thoughts on violence. The words are fire, leaven, seed . . . They indicate the clear directions in which

---

purifying (Is 1: 25). This dreadful character of fire still prevails in the New Testament (II Cor 11: 2) but to it is added the merciful love of Christ, of which fire is the symbol.

---

[16] Prov 30: 16
[17] Mt 13: 3
[18] I Pet 1: 23
[19] Mt 13: 32
[20] Mt 5: 15
[21] Mt 5: 13
[22] Mt 13: 33; I Cor 5: 6
[23] Mt 17: 19; Lk 17: 6
[24] Mt 5: 47
[25] Mt 5: 48

Christ has launched us and in which we have to go forward *as far as we possibly can*. If we do not see them in this light, we cannot escape the dilemma of irreconcilably opposed principles. One either takes their words to be precepts in the strict sense and imposes upon Christians the obligation to take the heroic, the strait and narrow way, or on the other hand one treats them as extraordinary counsels which everyone can take as not applying to himself. We thus extinguish the fire which Christ came to kindle in our hearts so that the world perishes through lack of the warmth of love. In either case the gospel is ineffective. Christians of good-will feel a vague uneasiness between these two positions and allow themselves to be carried along by prevailing currents.

Some take an uncompromising view of the precept "Thou shalt not kill". It is useless telling them that God in fact does not make it absolute, since in the very next chapter in Exodus which follows this the precept recurs like a refrain: the man who does such or such a thing *will be put to death*.[26] They will answer: Christ abolished this out-of-date law; he re-established the law of God in its fullest strictness, since he even goes so far as to forbid bad inner attitudes and even insults. This is the line taken by many conscientious objectors. At the other extreme, accommodating minds simply evade the obligation, explaining – quite correctly in fact – that the interdiction of killing is strictly concerned with murder; but at the same time they give way, without spiritual misgivings, to the prevailing climate of opinion however lightly it may regard the value of human life.

With regard to going beyond the old law of revenge, of "an eye for an eye", the rigorists take the line that one should "not counter-attack the wicked";[27] they would forbid all recourse to violence.

---

[26] Ex 21: 12–17 ff.

[27] M. le Pasteur Roser in his pamphlet *Le chrétien devant la guerre*, pp. 30–31 (Labor et Fides, Geneva, 1953): "Christ's words were μὴ ἀντιστῆναι – *do not take up an 'anti' position: do not reciprocate, inflict reprisals, give blow for blow, an eye for an eye, atomic bomb for atomic bomb.* Does this mean passivity, *laisser faire*? That is not like the behaviour or still less the spirit of him who, faced with the enemy in the temptations, conquered him. If it means non-resistance it is in the sense of not letting oneself be led into adopting the attitudes of the

The realists on the other hand, who want to get to grips with reality and refuse to give a free hand to the wicked, take no notice of the law of the gospel. They argue that it is illustrated by manifestly exaggerated examples and couched in oriental language which takes away its binding force; for instance: "to turn the other cheek".[28] Christ himself, when he was struck during his Passion, did not turn the other cheek, and as for St Paul, he could hit back with strong language.[29] Can you seriously imagine anyone giving up his coat as well when somebody had already taken his overcoat?[30] All these are counsels whose meaning eludes us because of the exaggerated imagery. In practice, a clear field is left for any kind of violence, and good reasons are brought forward for its justification. But what about the love of our enemies? It can degenerate in people who are too formalist into abdication or betrayal. It can fail to appreciate the true nature of charity which is modelled on human relationships, especially with our nearest and dearest. It can be the aberration of a mind thinking in the abstract, or even bitter resentment against the society in which one lives. On the other hand, the great majority of Christians cannot conceive how such a love is possible, or how it can avoid being unjust. For them Christ's teaching is simply a dead letter. Did not Jesus himself tell us that this was an *extraordinary* way? Are there not many Christians who consider it their duty to hate their enemies? In wartime or times of social upheaval, there are some who even canonize this hatred.

In effect, the rigorists make the demands of God untenable. They are unaware of the consistency and complexity of the realities of nature. Faced by them, the majority simply slip into the service of Moloch and Mammon; they even go so far as to do so in the

----

adversary. Jesus in fact would refuse to take up a position chosen by the adversary where he could not decide on or be free to examine the means, where God would not intervene because his help would be on such very different lines."

----

[28] Jn 18: 23
[29] Acts 23: 3, 4
[30] Lk 6: 29

name of Christ. Whereas the rigorists, with their intransigent attitude, turn God into Moloch.

There is not the slightest doubt that Christ puts us under a threefold obligation regarding violence and the positive pursuit of gentleness. He treats of these obligations under two general headings, which cover a whole section of the Sermon on the Mount. He begins with these words: "If your justice does not abound more than that of the Scribes and the Pharisees, you shall not enter into the Kingdom of heaven."[31] He then goes on to oppose this "more" that is required of his followers to the "justice" of the Pharisees – and Christians are usually satisfied with even less than this "justice". He ends with the words: "Be ye perfect as your heavenly Father is perfect."[32] Such expressions bring us to a consideration of what he requires of us on these three points.

The non-violent are quite right in thinking that the prohibition of killing is an absolute command. They have reason to claim that it is usually ignored. But it is not a prohibition to kill in any circumstances. It flows from the sacred character of human life, from the fact that man is made in the image of God – and thus he has power over all living things.[33] God requires that he should give an account of all blood, of the soul of every man, for man is made in the image of God.[34]

To kill a man can never be a purely secular act; it is either an act of sacrilege, or it is an act of God's justice which he effectively delegates to men.[35] In exercising it, man is expressly given the role of one who sacrifices for expiation, the role of a liberator and, fundamentally, of a protector.[36] This sacred function cannot be assumed lightly. It does not authorize the glorification of the soldier, the judge, or the torturer (as is sadistically done by some Catholic writers). It requires, on the contrary, a great humility and integrity in questioning the legitimacy of what is being done. This should be the spur of conscience throughout history.

---

[31] Mt 5: 20
[32] Mt 5: 48
[33] Gen 1: 30
[34] Gen 9: 5, 6
[35] Jn 19: 11
[36] Ruth 2: 20; Ps 19: 15; Is 41: 14

Why does the humanitarianism of so many men of goodwill prove more effective in this matter than the conscience of Christians?[37] Christians are not sufficiently concerned about this. When an absolute principle is really effective throughout a lifetime – whether of a man, a human community, or the Christian communities – it increases its hold on that man, community or the historic Church. It will come up against difficulties, setbacks may even occur without there necessarily being any culpability. But fidelity to the principle must become all the more deliberate and strict. How can this principle not predominate in hearts whose law of life is the *new commandment*, the law of a merciful and redemptive sacrifice, the sacred character of the divine image shining forth in our neighbour?

We must try increasingly to reduce the number of death sentences, which are still not considered murders. We must – in so far as Christians wield power in the world – help the evolution of mankind to the point where all forms of deadly violence and wars are totally excluded from the world.[38]

If Christians knew intimately the Heart of Christ, his anguish and his longing to overcome death,[39] they would have no difficulty in imagining the violence and the supreme peace with which he recalled the precept of the Duologue "Thou shalt not kill". They could never bear to think of anyone being put to death, still less of taking part in it, without seeing before their eyes the figure

---

[37] It is the humanists rather than practising Catholics who are particularly concerned about capital punishment. (In France, people like Albert Camus strongly opposed the guillotine.) In the last books of the Old Testament a realization of the sacred character of life, of which blood was the symbol and expression, led the Jews to consider the shedding of blood as a disqualification for leading the full liturgical worship of God. Thus the Book of Chronicles gives this as a reason for the fact that David was not allowed to build the Temple. It was Solomon, whose name is associated with Peace, who was to build it. I Chr 22: 8, 28: 3

[38] Our awareness of and obedience to the demands of the Sermon on the Mount should become increasingly strict, whatever the world thinks or does. There must be no limit to this striving for perfection in implementing the teaching of Christ in history.

[39] Lk 12: 50

of Christ standing before Pilate, crowned with thorns, and covered with blood, while he solemnly reminded his judge that his power was from above.[40]

In warning us not to "counter-attack the wicked", Christ is instructing us to do everything in our power not to let ourselves be caught up in the methods of our enemies; and let us face it, now certain methods are never legitimate. For instance, Pius XII condemned the use in war of methods of destruction which destroy all life indiscriminately within their range of action.[41] Christ wants us to escape the fatal, ambiguous position in which evil generally overcomes good, even in the very victory of those who are fighting for a just cause. St Paul teaches that *we must overcome evil by good*,[42] and we shall see later to what extent this law is essential, and organically connected with what has gone before. No doubt Christ wishes to stir us to a deep concern; if his warnings seem exaggerated it is that he is vigorously urging us to set out along the way. This exaggeration is much more than just oriental imagery – it turns us in a particular direction, along which our progress can have no limit. As if he said to us "Become the sort of person who will one day be able to turn the other cheek in all sincerity, without cowardice, without betraying the claims of justice; in as much as you love, you will have the simplicity of the dove and the cunning of the serpent".[43]

Resistance to evil inevitably must adapt itself to the working of human affairs; and the greatest skill and purity of heart is needed if it is to be free of all violent methods. Christ cannot forbid us to accept the inevitable subjection to human nature. What he does ask is that we should reduce them as much as possible and to continue to do so. The upholders of non-violence often make the gospels into a vague doctrine. They say, for instance, "No text of the New Testament gives a right to legitimate self defence" (that is, armed defence). Even if this were a fact, what does it matter? There is no need for a text to legitimize it for *it is a natural right*. Yes, we know about the danger of substituting our human wisdom

---

[40] Jn 19: 11
[41] 30 Sept., 1954
[42] Rom 12: 21
[43] Mt 10: 16

for that of Christ; this risk has to be taken. When one is conscious of it, one is in less danger of falling. A bogus Christian wisdom which forbids the coming to grips with human realities betrays the great laws of the incarnation and redemption. One has to be very self-critical, of course, in one's desire to get results, and the drama of adapting the means to the end will never have a completely satisfactory solution. One will have to be continuously reconsidering one's methods, which are always mixed. But, except in extreme cases, they will not normally consist either in a simple rejection of violence, or in simply answering evil with evil. It is precisely this latter course of action which Christ proscribes. He puts us under an obligation of always seeking to resist without reprisal, and he also requires certain inner dispositions. A whole education of the heart and techniques of action are required of us,[44] in order that we may in every case judiciously reconcile an effective goodwill towards our assailant with the defence of right. It is most remarkable that Jesus should have made the love of our enemies a condition of our divine adoption: "Love your enemies . . . that you may be the children of your Father who is in heaven."[45] This love will be its greatest sign, the most extraordinary fulfilment of the supreme beatitude put into words that link it with the former saying: "Blessed are the peace-makers, they shall be called the sons of God."[46]

A peace of such fullness that it succeeds in overcoming enmity, this is truly the sign of regeneration through the grace of Christ. But it consists in more than a sign: an effective striving for this overcoming is required of us, however *extraordinary* it may be, or rather because it is extraordinary, so that we may truly become the children of God that we claim to be in theory. We must, each one of us, purify our hearts. The instinctive hatred we feel towards those who hate us or do us harm must be changed into love. What form will this love have to take? We need to be more specific about it.[47] In every case it will have to imitate the love of our Father in heaven who makes his sun to shine on the good and the bad, and his rain to fall on the just and the unjust.

---

[44] These will be dealt with in the second and third sections of this book
[45] Mt 5: 45
[46] Mt 5: 9
[47] See Chap. 8

What exterior action will manifest this interior disposition? Christ does not state this precisely. What is possible will vary indefinitely according to different situations and people's state of conscience. An evangelical command must never be treated in isolation from the others. The requirements of justice, in all its forms, will always be binding. It is for us to discover what we are capable of doing in order to manifest our love for our neighbour without betraying the values we have to defend.

The parallel text from St Luke offers us certain details which enable us to see more precisely the spirit which must actuate us. It is here we find the golden rule "As you would that men would do unto you, do also to them in like manner".[48]

In Matthew the whole drift of the Sermon on the Mount leads up to it as a conclusion. Luke seems to have thought that its connection with the subject we are considering was more immediate and he wished to make this clear. He links it up with Christ's teaching that we have to show love to those who have no love for us. He emphasizes the formal command that we have to love our enemies by saying: "Do good to those who hate you." He adds some difficult words which can be interpreted in two ways and both are striking. One: *"Do good and love*, hoping for nothing thereby", which goes beyond the care of enemies, and underlines the supremely positive character of this moral teaching. Here we have the plenitude of good which we have to spread abroad creatively, like the Father in Heaven of whom the sun is a beneficent image; doing good to enemies (once again within the limits of the possible, having considered all the claims of justice) appears as the supreme example of this essential generosity. The spontaneity of this action must in no way be determined by the behaviour of its beneficiary, though such spontaneous action will, alas, inevitably be restricted by his limitations. The other interpretation is as follows: "Never despair of anyone (or, never make anyone despair) or, never despair of anything", which emphasizes the supreme nature of a love which is optimistic enough to count on the conversion of the unjust enemy by means of a superabundance of love on our part. The whole of this passage ends with this command: "Be ye therefore merciful as your Father is

---

[48] Lk 6: 27–35

merciful", whereas in Matthew we find "Be ye perfect". It is therefore in the direction of bringing relief to one in need that Luke
orientates all striving for perfection. He concludes *"Judge not and
you shall not be judged"* which, as we shall see shortly, is particularly germane to our subject.

We have seen in these three cases what is meant by the "evangelical law" and what is the nature of its obligation. It is hardly a
law in the juridical sense of the word. As Fr Lagrange[49] says, "Jesus
never used the term 'New Law'. What he preached was not a law,
but an indefinite perfection". Indefinite since it will never reach
the perfection of the Father, but very definite in its orientation..

> The "superabundance" which the disciples of Jesus must give
> is the *supernatural in the practical sphere*. They are called upon
> to lead a divine life; they have to behave as sons of God. They
> are the inheritors of limitless riches: they will therefore have to
> give without measure. What seems to be beyond the claim of
> justice from a human point of view is simply justice in the eyes
> of God . . . Jesus has engraved a new covenant in their hearts
> as was predicted by Jeremiah.[50] This new interior law can only
> be suggested, it cannot, properly speaking, be expressed in
> human language.[51]

---

[49] *l'Evangile selon saint Mattieu*, 1923, p. 76, n. 8; and the remarkable
article by Fr Lyonnet S. J. on Paul and the Law in *Christus*, no. 4.

[50] Jer 31

[51] This excellent paragraph is taken from a study by Fr. A-M
Dubarle on St Matthew, Chap. 5. Cf. by this same exegist *Les Sages
d'Israel*, p. 248. "Jesus uses a way of teaching the object of which is to
lead the heart and mind to *strive without ceasing to go beyond its present
state.*"

Fr. Lyonnet, S. J. *Liberté chrétienne et loi de l'Esprit selon S. Paul*
in *Christus*, No. 4, p. 16, "Christ has not replaced the Mosaic code
by a less complicated one of the same kind, so keeping the Christian
under a legalistic régime": *he himself takes the place of the law*. That
is the meaning of Col 2: 3. "In whom are hid all the treasures of wisdom
and knowledge", these treasures which for the Jews consisted in the
commandments of the Law (thus Ecclus 24: 9–22).

P. 25: *"The external law does not normally give the Christian an ideal
which he is content to reach but merely a limit beyond which the dynamic
force which makes him a Christian will assuredly be lacking."*

Aquinas has expressed this singular dispensation of the law of the gospel with the greatest profundity. This law is nothing other than "the grace of the Holy Spirit given to the faithful".[52] We need definite precepts, put into formulas, because we are rational beings, who must have clear and distinct ideas both in the speculative and the practical realms. But the formulations are *secondary* in relation to the grace of the Holy Spirit.[53] Without it the written law becomes a letter that kills, and one has to say, with Augustine, that this also applies to the letter of the gospels.[54] On the other hand, if we are responsive to "the grace of Christ which justifies us",[55] then the *letter* predisposes us to that same grace, by indicating to us what has to be believed and what has to be done.[56] It leaves a lot to be determined, and this is one of the reasons why the gospel is known as the "law of liberty".[57] The grace of the Holy Spirit acts in us as an inner nature which inclines us instinctively to do what is in conformity with it and to reject what is against it[58]. It interiorizes the exterior law in such a way that we conform to it spontaneously, freely and joyfully.[59]

Thus the evangelical obligation, directed by God's word, and by a corresponding grace in ourselves, and of course, under the direction of the Church, means far more than simply obeying the letter of the law. It is, as Fr Dubarle puts it, "an obligation to

---

[52] Ia, IIae, qu. 106, art. 1; cf. qu. 107, art. 1

[53] Ia, IIae, qu. 106, art. 2

[54] ibid.

[55] ibid.

[56] Frequent mention of the part played by faith in matters touching the evangelical law and the conjunction of "things to believe and things to do" underlines the striking parallelism in St Thomas's teaching about the *object of faith* and *the obligation of the law*. The object of faith is nothing less than God himself in his infinite mystery, as prime Truth, but we can only attain to this through formulas of faith which direct us to him (1a, 2ae, qu. 1, art. 1 and 2). Similarly the law of the Christian is nothing less than the grace of the Holy Spirit but to put ourselves in a right disposition for it we must obey the commandments to the letter for it kills unless given life by this grace and only through it is our obedience of value (1a, 2ae, qu. 106, art. 1 and 2).

[57] ibid., qu. 108, art. 1

[58] ibid., ad. 2

[59] ibid., cf. II Cor 4

respond to the love of the heavenly Father". It will stimulate
originality. In the words of Romano Guardini: "it is a question of
doing what freedom is able to do . . . initiating a movement which
will be constantly developing".[60] "What freedom is able to do."
It is conditioned in its exercise. The directions indicated by Christ,
and in which the Holy Spirit is spurring us on, are conditioned
by *the state of our conscience and by external circumstances.* The
determination of what is possible will vary greatly even along the
same lines of conduct. One will not only have to take account of
situations but of states of conscience, of the different degrees of
assimilation which the gospel will have reached in different hearts
and human settings. For these actions are not virtuous unless they
are subjectively sincere as well as objectively true. It is a duty to
rectify these states of conscience and to bring them into conformity with an objective order embodied in law. But they are
as they are, and it often takes centuries to correct consciences;
think of slavery or torture.

It is customary to insist on the individual nature of the perfection
preached by Christ. As Fr Lagrange wrote with regard to the love
we owe our enemies: "Jesus gives no orders or advice to public
authorities, the influence of his gentleness on them being left to
time."[61] Admittedly public authorities have the duty to care for the
common good, which they have no right to abandon to the attacks
of unjust enemies. But when the Christian spirit has "influenced
with its gentleness" a whole human institution, the latter is under
the same obligation as a private person to strive for effective means
of manifesting a merciful love for its enemies. The Christian leaven
must seek to leaven the whole lump. The fire which the Lord
came to cast on earth must strive to overcome public as well as
personal enmities. It must enlighten and enkindle the common
man, the common outlook. Alas, our hope for progress in this
direction may seem quite illusory in this cruel world which is
becoming increasingly hard. At least we should keep the gospel
open and receptive to every possible development. The evangelical
obligation is to extend the area of light and zeal to the utmost, that
it may conquer the cold and darkness of this world.

---

[60] *Le Seigneur*, Vol. I, pp. 88, 107; *The Lord* (Longmans, 1956)
[61] *l'Evangile selon saint Matthieu*, p. 112

GOING BEYOND THE REALM OF JUSTICE TO THE REALM OF CHARITY

If the love which the Father has for the Son is in us,[62] it will make us zealous to carry out the literal precepts of the law, every jot and tittle of it.[63] True peace is the fruit of love, since the divine order is the order of love, but it is also a work of justice.[64] Peace and justice have embraced each other.[65] Love requires justice as its basis, its defence and its witness. Consider the perfect conformity with the will of his Father in the Heart of Christ. His continuous reiteration of the words "He must . . . Must he not"[66] is not simply the expression of the driving power of his love, but its precise determination concerning himself which he found in the law and the prophets.[67] "Love, and do what you like!" Augustine tells us. He knows that if we truly love we shall want to keep the commands of the Loved One. We shall conform with all the more strictness and minuteness, because God's ways contain a twofold mystery: they are supernatural as well as a mystery of love. We are solicitous about every indication which will reveal to us the ways of God. We cannot insist sufficiently on this aspect, particularly at a time when a superficial attitude of "anti-legalism" is fashionable. To go beyond the law is a necessary condition of evangelical gentleness. It goes without saying, of course, that this can never be taken as a rejection of the law; it presupposes a fidelity to the letter itself and includes the order of justice. The harmonization of these two orders is best expressed in the traditional doctrine of the relationship between *precepts* and *counsels*. One hears it said: "These excessive demands which Christ seems to ask of us are only counsels", and so only to be treated lightly. But the tradition of which Augustine and Aquinas are the greatest exponents gives a special urgency to evangelical "counsels". It does not treat them as *de luxe* optional extra, or fine supererogatory expressions. They are necessary norms for the life of the soul. They are warnings from

---

[62] Jn 17: 26
[63] Mt 5: 18
[64] Is 32: 17
[65] Ps 84: 11
[66] Mt 16: 21; Lk 18: 33, 17: 25, 22: 37, 24: 44, 46
[67] Mt 4: 14, 8: 17, 13: 35; Mk 9: 12; Lk 4: 21; Jn 15: 25, 18: 9

the Master of life, who alone knows where it leads and what the conditions of salvation are. It is true that a counsel is not a precept,[68] but it indicates the spirit in which the letter of the law has to be kept and which the soul must prepare itself to accomplish in a literal sense, if a particular situation or an impulse of grace requires it.[69]

We recall this doctrine because we have frequently heard people appealing to the distinction between precepts and counsels in order to exclude in practice the majority of Christians from a line of development which finds its origin in the teaching of the gospels. The distinction is of course legitimate and even necessary, but one cannot invoke it in faithfulness to the gospel if one does not understand it in the sense we have just indicated. It alone expresses accurately in terms of legal obligation the vital character of the gospel. The evangelical law is essentially "a going beyond the law", since the precept of all precepts is to love in a supernatural way. Let us be on our guard against two sorts of betrayal which are committed against the gospel. One is to give to the strict order of justice without love a sufficiency which Christ denied it. The second is to treat with a juridical mentality the evangelical realities which spring from love. For instance, there have been theologians who have tried to decide how frequently acts of charity are required by the commandment of loving God with all one's heart. Once a

---

[68] A "counsel" is of a different nature from a "precept". It is not just a precept which is less binding, so that obedience to it would be reckoned more perfect, by conferring upon it, by way of supererogation, a value of stricter obligation, which it would not possess in itself. No; "precepts" and "counsels" are different in kind. The one who gives a counsel does not intend to *bind* in the legal sense of the word. He must not allow it to be said: "Your counsels are orders as far as I am concerned." if he gives them, it is precisely because he considers that the interested party is alone in a position to judge his personal possibilities, or what the objective situation presents. Anyone who receives a counsel is under a moral obligation to ask himself whether the guidance given to him should be *binding* on him. Whatever he decides, if the counsel comes from a competent authority, he will have to take it seriously and let it influence the general direction of his behaviour, and the spirit in which he considers his own particular case. There are certain cases where a competent authority may impose as an obligation what in other circumstances would simply be counselled.

[69] Ia IIae, qu. 108, art. 4, ad. 4; IIa IIae, qu. 40, art. 1, ad. 2

year, says one, every six years, according to another. . . . This type of Christian pharisaism takes all sorts of forms, from barely offensive but thoroughly boring mediocrity (there is a smug mediocrity which is a ludicrous form of pharisaism) to the most deliberately cruel aggressiveness. In these two ways and in all its manifestations, the self-sufficiency of a closed system which refuses to open itself truly to love, extends from irony to downright cruelty towards any attempt at evangelical gentleness and love of enemies.

The Kingdom of God is as it were a sphere which one has to try to enter, into which one must be assimilated. It has its own climate and way of life, which are those of the Heart of Christ. It is infinitely above the "order of spirits", according to Pascal, who calls it "the order of charity". Its transcendence of the "order of spirits" is as great as that order's transcendence of "the order of the body". Justice is in the sphere of the "order of spirits" but it has a tendency to degenerate into "the order of the body", by treating all things in a quantitative way because it tends to deal with them in fixed relationships. The passing into the order of charity is manifested by surprising reversals of attitude which Christ stresses in some of the parables. Take one, for instance, which is particularly apposite in the context of this work. We find in the parable of the Good Samaritan,[70] that Jesus substitutes for the question: "Who is your neighbour?" the obligation of making ourselves a neighbour to anyone in need. We find ourselves determined by a certain situation which we transform by introducing a factor of pure gratuity and generosity. This reveals the positive character, the source from which the gentleness of the gospels emanates. Jesus chose the example of an enemy in need; it is precisely in the love of our enemy that this creative reversal is most apparent. It is in this context that St Paul formulates his great precept "Be not overcome by evil, but overcome evil by good". When "love is lacking", it often seems just and meritorious for us to take a stiffly correct attitude, and even to be hard and violent out of a sense of duty. Christ, St Paul and St John of the Cross urge us to make good this *deficit* of love with an excess of love: "where love is lacking, let us pour in love".[71]

---

[70] Lk 10: 29 ff.
[71] *Oeuvres spirituelles*, ed. Lucien-Marie (1945), p. 1160

This reversal is emphasized in the Christian state by a simile of coals of fire which St Paul borrows from the book of Proverbs: "Bless those who persecute you, bless and curse not. To no man rendering evil for evil . . . If it be possible as much as is in you, have peace with all men. Revenge not yourselves my dearly beloved, but give place unto wrath"[72] – obviously the wrath of God, who alone has the right to punish – "for it is written 'Revenge is mine, I will repay' saith the Lord.[73] But if your enemy be hungry, give him to eat, if he thirst, give him to drink. For doing this thou shalt heap coals of fire upon his head.[74] Be not overcome by evil; but overcome evil by good."

In the book of Proverbs the "coals of fire" were an image of God's wrath which would only be increased by sparing the enemy.[75] In the mind of St Paul it certainly retains something of

---

[72] Rom 12: 14–20

[73] Deut 32: 35

[74] Prov 25: 21–22

[75] The Christian feeling of love towards enemies was so strong in St Augustine, many of the Fathers, certain saints and particularly St Francis of Sales, that they interpreted Prov 25: 21–22 in a Christian sense. St Augustine said, "The Scriptures never command anything but charity." It is true that it is always just over the horizon but the Old Testament leads us to it by strange detours. We must not underestimate the progress of revelation and morality. Christ underlines them by almost exaggerating the opposition between the New and the Old. "You have heard that it hath been said: Thou shalt... hate thine enemy." In fact he spoke in Aramaic, a poor language which used strong contrasts. The words given crudely in the Greek of the New Testament mean nothing more than "You have not to love them". However that may be, it was the sense of the avenging justice of God, and the jealousy with which he kept punishment in his own hands, that led to a whole tradition of which our quotation from Proverbs is an extreme example. When the wrong done by an enemy is called iniquity and in it is seen something prejudicial to God's justice, piety itself makes goodness implacable. Such is the divine jealousy that for man to take a hand personally in the punishment of the enemy, or even to associate himself with God's joy in punishing the sinner, would offend him to whom alone belongs vengeance. "When thy enemy shall fall, be not glad: and in his ruin let not thy heart rejoice. Lest the Lord see, and it displease him, and he turn away his wrath from him" (Prov 24: 17, 18).

this original meaning: the conjuring up of divine wrath is certainly explicit in the given context. These coals are still burning by this wrath, if it is necessary where the unjust man does not repent. The hardening of the culprit who is impervious to kindness obviously makes it worse. This mystery is God's concern. But in the order of divine love the great theme of justice manifestly takes on a new meaning, in many ways contrary to the one it had under the Old Law. In the lapse of time between Christ and the parousia, it is merciful love which dominates a process of which the Judge-

---

It would seem that a certain current of divine anger is concerned and that it is dangerous to pass into the circuit from God to the guilty man; it would be deflected from him to the intruder. This reveals what patience the divine teacher needed to deal with the most strange views of men, instructing them gradually in behaviour less unworthy of their calling. "God," said Fr Sertillanges, "makes the pattern strokes for us." The mother guides her child's hand to teach him to write: the result is terrible; the strokes are distorted through the child's clumsiness. But this must be attributed to the childish hand *and to the one which guides him.* We should at any rate hold to the deep inspiration underlying the bizarre form it takes in the two texts from Proverbs – that is the sense of the mystery of the Judgement that God so jealously keeps in his own hands. "Judge not that ye be not judged." The "coals of fire" evoke this terrible judgement – cf. II Sam 22: 9; Ps 120: 4; 140: 11; Is 47: 14. The original meaning of the text quoted by St Paul is only too clear. It carried to the extreme the logic of the system: not only should one restrain one's joy at seeing the suffering of the enemy so that he may suffer to the bitter end, but one should go so far as to act beneficially in the expectation that he will be hardened, and so God's anger against him will be increased. But as quoted by St Paul the words pass into the climate of Agape as the conclusion of the passage shows (Rom 12: 21). Diadochus of Photike in *Centuries*, ch. 64 (des Places, 1956, pp. 124–5) speaks along the same lines: "It is good to bear with the violence of those who wish to do us harm and to pray for them so that through repentance (this is what the 'coals of fire' have become) and not by restoring what they have taken from us, they may be absolved of their sin. That is what the Lord requires: not that we should recover the goods but the thief *freed from his sin through repentance.*" St Francis of Sales in *Traité de l'amour de Dieu*, book 8, ch. 10, says: "Lead him to the good, render to him good for evil, cast on to his head and his heart coals of fire by showing such charity as will burn him up and drive him to love you."

ment will be the outcome. Wrath will then manifest itself to the
extent that we have stifled the power of love in ourselves and in
others. At present, the "coals of fire" which we wish "to heap on
the heads of our enemies" should be called down only in order to
awaken their consciences, that they may be converted and live.
Our hardness and violence would certainly not contribute to it,
but merciful kindness might have a chance. It must, of course, be
sufficiently subtle to appeal to what is still pure in him. It is thus
that the "Golden Rule" is applied in extreme cases. Goodness
must be so powerful and efficacious in the sinner to whom injury
is done, that it may lead to his conversion and end in turning him
into a friend. In his famous hymn in praise of charity, St Paul
speaks highly of this virtue in that it takes no account of injury
"hopeth all things, endureth all things".[76] He expresses his distress
at seeing the Corinthians going before pagan judges to settle their
quarrels – how can there be *jealousies and quarrels* between
Christians? Would it not be better *to suffer injustice, to let oneself
be defrauded?*[77] In passing, note that Paul, the great realist, is
considering the paradoxical and extreme teachings of the Sermon
on the Mount as quite normal, in a concrete instance and for
people who were recently converted. It must be added that he
does not enforce his teaching. If charity sets out to overcome enmities, all the more must it strive to penetrate every good human relationship. The art of living is to contrive to introduce this love into
every possible channel of communication that links men together.
Jesus has given us a simple rule which we often overlook and rarely
practise, and which should have priority in our instructions:
"When you enter into a house, first say: 'Peace be to this house'."[78]
This is not meant to be a mere ritual which we perform by con-
vention. It is not an empty saying. This customary greeting among
Jews takes on an immense significance on the lips of the Prince of
Peace as well as for us upon whom he has bestowed the *ministry
of reconciliation.*[79] It is the supreme law in human relationships
according to Christ. Whenever we meet someone our main concern

[76] I Cor 13: 7
[77] I Cor 6: 7
[78] Lk 10: 5
[79] II Cor 5: 18

should be to bring them to that Peace of God which is the sum and summit of all spiritual good. Things being as they are, how can we accomplish this divine work of peace, which springs from love? "*Peace be unto you*"[80] – this is the greeting with which the risen Christ always saluted his disciples just as at his birth the angels sang: "Peace on earth."[81]

THE USE OF SUPERNATURAL POWER

The realm of charity is invigorating. Anyone who enters into it should experience in all his contacts that he is endowed with strength from above.[82] He learns "What is the exceeding greatness of God's power towards us who believe, according to the operation of the might of his power".[83]

We see it at work in his saints who were deprived of all earthly resources, beginning with St Paul: "Wherein also I labour striving according to his working which he maketh in me in power."[84] In the midst of terrible trials he tells us: "I can do all things in Him who strengthens me."[85] We must therefore ask ourselves this question: why have we so little experience of this divine power? It seems to us that the word of God itself gives us the answer, and that we fail to respond to the laws of the supernatural world in at least four ways.

Firstly, Christ only gives us his power in order to do *his work*.[86] Do we not, in fact, fight for other objectives than the Kingdom of God – even when we pretend to ourselves that we are fighting for him? We have grounds for believing that when St Paul says to us: "Our wrestling is not against flesh and blood"[87] he is warning us that Christians should not be fighting these battles; that they should leave them to the worldly-minded.

---

[80] Lk 14: 36; Jn 20: 19, 21, 26
[81] Lk 2: 14
[82] Lk 24: 49
[83] Eph 1: 19
[84] Col 1: 29
[85] II Cor 11: 23–29
[86] Jn 14: 12
[87] Eph 6: 12 (C. Spicq translates II Tim 2: 24–5 "A servant of God should not fight," *Rev. Bibl.*, 1947, p. 330).

Secondly, the source of this strength lies in faith, which, Christ assures us, will be accorded to us *to do even greater works than his own*[88] because he is glorified with the Father. We shall only "be strengthened with all might if we draw it from the power of Christ's glory".[89] If we are to benefit from it we must grow in all wisdom and spiritual understanding.[90] We are too much concerned with purely human means. Yet it is in our very weakness that God's power is manifested. St Paul heard this from Jesus himself.[91] Is it not a remarkable fact that the man who was bound and plundered in the Lord's parable,[92] seemed so strong and well armed in the eyes of the world? Should not this encourage us to rely upon power of a different order, a power that never fails us? There is little doubt that this is a way which Christians rarely venture along, although it is revealed to them – the way of weakness according to the world and the flesh, but of the power of God. A few saints dared to trust themselves to it, when placed in extreme circumstances when the spirit correspondingly worked with extraordinary power in them.

Thirdly, the Word of God makes clear to us the weapons we ought to use. The New Testament enumerates them in the famous "panoply" of St Paul. He says to the Ephesians "Stand therefore having your loins girt with truth, and having on the breast-plate of Justice",[93] and to the Thessalonians he speaks of "Faith and Charity",[94] which comes to the same thing, for the one is the virtue of supernatural Truth and the other the plenary "Justice" of Christians. He goes on, "have your feet shod with the propagation of the Gospel of Peace; in all things taking the shield of faith,[95] wherewith you may extinguish all the fiery darts of the most wicked one"; and, finally, "take unto you the helmet of salvation" – in the epistle to the Thessalonians it is Hope which corresponds

---

[88] Jn 14: 12

[89] Col 1: 11; Rom 1: 16; I Cor 1: 24

[90] I Cor 1: 9

[91] II Cor 12: 9. Cf. ibid. 12: 10 "When I am weak, then I am strong"

[92] Mk 12: 29; Lk 11: 21

[93] Eph 6: 10, 14–17

[94] I Thess 5: 6

[95] Cf. I Peter 5: 9 "Resist him (the devil), firm in your faith" and I Jn 5: 4 "the victory that overcomes the world is our faith".

to this – and the "sword of the Spirit" (which is the word of God). In making an inventory of this equipment, St Paul is obviously inspired by words from Isaiah and the Book of Wisdom; but he leaves out "the garments of vengeance" as well as "the spear of severe wrath".[96] We are "like lambs among wolves"[97] but instead of encouraging us to imitate the wolves in their ferociousness, Christ bids us to have the purity of heart and clarity of judgement which is "prudence" inspired by the Holy Spirit. "We have put on the armour of light.[98] We have been strengthened in the Lord and in the might of His power."[99]

For all this, and this is the fourth aspect of the problem, Christ wants us to take great pains. What he deplored in the parable of the unfaithful steward is that in his end and his means he showed so much more determination and strength than the children of light do in the things of God. The children of this world are wiser in succeeding in their sordid affairs, than the children of light in the things of God.[100] They put great vigour into it. But the Kingdom of God suffers violence, the violent will take it by force.[101] The idea is certainly this: since the Kingdom has come upon us we cannot just wait passively for it; we have to show great determination in entering into it. One has, so to speak, to force one's way in.

In the final Beatitude: "Blessed are they who are persecuted for justice' sake", Christ seems to be merely hinting at the possibility of persecution.[102] Later on he explicitly promises them to his

---

[96] Is 59: 17; Wisdom 5: 17

[97] Mt 10: 16

[98] Rom 13: 12

[99] Eph 6: 10

[100] Lk 16: 8

[101] Mt 11: 12. In Luke 16: 16 we find "Since (John) the good news of the Kingdom is preached and everyone enters it violently". Various interpretations of these words are possible in the light of the circumstances in which they were spoken, but they are valid at all times and this is what concerns us here. A. M. Dubarle, in his unpublished lectures on St Matthew, says: "The efforts made are like those of a crowd struggling for places or for largesse. The successful ones are the most determined and vigorous."

[102] Mt 5: 10–11

witnesses[103] and to all those who leave everything to follow him.[104] St Paul is definite about it: all those that will live godly in Christ Jesus shall suffer persecution.[105] The servant is not greater than the master.[106] Anyone who tries to love his brother in this present world, as Christ loves us, is asking for trouble. One hesitates to say these things, because there are presumptuous and indiscreet people and those whose faults make them insufferable, but who are only too inclined to think of themselves as being persecuted for their faith. But such men must not be allowed to stand in the way of encouraging true Christians in their endeavours. And it is of major importance to observe that these persecutions are foreseen as a blessing and one which results from the preceding ones. If we are to "be glad and rejoice"[107] clearly we must live in the spirit with a special intensity, particularly in showing pity towards those who inflict suffering, with poverty of spirit, happy to be despoiled and bereft, with a gentleness which turns the edge of bitterness and with the peace that comes from God.

Obviously, if one accepts the likelihood of persecution as a blessing,[108] Christianity will regain an aspect which has been forgotten. Christians have now come to expect the goodwill of the world.[109] They have become so impregnated with its thoughts and ways that even when they are at odds with it they may still, in the eyes of God and the angels, be using its methods. The so-called good seed hardens itself into an aggressive faction. Even in its victory over the tares it is not conscious that it has itself turned into tares. No doubt it became such as soon as it judged itself to be pure seed. Manifestly the true struggle of Christians is "the most

---

103 Mt 10: 24

104 Mk 10: 30

105 2 Tim 3: 12; cf. Mt 10: 22; Jn 15: 19

106 Mt 10: 24

107 Mt 5: 12; Cf. I Pet 4: 13

108 Acts 5: 41, 16: 25, 21: 13; Phil 1: 29; I Pet 3: 14, 4: 13–14

109 But we must not carry this to extremes. St Paul does not say "If I please men I am no true servant of Christ," but "If I still wished to please men . . ." (Gal 1: 10). This does not mean that Christ's servants should not show general goodwill. See also Rom 12: 17; II Cor 8: 21 and Phil 4: 8; Lk 2: 52.

terrible of all human struggles".[110] It is not simply fought on the
exterior front between themselves and the world but also within
themselves; the demarcation between the two can never be fixed.

It will also be finally obvious that when our consciences awaken
to certain injustices in an "established disorder" in which we are
necessarily implicated, a point is reached when we feel we have to
break away from it if we are not to be accomplices of this disorder.
We shall have to pay a terrible price for such a break. When, on
the other hand, the world seeks for the backing of the Spirit and
his love in forwarding its schemes, it soon turns against us in the
face of the hesitancy or refusal which springs from our faith and
becomes a persecutor. At all times it has been a great risk to play
the world's game, as one may easily find without oneself playing
the game of the "Prince of this world".[111] This is not more than a
risk, for the world is spiritually ambivalent.[112] It is like a key which
either closes or opens the door of charity, according to the way we
turn it. The risk has always been very great. At the last Judgement
we shall find out how often we have succumbed to it under the
illusion of doing a work of piety. Whatever may have been the
case in the past, we have now entered upon an epoch when we are
likely to be faced with the sort of situation with which the early
Christians could only come to terms by a very precarious form of
life, or even by martyrdom.

---

[110] This is one of Rimbaud's sayings but is even truer of the spiritual
life than of the poetic. Evagrius Ponticus said: "The spiritual war is
more difficult than the material one" (*Rev. d'Ascet. et de Myst.*, 1934,
p. 52).

[111] Christ gives this name to the devil (Jn 16: 11). The Temptations
in the wilderness show how cleverly the devil makes use of the things
of this world (Mt 4: 8–9). Christ frees himself from the devil's toils
(Jn 14: 30) and he frees us from them (Heb 2: 4). But since we live in
the realm of expectation and hope this means that we for our part
must make real this "setting free". What we must discover is precisely
this – whether our actions will give the devil power over us, or whether
they conform to Christ's commands and so are proof of our liberation.

[112] Contrast I Jn 5: 19 and Jn 17: 9. On the other hand, "God so
loved the world that he gave his only begotten Son . . ." Jn 3: 16.

CHAPTER
FIVE

"If thou hadst but Known the Things that are to thy Peace"

CHRIST WEPT OVER THE WORLD: "IF THOU hadst but known the things that are to thy peace: but now they are hidden from thy eyes."[1]

The case of Jerusalem on that day of palms,[2] when the people of the holy city did not understand the message of the Prince of Peace despite their acclamations, is not the same as that of the world in its present era, between Pentecost and the Parousia.

The people of the Old Testament were assured of peaceful prosperity if "they walked before him with all their heart"[3] and "walked in the way I commanded you that it may be well with you".[4] This is the profound significance of the history of the chosen people: what makes it a "Holy History". "If you will not believe, you shall not continue"[5] was the warning of the prophet of God, but the *whole people had life on account of its fidelity*.[6] Bitter trials

---

[1] Lk 19: 42

[2] ibid.

[3] Deut 28; II Kings 8: 23

[4] Jer 7: 23. Cf. Hos 14: 3

[5] Is 7: 9

[6] Hab 2: 4 (Rom 1: 17; Gal 2: 11). Habakkuk is speaking of the whole Kingdom of Judah; St Paul of each of the saints.

and spectacular interventions of God brought out to them at one and the same time the disastrous effects of infidelity and the effectiveness of divine help even when everything seemed lost from a human point of view: as for instance in the overthrow of the army of Sennacherib.[7]

The coming of God in person is the supreme attempt of mercy in the plan of universal salvation, to obtain happiness for the chosen people, *even on the temporal level*. Humanly speaking, one can well visualize how the awakening of this people to the significance of the Good News could have secured their earthly happiness. A truly spiritualized messianism, such as was prepared for by Deutero–Isaiah, Zachariah, Malachi and Joel and such as Christ came to establish, if it had been fully accepted and lived up to, would have had all sorts of repercussions not only on personal morals but on political, economic and sociological problems. Jesus would have solved them gradually and in ways which would not necessarily have involved conflict with Roman authority. The conflict between God's living initiatives and the hardness of human hearts had made of the Holy History a long, tragic process. The obstinate clinging to a purely *carnal* conception of messianism resulted in irremediable *tragedy*. The anguished cry of Christ on the evening of his pathetic triumph, is the last outburst of God's long lament: "But my people heard not my voice."[8] "What is there more that I should do to my vineyard?[9] Return O rebellious Israel.[10] And I said 'Thou shalt call me Father and shalt not cease to walk after me.'"[11]

The people had neither danced to the sound of the pipe, nor lamented in songs of mourning.[12]

The hardening of hearts always results from a so-called "realism" which refuses to put complete trust in divine promises: it prefers to find support in compromise by relying on godless powers.

---

[7] II Kings 18, 19; II Macc 8: 19

[8] Ps 81: 12

[9] Is 5: 4

[10] Jer 3: 12

[11] Jer 3: 19

[12] Mt 11: 17; Lk 7: 37

Therefore thus saith the Holy One of Israel: Because you have rejected this word and have trusted in oppression and have leaned upon it. Therefore shall this iniquity be to you as a breach that falleth and is found wanting in a high wall. For the destruction thereof shall come on a sudden, when it is not looked for. And it shall be broken small as the potter's wheel is broken all to pieces with mighty breaking: and there shall not a sheard be found of the pieces thereof, wherein a little fire may be carried from the hearth, or a little water drawn from out of the pit.

For thus saith the Lord God, the Holy One of Israel: If you return and be quiet, you shall be saved. In silence and in hope shall your strength be. And you would not. But have said: No, but we will flee to horses. Therefore shall you flee. And we will mount upon swift ones. Therefore shall they be swifter that shall pursue after you. A thousand men shall flee for fear of one . . .[13] And I will not save them by bow, nor by sword, nor by battle, nor by horses, nor by horsemen . . . They called upon Egypt, they went to the Assyrians. And when they shall go, I will spread my net upon them: I will bring them down . . .[14] I carried them in my arms: and they knew not that I healed them.[15] Cursed be the man that trusteth in man and maketh flesh his arm and whose heart departeth from the Lord . . . *he shall not see when good shall come.*[16]

The Beatitudes are a shining light. But they are not taken seriously even by serious people. Where would they lead to if one followed them? The humble, who detect their messianic tone, insist on seeing in them the foretelling of a political upheaval: to the very end "they thought that the Kingdom of God should come immediately"[17] needless to say as an earthly kingdom. The better informed are anxious about the difficulties that popular enthusiasm might create with the occupying power: "It is better that one man should die for the people rather than the whole people should perish."[18]

---

[13] Is 30: 12–17; cf. 31: 1
[14] Hos 1: 7, 7: 11, 12. Cf. Ps. 20: 8, 33: 16, 52: 9, 146: 3–4, 147: 10
[15] Hos 11:3
[16] Jer 17: 5; cf. Is 1: 3; Jer 8: 7
[17] Lk 19: 11; cf. Acts 1: 8
[18] Jn 11: 50, 18: 14

Entering Jerusalem "riding upon an ass and upon a colt, the foal of an ass", Jesus fulfils for his part the prophecy of Zachariah.[19] But as a result of the vision men had of him, he is forced to give a symbolic value in terms of the nostalgic aspirations of his people to project it into the Second Coming: "And I will destroy the chariot out of Ephraim and the horse out of Jerusalem: and the bow for war shall be broken. And he shall speak peace to the Gentiles."[20] How many words of the prophetic tradition converge upon him:

His empire shall be multiplied, and there shall be no end of peace.[21] In those days Israel shall dwell confidently.[22] And the work of Justice shall be peace: and the service of justice, quietness and security for ever.[23] And I will make a covenant of peace with them.[24] And they shall beat their swords into ploughshares and their spears into spades. Nation shall not take sword against nation: neither shall they learn war any more.[25] Jerusalem, Jerusalem that killed prophets and stonest them that are sent to thee, how often would I have gathered thy children as the bird doth her brood under her wings, and thou wouldest not?[26] If thou hadst known, and that in this thy day, the things that are to thy peace . . . For the days shall come upon thee: and thy enemies shall cast a trench about thee and compass thee round and straighten thee on every side. And beat thee flat to the ground, and thy children who are in thee. And they shall not have in thee a stone upon a stone: because thou hast not known the time of thy visitation.[27]

Thus the "living stone,[28] the cornerstone, the precious one,[29]

---

[19] Zach 9: 9
[20] Zach 9: 10
[21] Is 9: 6
[22] Jer 23: 5
[23] Is 32: 17
[24] Ezk 37: 26
[25] Mich 4: 3
[26] Lk 13: 34
[27] Lk 19: 42–4
[28] I Pet 2: 4
[29] Is 38: 16

has been rejected".[30] The building in "which we were also built together into an habitation of God in the Spirit"[31] remains conditioned in its growth by the law that governed its foundation: the Kingdom of God does not start with a successful Saviour, "received by his own",[32] but is an extension of the reign of the crucified one. Whereas peace and happiness would have been the lot of the chosen people had they received the Messiah, there is no promise of earthly success linked with supernatural fidelity, now that it means following one who failed from an earthly point of view. The Church has not grown out of a people who had gradually spread the realm of the Beatitudes into public affairs: it had to start from a community of believers who were solidly committed to human institutions and outlooks that were both antagonistic to the gospel. We are inevitably weighed down by this. To what extent can we accept the mixed standards of the world as a starting point for its transformation and renewal? At what point does this subjection to evil, this betrayal, arise? In the very first Christian Churches, we see from the epistles of Peter, Paul, James and John that principles of violence were at work, and that the apostles and the faithful were more adaptable in their methods than rigorous.

How can "we prove what is pleasing to the Lord"?[33] In the infinite variety of contradictory situations, which become increasingly worse with the growth of means of power, which of our actions will provoke the tears of Christ? He cannot give us a precise and invariable rule; he wishes to give us a certain spirit by our sharing of his Holy Spirit. What he requires of us is that we should never cease to be "renewed in the spirit of our mind and put on a new man, who according to God is created in justice and holiness of truth."[34]

With regard to peace and gentleness, this renewal enables us to share in certain indubitable dispositions of his Heart which become the guiding principles of our own minds.

The first is the obligation to do his work of peace in the world,

---

[30] Ps 118: 22; Mt 21: 42
[31] Eph 2: 22
[32] Jn 1: 11
[33] Eph 5: 10
[34] Eph 4: 23-4

to go as far and effectively as our lights and our means of resistance to the world permit. We in fact refuse his message of peace and we tempt God if we do not go beyond a theoretical and sentimental desire for peace. We have to give ourselves totally to the violent process of creative love, such as we have outlined in the last three chapters.

Let us add that Christ certainly intends that we should do everything in our power to work for peace only by peaceful methods. For he "who knows what is in man"[35] sees the dreadful effects of violence in the world; they are patent to all those "who have eyes to see".[36] For he sees the nations "labour in vain".[37] We too see how pointless and horrible are these human conflicts. But usually we see it too late. How much time has to elapse before we grasp the folly of the conflicts in which our passions involve us? When shall we rejoice like him in what "is not the will of the flesh and blood, but of his Father who is in heaven"?[38] "Walk in love," he tells us, "according to my example."[39]

His view of violence goes even deeper than what we have just said. His judgement of it must become one of our guiding principles. He sees in violence a ransom that has to be paid to death and the empire of the devil.

Yes, even in the case of what we call a "justifiable", because inevitable, use of violence, we are still in the realm of the "elements of this world":[40] compulsions which the spiritual man must increasingly strive to rid himself of, for these are in the realm of the flesh, "and the wisdom of the flesh is death".[41] "For the anger of man worketh not the justice of God."[42] Everything, in the last resort, fulfils this justice. Even "when iniquity shall bring all the earth to a desert and when wickedness shall overthrow the thrones

---

[35] Jn 2: 25

[36] Mt 13: 13; Rom 11: 8

[37] Hab 2: 13

[38] Mt 16: 17

[39] Eph 5: 2

[40] Gal 4: 3; Col 2: 8, 20

[41] Rom 8: 6; cf. above, p. 60 f

[42] Jas 1: 20

of the mighty",[43] it is still the breath of the Almighty at work within it. Iniquity and injustice also do the work of God and ultimately contribute to his glory. But, as far as we are concerned, let us not carry out what seem to us to be works of righteousness by unleashing forces of destruction which are under "the power of wickedness" and lead to death.[44] How often do we not deserve Christ's rebuke to the "Sons of Thunder" when we claim to be righteous in inflicting punishment "You know not of what spirit you are"?[45]

Is God less affected by the overflowing of violence in the modern world than Yahweh was at the time of Noah? "And God seeing that the wickedness of men was great on the earth, and that all the thought of their heart was bent upon evil at all times . . . And the earth was corrupted before God and was filled with iniquity. God said to Noah 'The end of all flesh is come before me: the earth is filled with iniquity through them; and I will destroy them with the earth.'"[46]

God does not send his flood upon the earth; he weeps over it. But these outpourings of violence are in themselves like a flood in which many human values perish, "Folly is the chastisement of fools",[47] "Destruction is thy own O Israel: thy help is only in me".[48]

Unhappily men seek their own destruction so inexorably, that they preclude any help. It is not so much suffering that Jesus deplores in the growth of violence as "the perversity of their hearts"[49] which consigns them to their own hell, by refusing to find a way out of their self-made vicious circle. They only "go according to the desires of their hearts"[50] without allowing the light and the strength of God to affect this fatal trend. "They shall eat the fruit of their own devices."[51] Our Lord grieves over our

---

[43] Wis 5: 23
[44] Jn 5: 19; Wis 1: 12–13
[45] Lk 9: 54
[46] Gen 6: 5, 11–13
[47] Prov 16: 22
[48] Hos 13: 9
[49] Jer 3: 17
[50] Ps 81: 13
[51] Prov 1: 31

deafness.[52] All our violence, whether it springs from virtuous or evil intentions, is in his eyes but the outcome of our habitual unconcern and refusal to overcome the sordidness of our lower nature, by a recourse to his grace. In its lowest depths it only consists in lies and sin.[53']

If God were capable of irony he would be continually asking us: "What do you think you are doing?" We deceive ourselves as to the real significance of our own actions, we only realize this after a lapse of time. What view must we take of the actions of others? "Do not judge" is a third principle which should certainly reduce violence to a considerable extent. Violence is frequently a spontaneous reaction of a subhuman quality; therefore it should be taboo. At other times self-interest is its motive and it is therefore suspect. We shall see that it is even more than suspect; it is a kind of sacrilege.

We are, of course, bound to regulate to some extent our human relationships. Human justice in various forms is therefore a necessity. But it should be strictly limited. To claim to assess the real culpability of our fellow men is to usurp the right of God. It is no less stupid and impious an usurpation of authority to inflict punishment beyond what is required for the correction of the culprit and the restoration of order. "Revenge is mine, saith the Lord, I will repay."[54]

In this respect the "jealousy" of God fills the Heart of Christ. His terrifying majesty of which the prophet Daniel and the seer of Patmos caught a glimpse,[55] expresses to us his eternal attitude to this type of usurpation. We cannot authorize ourselves to make use of the severity he manifested upon earth; he could rightly see wickedness in men's hearts.[56] God alone sees the heart. "The heart is perverse above all things and unsearchable. Who can know it? I am the Lord who searches the heart."[57]

---

[52] Mk 7: 34

[53] *Nemo Habet de suo nisi mendacium et peccatum* (Denzinger p. 195)

[54] Deut 32: 35; cf. Rom 12: 19. This is a major theme running throughout the Scriptures.

[55] Dan 7: 13–15 and Rev. 1: 13–18

[56] Mat 22: 18

[57] Jer 11: 20, 17: 9–10; I Kings 8: 39

It is even more serious than that. "Our acts of justice are like the rag of a menstruous woman",[58] to use the daring image of the prophet. We judge according to the flesh;[59] we are harsh towards faults from which we think we are exempt when only too frequently we attack in others the very faults whose seeds lie hidden but germinating in ourselves. Our sins put us out of court as suitable advocates of God's righteous vengeance. It is as inevitable as it is mysterious. Would-be accusers will slink out one after the other if they reflect on the words of Jesus: "Let he who is without sin among you, let him first cast a stone."[60]

You castigate some wrong-doing. Granting even that you judge rightly, watch yourself! Another evil is in you, and you project it on to others in your severity. What a splendid figure you cut when you flatter yourself that you are getting rid of the evil you condemn. But in most cases – let us be honest – you only make a pretence of punishing. In either case, your action is very impure and you take little heed of the risks it involves. You will have to wait for the last Judgement to see whether you merely replaced one evil by another or even made matters worse. What is quite certain is that you are rash and presumptuous. All the more so if you are self-righteous in maintaining your right to judge. As David cried out: "It is better that I should fall in the hands of the Lord (for his mercies are many) than into the hands of men."[61]

There is a still more serious aspect. The Son of Man did not come into the world to judge the world, but to save it.[62] The time which elapses until his return to Judge, which is the time of the Incarnation prolonged in us, is thus a time of mercy.[63] When we

---

[58] Is 64: 5
[59] Jn 8: 15
[60] Jn 8: 7
[61] II Sam 24: 14
[62] Jn 3: 17
[63] Christ inaugurates the time of mercy. It is not sufficiently realized that by applying the prophecies to himself, he expurgates them of everything that is concerned with revengeful justice. In the synagogue at Nazareth he quoted Is 61: 1, 2, but dropped the words "the day of vengeance of our God". When he showed John's disciples how he fulfilled the signs of Messiahship given in Is 29: 18–20 he omitted "the ruthless shall come to nought, etc." (Lk 4: 18–19 and 6: 22).

exceed what is strictly necessary in our severity and the subsequent violence, we usurp the office of the supreme Judge. It is an intrusion of our hardheartedness upon his merciful gentleness. It is an unwarranted substitution of punishment such as is "given with the rod of man, and with the stripes of the children of men"[64] for the ministry of reconciliation[65] which Christ has committed to us. Whereas sin disqualifies us from exercising God's avenging justice, it entitles us to be bearers of his mercy. Merciful salvation is so much the dominant law of Christianity that judgement is only legitimate or even conceivable to the extent that it leads to this salvation. *To have the right to judge, we must have the power to save.*

As St James puts it "There is one lawgiver and judge that is able to destroy and deliver. But who art thou that judgest thy neighbour?"[66]

In fact, the supreme principle for the extension of the Kingdom of God in the world, and for the discernment of its opportunities of success in such an antagonistic climate, is to establish it in our hearts. The Kingdom must come in us for it to shine forth in the world. We must therefore go on to examine the functionings of Christ's peace and gentleness within the soul. "We shall only overcome because of him that loved us."[67] In him we find victory.[68]

"Be thou faithful unto death, he tells us, and I will give you the crown of life."[69] "In the world you will have distress. But have confidence, I have overcome the world."[70] These are infallible promises. Salvation is assured to those who remain faithful in the fight. But is not this faithfulness "unto death" similar to Christ's "faithful obedience unto death"?[71] Does this mean that salvation as expressed in our supernatural hope, must wreck all our human hopes? There is no answer to such a question. Go

---

[64] II Sam 7: 14
[65] II Cor 5: 18
[66] Jas 4: 12
[67] Rom 8: 37
[68] ibid., trans. of C. Spicq, *Vie Morale et Trinité Sainte*, p. 29
[69] Rev 2: 10
[70] Jn 16: 33
[71] Phil 2: 8

forth![72] Cast your seed, kindle the fire, bear fruit! As to how you are to fight, that has yet to be determined. Find the weak spots where you can plant the Sword of the Spirit. Engage with the forces of this world with your own feeble strength, but do it rightly so that the power of God can work through it.

---

[72] Lk 10: 3; Mt 28: 19

PART II

The Gentleness and the Holy
"Violence" of a Christian Heart

THE GENTLENESS AND THE HOLY "VIOLENCE" OF A CHRISTIAN HEART

MANY OF OUR CONTEMPORARIES NO LONGER seem to know what is meant by "keeping the word of God".[1] For them it merely consists in a reasonable conformity of external conduct with laws which a rational study has enabled them to extract from God's teaching.[2] What more is required? One has, of course, to get down to concrete action, and it has to be reasonable. But if the mind is simply seeking for beautifully clear and distinct rules of conduct, it will be deaf to the Word of God (particularly when it dissects it hastily and crudely or under the sway of emotion). The Word of God is a mystery; it must be understood over and above rational ideas and sentimentality. It springs from the Heart of God and it requires to be assimilated slowly, silently and with all one's "heart".

What thousands of years of human tradition, and notably biblical tradition; call the "heart" is jointly the depths of the will open to the good and a profound feeling for truth. Rational ideas and emotion diverge, frequently in opposite directions; this inner sense, the "heart", lies deeper than these; it is at one and the same time the expression of love, a seeking for fulfilment and transcendence of self, and the simple perception of the spirit.[3]

---

[1] Lk 11: 28; Jn 14: 23

[2] Lk 11: 28 is often rendered as "Blessed are they who hear the word of God and *put it into practice*" – particularly if we compare it with parallel text of Lk 8: 21. That is how we would have our readers understand it. But they must also understand what they have missed – i.e. the presence, the life of the divine Word *in our hearts*, as Mary "kept all these words, pondering them in her heart . . . And his mother kept all these words in her heart" (Lk 2: 19, 51).

[3] Kittel enumerates the various meanings of the word "heart" in the scriptures thus: "It is the mainspring and organ of a man's personal

It demands self-commitment. The "heart" only achieves righteousness through action. "To keep the word of God" is "to put into practice", it is "to *do* the Truth". This is the only way to come into the light.[4] There is therefore a drawback in studying the evangelization of the heart before considering the problem of action. We must be conscious of the risk of being led astray. How many declared seekers after "perfection" imagine that they are acquiring gentleness of heart while remaining a prey to violence in their behaviour and words? Sometimes over serious matters and in terrifying ways. Torturers have been known to find pleasure in meditation on the Beatitudes. Gentleness can be a means of making feelings appear respectable in our own eyes, whereas they are in fact a cover for the most wicked desires. This is precisely why we need to pay close attention in this second part to the need for the correction of our attitudes, which will only have profound repercussions to the extent that we are exteriorly committed.

As Mounier wisely pointed out:[5] "Feelings without roots or density, of the type possessed by those who want to climb high without effort, are not developed without impunity. Generous feelings are only made tough by tough commitments."

The complementary truth must not be overlooked and it justifies the order we have chosen: the truths of the heart also have their own consistency. And above all, the exterior acts in which they need to be expressed must bear their stamp. They have to be worked out in the Kingdom within us. This intimate

---

life, that most intimate meeting point between his 'being' and his 'doing', and hence the centre and source of his religious and moral life. It perfectly expresses the idea of courage, profound understanding, the power of decision and the will. In a word, it sums up the finest and most personal qualities of a man." (Quoted by Stierli in *Le Coeur du Sauveur*, p. 131.) Hugo Rahner in the same work says, "Whenever we lose the authentic understanding of this eternal, unchanging reality, the heart, the spirit suffers catastrophically. And whenever a deep and real understanding of the heart of Christ revives in us (fed by the Word in the scriptures) something decisive takes place in the realm of the Spirit. *God is apprehended in the way in which he revealed himself to men – heart to heart – the heart of God to the heart of men.*"

---

[4] Jn 3: 21
[5] E. Mounier, "Les équivoques du pacifisme", *Esprit* (Feb., 1949), p. 190

evangelization is a spiritual conversion. But we are not pure spirits. The psychological aspect of this new life is of essential importance; in this too the need to dissect and consider successively the various elements involved has its drawbacks.

In us the gentleness of Christ shows itself in a kind of general moderation.[6] As in every case of temperance (with its connected virtues of modesty, sobriety, meekness, chastity) it is not a virtue unless it also controls the emotions. For the emotions themselves have to work in spontaneous and joyful harmony with what the spirit demands. As long as this is not achieved, the soul suffers violence: either the emotions triumph over the spirit, or the spirit holds them under, but they remain untamed beneath its yoke. There can be no true gentleness, no action purified of harmful violence, when the spiritual equilibrium is seriously threatened. The world within us can only find peace once it has evolved out of the "despotic" stage and into the "political" stage of prudence, rational discussion and agreement.[7]

To a greater or lesser extent, and either consciously or unconsciously, we resemble those atmospheric conditions in which various superimposed air currents move above one another in opposite directions. But we must work towards integrity if we are to become balanced and useful persons who fulfil their vocations and do something of value in the world. How precarious and ineffectual are spiritual forces which have not been reconciled with and harnessed to our instinctual drives; they often produce the worst types of violence. We must therefore do all we can to maintain the right balance – psychological, spiritual, and even physical – which underlies and sustains Christian peace and gentleness.

---

[6] It is permissible to speak of "general virtues". Each of these is, as it were, a form imprinted on all the special virtues going beyond the particular field of the special virtue of the same name. For instance, temperance is, literally, moderation in eating and drinking, but discretion in other matters is also a generalized form of "temperance" (*Summa*, IIa, IIae, qu. 142, art. 2; qu. 143).

[7] The simile of the interior city is of Aristotelian origin and it was incorporated into Christian philosophy by Aquinas. The latter frequently insisted on this pacification of the emotions. Instinct must be brought under the guidance of reason without destroying it. (III Sent. dist. 23, qu. I, art. 1; Ia & IIae, qu 56, art. 4.)

CHAPTER
SIX

The Harmony of Gentleness and Holy "Violence" within Love

THE WHOLE WORLD OF THE EVANGELICAL virtues and beatitudes is immensely rich. This is so little known even to believers that one is tempted to dwell on it at great length. Let us, however, restrict ourselves to two points which will throw light on our subject: firstly, what are the characteristics and inner dynamics of true Christian gentleness? Secondly, how can it be acquired and developed? This, however, will not be the order of our inquiry; the first question is so intimately bound up with the second that we shall have to examine them both together.

SPIRITUAL LOVE

Gentleness is an inevitable consequence of supernatural love, the love of God and our neighbour, as long as it is sufficiently active in our lives to give them a truly Christian form. Our contemporaries oppose our point of view on four counts; these help us to see in a fresh light how radically gentleness is compromised in the modern world and how urgently we need to be made aware of this fact.

"Love?" they cry; "but can one love to order?" Love is the first and great commandment[1] but it is precisely something which cannot be done at will. What we make ourselves do may be devotion, courage, obedience, but it cannot claim the name of love, and it certainly has no gentleness about it. One is tempted to give the old answer that it is not "*affective*" but "*effective*" love which is commanded. It will quite justifiably be objected that this is too convenient a distinction. Our objectors are quite right in thinking that love is either *affective* or non-existent. But only emotional affectivity is considered. The idea of spiritual affectivity is lost. This impoverishment which has such grave repercussions in the whole of our spiritual life, is particularly important in relation to our subject-matter.

Certainly God can require us to love him and to love our neighbour, not in the sense that we are able to command love by acts of will, as the heroes of classical tragedy seem to do, but because we can put ourselves in certain dispositions in which we shall certainly love. We are going to consider how this can be done but we must first of all inquire as to the source of love.

Basically, it is because God has made us for himself and from his grace love flows. "Made for himself": these words express too little. When St Augustine says: *Fecisti nos ad te*,[2] these two last words in Latin are concise and dynamic and mean that God has made us in such a way that inclination towards him is in our very being. His grace refashions us from within, enabling us to break out of the stranglehold of egoism, which constantly leads us to set ourselves up as the beginning and end of everything. It puts us back in a Godward direction and awakens in us an instinct for God, not as an abstract principle, but as "the life of our life". It reverses the terrible saying of Rimbaud "The true life is absent; I am an 'other'". The infinite Other becomes "more ourselves than ourselves"[3] and gives us back to ourselves in giving himself to us; and his life, the true life, becomes so present to us that our own

---

[1] Mt 22: 38–40
[2] *Confessions*, 1
[3] From a poem on youth by Claudel:
$$\ldots \text{ "un autre}$$
Qui soit en moi plus mois-même que moi".

life is but a participation in his.[4] Supernatural life can indeed well up in us from this source with a spontaneity and affective vitality without which it is quite rightly argued that there is no *love*.

In practice, what is required is that we should renew our choice of him as the First and the All. The name given traditionally in the Roman tradition to the act of charity is most significant in this respect; it is called *dilectio*, which essentially implies the idea of "discernment". The best modern equivalent would be "predilection", but let us use the old form as often as possible to make it familiar again. This exclusive choice of the One and Only Beloved excludes no one; on the contrary it is the foundation stone of all loving: God is the creator of all men, their Father, their Saviour, their eternal joy. In this predilection for him we can find utter satisfaction. This remembrance conjures up a presence.[5] If we welcome his Word it awakens an echo in us. Therefore we can summon up in ourselves the love of God and our brethren; it depends upon us to get rid of those things which hinder us. The source is blocked, but we can clear it and it will flow at once. It rests with us to give ourselves a "heart". What springs anew in us, then, is a vital desire for our fulfilment, for our beatitude, which instead of dissipating itself upon objects unworthy of it, recognizes the infinite goodness for which it is made. Through grace this attraction can awaken our capacity for loving. Even without emotional feeling, or in aridity, this is what is meant by true spiritual affectivity; through grace our heart is moved, attracted by God's goodness; it is comforted by it, and invigorated in its work. These are two characteristics of affection. The spirit or mind is a capacity to love as well as to know. Our interior being has all it needs to renew itself day by day in charity.[6]

---

[4] Jn 1: 12; II Pet 1: 4

[5] "Remembrance of the Lord" is a devotion that needs reawakening among the faithful. It is a constant liturgical theme, by which we are called upon to remember some attribute or great work of God. It is particularly prominent in Eastern liturgies and the Eastern Fathers. In the West in medieval times, especially in the twelfth century, it was well to the fore: according to St Bernard the "remembrance of Jesus" made him *present* to us. The first verse of the hymn *Jesu dulcis memoria* sings of this. In those days men knew what it meant to keep the things of God in one's heart.

[6] II Cor 4: 16

This charity extends to our neighbour, since it enables us to enter into the outpouring of God's love upon all men. But it is only within this divine love that we can find what is required to love our neighbour. As we read in the incomparable words of Diadochus of Photike: "When we begin to experience the overwhelming riches of God's charity, then we also begin to cherish our neighbour with a spiritual love."[7] Even when he has inflicted on us "great injuries and insults, in the gentleness of God, the soul completely absorbs the bitterness of the quarrel. He who has experienced this love, even if he is insulted and injured in a thousand ways, does not rise up in anger against the offender: he remains, as it were, inseparably bound to the soul of the one who has insulted and injured him".[8]

The ancient writer may seem over-optimistic and therefore rather discouraging. Alas, many of us sigh, if we began to feel "the overwhelming wealth of the charity of God" we should no doubt absorb in this gentleness all violence and antagonism. All we seem able to do with regard to those who do us harm and are the instigators of violence, is at most to manifest some pity, and to try to be as just as we can in our judgements about them. This faint-heartedness in no way mitigates our hostile feelings, which are dictated by justice. No doubt if our feelings could be transmuted into a mystical state by divine love, they would become, in the words of the old bishop, like iron incandescent in the fire. But Diadochus himself admits that "to taste the gentleness of God in all its intimacy and plenitude" is a passing favour of the Holy Spirit.[9]

This discouragement must be met by an invitation to move always more and more towards the experience of "dilection", to this spiritual *affectus*. It need not take an emotional form, or reach a high mystical level. We have, in fact, indicated three ways in which the grace of God brings forth love in hearts which are open to it. They are the same as those through which we love our neighbour. We must listen to the Word of God, and if we *keep it in our hearts* it has an infallible power to move us towards brotherly love: we must constantly remember God with all our heart, for it is

---

[7] *Centuries*, 15 (Ed. des Places, 1956), p. 92
[8] ibid., 91, p. 152
[9] ibid., 90, p. 151

through us that he wishes to save others; and if it is truly in him that we are well pleased, our joy is in the God of the new commandment. Finally we must constantly and continually pledge ourselves to God by rejecting all that is perishable and in our predilection of him include, as he did, all who were responsible for his Passion which continues in the world.

As long as we do not commit ourselves to these three ways, we cannot even begin to imagine the experience of spiritual peacefulness towards men of violence. It is experienced only in the love of a crucified, suffering God which transforms our hatred. It is unfortunately quite natural that most of our contemporaries do not believe in such an experience, since they exclude themselves from it throughout their lives. In their thoughts they even go so far as to condone the violent policies of the world. Since they have no peace in their hearts, it is vain for them to make a pretence of non-violence in their behaviour. It is in this experience alone that non-violence finds its "virtue", by which we mean its efficacious power, its charm and even its moral value, to which the efforts of grim duty will never attain.

Unfortunately our contemporaries frequently stultify the power of charity by the sluggishness and infrequency of their acts of charity. We have already castigated a purely juridical and negative approach to the obligation of love:[10] being content with a bare minimum considered necessary to keep within the letter of the law. It is senseless to ask how frequently the ordinary Christian should perform his acts of charity and equally senseless to answer this question by indicating a time scale. These acts are as necessary to life as is sustenance and growth. All kinds of functional processes take place in physical organisms; and all sorts of mechanical operations come automatically into play as soon as they are required. Shall we deny this law of spontaneous reaction in the functioning of divine love? Reactions which are at times fervent and at times slack according to vocations, situations and opportunities.[11] It is

---

[10] pp. 110 ff.

[11] The word "slack" should not surprise us. The spiritual life of a Christian cannot always be at full stretch. Normally there must be times when it is relaxed, economizing its reserves, so to speak, for occasions of exceptional effort. Aquinas laid this down in his teaching on *actus remissi*. Cf. Deman, *Dict. de Spiritualité*, Vol. I, Col 145.

very necessary to have a true conception of the part charity has to play in the general functioning of love. Our charity would be very sluggish indeed if it were thought satisfactory for Christians to respond to the demands of the world like unbelievers, and merely to colour their behaviour by some pious intentions. Such Christians flatter themselves that they have "habitual charity" such as they were taught at school, that it gives a Christian value, "a whiff of incense", to a life which is in fact impregnated with the sourness of the old leaven. But if the Kingdom of God is to be an effective reality in our souls, if the mind of Christ is to have a bearing on the way we live, it is imperative that the love of God should influence our actions and that with great force. It finds its full scope and growth only through such acts. In particular, gentleness is one of the evangelical beatitudes. The great Western tradition, of which Augustine and Aquinas are the foremost exponents, recognized in the beatitudes the action of the gifts of the Holy Ghost, the functioning of which is proportionate in intensity with the degree of charity in the soul.[12] A special connection links gentleness with the gift of "piety". This means that gentleness is a quality of the soul in which the Holy Ghost conquers bitterness, violence and hardness by enabling it to share in the filial relations of the Son with the Heavenly Father.

"The gentle," wrote Guardini,[13] "are those who have become inwardly calm, who are humble and good-hearted . . . They stand simply and peacefully in God's presence." This is a specifically *filial* attitude. So much so that another spiritual writer, von Balthasar, who is not writing within the thomist framework of the gifts and beatitudes, defines gentleness as "The unreserved, pure, and naked acceptance of what comes from the Father".[14] However little the reader may be aware within himself of the realities we

---

[12] In *La Vie Spirituelle* (Oct 1956) I tried to show in "Esquisse d'un portrait spirituel du chrétien" the solidity and correctness of Aquinas's teaching on the gifts of the Holy Spirit and the Beatitudes, and especially how they correspond, as shown by Augustine, even though at first sight this harmonization might seem arbitrary.

[13] *Le Seigneur*, vol I, p. 82; (*The Lord*, Longmans, 1956)

[14] *Théologie de l'Histoire*, p. 37; (*A Theology of History*, Sheed & Ward, 1963).

have been considering, he will agree that this filial sense, the source of gentleness, is only conceivable in the light of a divine love which never sleeps, but which, on the contrary, comes to life and spreads out in intense activity. This life of charity must indeed be intense, particularly in our relations with others, considered as children of God; otherwise it will certainly not be that gentleness towards others which will prevail in our hearts over the unfavourable impression they make upon us and the aggressive feelings they provoke. The activity of supernatural love must be intense in order that gentleness may penetrate our feelings; we have already mentioned how necessary this is. In order to evangelize the depths of our heart and soul, do you really think it is sufficient to have an "habitual charity" which hardly influences our way of judging feelings or conscious volition?

In order to renew an act of "dilection", there is no need for tension. On the contrary, "dilection" is the secret of complete lack of tension, of any form of self-display. The more we give ourselves to a love which anticipates our own loving, the more we are refreshed by it.

But today evangelical gentleness is suspect. There are too many caricatures of it: slackness in action, complicity in established disorders (which can be, needless to say, very profitable), sanctimoniousness which readily conceals the worst betrayals, complacency in an inner smugness which can easily be narcissistic – simply the self-defence mechanism of the weak who lack virility in action. These deviations are only too real. They have certainly affected the behaviour of many Christians for whom the word "gentleness" evokes one or the other of these contemporary attitudes. All the more because their minds, particularly if they are genuinely sophisticated, have been deeply influenced by criticism in the naïve form by which American thought has triumphantly swept aside the dull routines of conventional Christianity, and by the radical criticism which Marx and Nietzsche have made of the gospel itself.

It is a very real problem to examine how far genuine Christian gentleness is a sign and example of weakness. It must be one of our chief concerns. Two kinds of answer can be given to this question, both of them factual. One is given in the example of the great saints, who have been obedient to the spirit of the gospel with such integrity. However many differences there may be between them, one of the constant features of their psychology is the gentleness and strength they manifested as complementary qualities. Take, for instance, the examples of St Paul and St John, and I do not hesitate to take Gandhi as exemplifying the same truth: he is the most striking instance in our age of someone who combined a most heroic and effective strength with the most integral gentleness.[15] We will explain later what we mean by his evangelical spirit.[16]

The second answer supports the assertions in the first and is found in a phenomenological treatment of Christian gentleness. We shall not be in possession of all the factors until we have examined the pacification of the psyche and human behaviour. But we are immediately given the secret of its success in a living experience of "dilection". If one of the caricatures of gentleness is but a camouflage of, and over-compensation for weakness, this is no doubt due to the fact that true gentleness is the outcome of a certain fulfilment, or at least a favourable disposition for progress towards such a fulfilment. Gentleness presupposes interior harmony; it results from it, manifests it and contributes to it. It presupposes and manifests an equanimity of heart and soul that have full control over their powers. We could not express this better than by quoting from a text which is in fact applied to God, which, *mutatis mutandis*, could be applied to gentleness: "great power always belonged to thee . . . and because thou art Lord of all, thou makest thyself gracious to all".[17] As Guardini[18] wrote: "Gentleness is a strength that has become gentle and can dominate by truth alone." Such a strength must find its source in a supreme love; supreme in the sense of capable of controlling all the powers of our being (taking into account, of course, with the realistic attitude of good government, the stage of development of a particular society and of the world in general). It must be understood that we are speaking of

---

[15] See L. Corman, *Une école d'héroisme: les campagnes non-violentes de Gandhi.*

[16] See below, pp. 191 ff.

[17] Wis 11: 22 and 12: 16

[18] See above, n. 14, p. 141. Note that in the list of the "fruits of the Spirit" (Gal 5: 23) *Gentleness* and *self-control* go together.

an ideal, since human nature is *wounded*, so that even with the help of grace, this mastery can never be absolute. Neither can gentleness have total integrity; love and its gentleness are, in a sense, militant. Is it not, therefore, more worthy for man to be working towards its attainment according to its own laws than to be destroying it further out of hatred for its counterfeits?

Finally, the supernatural character of gentleness is a source of much irritation to the contemporary mind. Some do not wish to have recourse to grace for something they consider can be achieved by purely natural means. Others blame God for the fact that they remain violent, hard and bitter, as if God were responsible for it and withheld his grace. With the latter, one can only try to make them understand that they do not know what they are talking about. They cannot be speaking of God if they think of him as one about whom complaints can be made. Further, his grace manifests itself only in our actions, which come to nothing if we undertake them as if we were their only cause. Christ wishes that we should become conformed to him, in an infinitely greater degree than we can conceive or will, and his grace does not fail us: it is we who fail it. If we Christianize our inner selves, purifying our actions from all violence, we shall grow into the mind of God, which will enable us to recognize in our innermost being that "every excellent gift comes from the Father of lights".[19] "A humble and gentle heart," wrote Isaac of Syria, "is the source of the secrets of the world to come."[20] As long as one has not got access to that world, one can only talk nonsense about the ways that lead to it. They seem absurd, but they have been shown to us, and we have only to proceed along them as if everything depended upon our own efforts for our progress – provided that we pray assiduously. In truth, it is grace which draws us on, which enlightens and moves us. If it were not hidden, it would not be divine, and neither would it treat us with the dignity that belongs to us as free beings. In this way we give an answer to the first kind of dissentients who claim that they can become non-violent and gentle without God's help. But they raise an important question which is of special interest.

---

[19] Jas 1: 17
[20] Quoted in N. Arseniev, *La Sainte Moscou*, 1948, p. 77

GENTLENESS AND VIOLENCE, IN RELATION TO THE HOLY SPIRIT, THE SPIRIT AND THE "FLESH"

We see in gentleness an effect of supernatural love[21] and, more especially, of a gift of the Holy Spirit, namely piety. Paul includes it among the "fruits of the Spirit".[22] But there are people who become gentle by purely natural means, even though temperamentally they are often hard and violent. Gandhi once declared: "The religion of non-violence is the law of our species, just as violence is the law of the brute."[23] Considering the question as a whole and reducing it to its essentials, gentleness can be found at three levels. Gandhi excludes it from the level of brute creation which he considers as the realm of violence; there is an intermediate human level of mind and spirit, which is the realm of non-violence; finally, Christian saints consider that to become "gentle" as the gospel describes it one must reach the level of the supernatural. "If in your love, O good Jesus, you did not make the soul gentle," cried out St John of the Cross, "it would continue in its natural hardness."[24] These words would seem to imply that without the intervention of supernatural grace, the spirit itself is hard and violent. It goes without saying that St Paul, St John of the Cross and Gandhi think along completely different doctrinal lines. Their doctrines cannot just be fitted together in the form in which they were originally put forward. But what we would wish to do is to recognize our own thoughts in their teaching, and to understand what is their true nature. We shall at once begin to see one of the most important tenets of Gandhi's teaching on non-violence in a Christian perspective.

We shall only see it clearly within the context of the pauline dialectic of the "spirit" and the "flesh". These two terms in St Paul designate sometimes the "superior" and the "inferior" parts of man; but, more often, the "spirit" and the "flesh" mean for him

---

[21] Not enumerated in I Cor 13, but qualities found there presuppose gentleness.
[22] Gal 4: 22, 23
[23] *Jeune Inde*, 11 Aug., 1920
[24] Maxim 47 in Lucien-Marie's edition, pp. 1301–02

man seen as a dynamic whole, in so far as he conforms with the life-giving laws of the Holy Spirit, or submits to those instincts which lead him to death. For instance, he writes to the Corinthians, "For you are yet carnal. For whereas there is among you envying and contention, are you not carnal and walk you not according to men?"[25] Yet these contentions are spiritual faults. Yes, but "fruits of the flesh":[26] if the charity of the faithful is troubled by them, it is because the attraction of passing things has the upper hand. Let us add that the action of the Holy Spirit through grace is generally hidden, and that conformity to the laws of the Spirit can be more or less implicit, unconscious, unreflecting – so much so that it is often an insoluble problem to decide whether St Paul means man's spirit or the Holy Spirit when he uses the word *pneuma* (spirit).

Let us leave aside for the moment the question of a religion of "non-violence".[27] The reality which Gandhi expresses in the phrase "Violence is (in man) the law of the brute"[28] is what Paul is saying when he speaks of "hatred, discord, jealousies, disputes, dissensions, factions, quarrels" and, *a fortiori*, wars in which these forms of violence reach their paroxysm, being all "fruits of the flesh". St James condemns similar forms of violence in even stronger terms, "But if you have bitter zeal, and there be contentions in your heart, glory not and be not liars against the truth. For this is not wisdom coming from above; but earthly, sensual, devilish."[29]

This is not the resentment of a false spirituality against the body itself: for that is the Temple of the Holy Spirit,[30] or capable of becoming it; the spirit in "its carnal condition" uses it as an instrument of sanctification[31] and it is destined to a glorious resur-

---

[25] I Cor 3: 3

[26] Gal 5: 20

[27] See below, p. 239

[28] We leave aside the whole question of violence and gentleness in animals. It requires minute observation, as well as a psychological capacity of seeing things from their angle rather than projecting human values and emotions into their behaviour.

[29] Jas 3: 14, 15

[30] I Cor 6: 19

[31] Rom 6: 19

rection. Sin, even in its most carnal forms, is only sin through the disordering of the spirit. It consists in a wrong use of freedom, which is a prerogative of the spirit. It involves the inner violence springing from a lack of harmony within oneself, with the voice of conscience. Hence in man, it is the spirit that is the instigator of interior states of violence, and therefore of exterior violence. Violence has, alas, become the law of our species. Our race is now "sold under sin" as St Paul puts it.[32] The revolt against God and what is best in our nature, and all the disorders that spring from this, have become a condition and, in a sense, the law of our being, "the law of sin, which is in our members".[33] This last expression must not lead us into error, as if the spirit were pure and innocent, and the members of our body perverted. The "law of sin" like "the law of our species" is an entirely spiritual violence; it has its profound roots in the spirit, it conditions it and leads it to all sorts of disorders. One has to add something to Gandhi's formula: non-violence is not purely and simply a law of our species. In man's fallen state, there is another law which is completely contrary to it.

As a genuine "experimenter with truth"[34] Gandhi was well aware of this. We do not contradict him in completing him. He was acutely aware of moral failure: he knew from whence it sprang and he believed, however vaguely, but with a profoundly religious spirit, in its divine repercussion. He was neither a theologian nor a metaphysician. He was certainly a theoretician, but his theories were the outcome of his personal experience. We must understand what he says as the teachings of a practitioner – a great spiritual practitioner who was at the same time a humble realist.

His formula is true in two ways. The "law of the brute" in us inclines us to violence. Our mind and spirit are out of harmony when the spirit no longer controls our whole being. One of the most essential factors of spiritual progress consists in the liberation of the spirit from instinctive impulses. They do violence to it. They are principles of violence, either by covetousness, or by an

---

[32] Rom 7: 14
[33] Rom 7: 23
[34] "Experiments with Truth" is the title he gave to his Memoirs

aggressiveness which disguises the death wish.[35] There is therefore an astonishing agreement between the spiritual and moral doctrine of St Paul and modern depth psychology, and both in turn throw much light on the intuitions of Gandhi.

His formula is also true in this respect: however much the spirit sins and is wounded by sin, and hence violent and causing violence, this is against its most essential inclination. Basically, violence consists precisely in this disharmony with what is best in the self. Its fundamental inclination, which St Paul calls "the law of the mind"[36] is "to be delighted with the law of God according to the inward man".[37] Whether we consider this law of reason as a simple dictate of conscience, or whether it be supernaturally fulfilled in "dilection", it tends to harmony with God, with oneself and with others, that is to say to peace and gentleness.

This is the profound basis upon which a collaboration must be built between those who work for peace and gentleness, whether they be such on account of their explicit Christian faith or because of their simple natural goodness and integrity. That is the bearing of the confusion in practice between Paul's use of "spirit" and "Holy Spirit".[38] This collaboration must not however be equivocal on the part of believers: they must first of all be quite clear in distinguishing between their strictly supernatural motives and the purely human reasons that also inspire them; and secondly they must not ignore the shattering "law of sin" which affects both man's spirit and his psyche.

CORRELATION OF GENTLENESS AND HOLY "VIOLENCE"

The evil violence, from which Jesus and Mary were completely exempt, emphasizes the distinction between the holy "violence" which is necessary in our gentleness, and that which we have considered in Christ. It is in us as in him an essential element in the

---

[35] Cf. Chap 1, pp. 60 ff

[36] Rom 7: 23

[37] Rom 7: 22

[38] See Rom 12: 11; II Cor 6: 6, 12: 18; Gal 6: 1 (which in fact deals with the "spirit of gentleness"); Eph 4: 3, 23, 6: 18; Col 1: 8, etc.

intensity of love, which is in conflict with a sinful world that rejects it. But our whole being is enmeshed in the sinful world.

"The work of the soul," said Aquinas, "requires a particular *tension*."[39] The intention which gives direction to all spiritual acts is not a mere mental directive. It is a vital impulse[40] of the will from within itself; and although in order that its action may be fully fruitful there must be an inner richness which comes from a degree of relaxation, nevertheless, too many constraints impede this impulse so that there must be some degree of acute tension. Man never obtains anything of value from himself without doing some sort of violence to himself. It is remarkable that in passing from the simple "order of the spirit" to the "order of charity", this necessary "violence" tends to become identified with gentleness.

Intellectual thought is strenuous. "The mind works furiously when attentive" remarked Malebranche.[41] Whoever strives to reach the truth, to grasp it at its most specific, to formulate it, to get hold of it and allow it to get hold of him, knows the almost intolerable tension of his solitary penetration into the unknown and what vital strength he requires. The ruthlessness that has to be meted out to anything other than the truth, the rejection of inadequate ideas, particularly those that we normally cherish and those that are the products of the automatic functionings of the mind. All our spiritual energies must be brought to bear "to see what one sees". This is surely the essence of heroism; if our life is to conform effectively to spiritual demands, it will have to grow continually in moral awareness and courage and venture along difficult paths. It will not only have to break away from the pattern of mediocre ideas: it will have to break itself and other lives. But what demands all this "violence" is the gentleness of truth: it is a concern not to do violence to reality by an improper use of reason, generally under the impulse of passion, which as we have seen happens so frequently and does such harm.[42] Delight in the truth is wonderful in its gentleness. The mind is made for truth.

---

[39] Ia IIae qu. 77 art. 1 (Bernard's translation)

[40] Ia IIae qu. 12 art. 1; qu. 180, art 1

[41] Quoted by Pierre Blanchard in *L'attention à Dieu selon Malebranche*, p. 47, n. 7.

[42] See pp. 66 ff

In truth it finds its rest and renewal, and a new impulse to further truth and it delights in the otherness of these truths. Of course it cannot *possess* the truth, which would be a violent assault upon it: the mind does all that is possible to be possessed by the truth. In disagreements, error always finally appears as a lack, and its only remedy is to become more submissive to the truth. Harmony between our spirits and the true framework of reality is "sweet", as is the harmony of our minds with others within its light.

Spiritual love is gentleness itself. Since it is alive to all goodness, it rejoices in it, welcomes it, seeks to spread it, and sees evil as a void it must overcome. It is in this, perhaps, more than in anything else, that one experiences a strange violence, out of which grace will bring heroism and holiness. The violence of the desire for good threatens to be exclusive;[43] it destroys selfishness, pride and inordinate attachments. In theory there should be no conflict between "a commitment" and "openness"; but in fact, love is torn, so to speak, between giving itself to people who induce it and remaining at the service of others; and on the other hand not letting the latter degenerate into a loan for which a return is expected.

To arrive at a state of mind and heart in which thought and love are sufficiently pure, so that they are felt as both gentle and violent, is a summit we can only glimpse, rather than pretend to attain. We experience this better in the supernatural order, which is gentleness itself, but is, nevertheless, made up of tensions, and which we adhere to in a supreme tension. The faith which gives us access to the supernatural does violence to our mind: for its law is to seek reasons for everything, and is only satisfied by sight and proof and only gives its assent according to the degree of evidence it receives; yet it is asked to give the complete *yes* of faith to what remains infinitely obscure, and which it will never see satisfactorily here below and not find intrinsically contradictory. How, for instance, to reconcile a Trinity of Persons within one nature, or to accept a small white wafer as the Body of Christ? But this very adhesion is the supreme repose of the spirit, for it is accomplished in the infinity of being and truth. A living repose which opens out an infinite field of searching, anxiety and discovery.

---

[43] See above, pp. 70 ff.

But we shall never come to an end, if we start describing the different forms which the act of faith can take with respect to its "violence" or "gentleness". Let us simply draw attention to a certain kind of evil violence and the false gentleness to which it can lead us. Gandhi cried out, "How can anyone who believes he possesses absolute truth, claim to be fraternal?" He thought that believers bound by definite dogmas could not be totally committed to non-violence. He was the victim of a misunderstanding, but that was the result of a correct intuition. Whoever pretends to "possess" the truth is a sectarian who closes his mind, and it is true that he will be led to the worst forms of violence, those that spring from fanaticism. We Christians *are possessed by* the truth, by a Truth, which is infinite and therefore infinitely mysterious. In it, all truth can find its foundation and fulfilment. We can never be sufficiently possessed by it. The more we give ourselves to it, the more it makes us open to others who seek; it makes us brothers. But it would be a false gentleness on our part to seek agreement with those who have not yet found the truth; it would be a betrayal, however slight.

The hope in divine help, the hope of salvation is sweet. But what violence there is in the tension it involves between its messianism, which urges us to fulfil, in Christ, all that is best in men's hopes, and a fundamental eschatological outlook, which among the ruins of human hopes forces us to live indefinitely and in all the detail of our daily lives in the light of the end of this world. The perplexities engendered by this mystery are insoluble.[44]

Divine love, inasmuch as it reigns in our hearts, is gentleness itself, but it is "strong as death".[45] The tensions that it multiplies are terrible to our nature, because they are supernatural; and together put pressure upon it to find its fulfilment beyond its own wishes. It is a violence to our nature to love Christ in such a wretched existence, but how sweet it is! One might well say with regard to all the teachings of faith "This is a hard saying, and who can bear it?"[46] and "How sweet are thy words to my palate! More

---

[44] See above, the conclusion of Chaps 2 and 5 and below, Chap 11

[45] Cant 8: 6

[46] Jn 6: 61

than honey to my mouth".[47] All growth in Christ involves inevitably a deeper "conformity to his death" and a higher experience of "the power of his resurrection".[48] The "consolation" of the Holy Spirit is communion with the power of God. Entry into the order of charity, and all progress made within it, involves *metanoia*,[49] a renewal of the heart and mind which demands heartrending penance and a deeper and livelier communion with the infinite goodness of our God.

The effects of this violence and gentleness which result from our coming into vital contact with the absolute, have repercussions throughout our lives. We have "to strive to enter in by the narrow door"[50] that leads to life. There is the violence of renunciation, the violence of "taking up one's cross"[51] and "losing one's life".[52] The violence of striving in God's battles, when the disciple of Christ becomes like him, "a sign of contradiction",[53] and when he has to push ever forward with the "sword" Christ has brought into the world.[54] This is the price of the gentleness of God.

Let us finally insist upon the fraternal character of this kind of ambivalence of violence and gentleness which lies at the heart of spiritual realities, and particularly of "dilection". The obstacles which our love meets in others force us to do violence to them, as we do to ourselves. We experience this in truly virile friendships, which are both worthy of ourselves and of our brethren. "If your friend is asleep," commands Saint-Exupéry, "thrust him away that he may become himself."

This is a dangerous precept. It will, of course, be frequently invoked by those who are not really qualified to apply it. It is a duty to be an ally of one's neighbours against themselves. Their goodwill is not sufficient to prevail against their own weakness,

---

[47] Ps 119: 103

[48] Phil 3: 10

[49] Etymologically: "thought in the hereafter". But it is a case of knowledge in the biblical sense of the word which is more than "thinking"; it is the vital commitment of the whole self.

[50] Lk 13: 24

[51] Lk 14: 26

[52] Mt 16: 24

[53] Lk 2: 34

[54] Mt 10: 34

their complacency, their ineffectualness in the face of conflicting tendencies; often they have not even got an insight into what ought to be the true purpose of their lives, and its discovery will imply a distressing renunciation of their present attachments. In the same way a gentle and holy violence in friendship – violent in its intensity, holy in its desire to promote their true vocation, gentle in its psychological awareness – needs to become violent in the proper and regrettable, yet necessary meaning of the word: a violence of opposition, which goes against their actual desire.

In order that we may dare to use this kind of violence towards our brethren, it is not sufficient that it should proceed from the love we have towards them, that it does not exceed that love, that it permeates it completely. It is not sufficient that we should really understand them, their possibilities and needs. It is not sufficient to appreciate what is their true vocation. (These are all points on which one can easily deceive oneself.) *They have to feel that they are being loved and understood.* How rare this is! It is an excellent thing to give a strict education, if the child experiences in the very strictness, a love and intelligence which are creative of the potentialities of his personality of which he is ignorant. If he reacts fully to the way in which he is treated, his personality will become rich; but the opposite will happen if the child feels rightly or wrongly that he is neither understood nor loved; he will then become inhibited and resentful. An admirable and creative severity such as exists among the truly *élite*, as for instance in certain religious orders (but how rare today) or in other close-knit organizations.

Discernment accompanies "dilection" both in regard to God and our brethren. To feel ourselves loved is to feel that we are being *discerned* with interest and goodwill. Life forces us to play a part and our worst failure is to succeed in doing this by betraying our true selves. A true friend is one who sees beyond the parts we play to the child of God, which we so often lamentably fail to be. Other people force us to wear masks and obstinately insist on only having dealings with these grotesque substitutes. They never really deal with *us*. Only occasionally someone joins us in this dereliction, which is the worst form of solitude. The worst violence we suffer is that of being misunderstood. For nothing is more contrary to our will, for it then feels itself denied in a form which does more than suppress it, for it substitutes some other odious personality for our true selves. One of the most cruel features of our age is its *contempt*.

We are therefore warned to become acutely aware of any signs that others give us of what they think they are. How many exhaust themselves by sending out messages which have no response from others! We must be completely open to all their approaches, see them as they see themselves. Then we shall see whether there is any need to oppose their present trend to use that violence that flows from our gentleness. Anything else would be harmful to them.

"PARRHESIA" AND "APATHEIA"

Can we discover the principle of this gentleness, in so far as it is, as we have already said, a sign and effect of a full interior life and of the strength which flows from this plenitude?[55] It is extremely important to recognize this principle, for gentleness is only virtuous if it is strong. This strength must be carried to the point of intrepidity. The victory of good over evil by using only good means[56] requires, then, that it must be well armed.[57] An athlete proves himself by the excellence of his performance. Gandhi was constantly making statements of this kind: "Non-violence is a condition in which one is in a position to strike . . . One must have the courage to resist violence . . . Fear must be conquered" . . .[58] "There is no greater sin than cowardice" . . .[59] Intrepidity was one of the vows he required from his disciples.[60]

"God," he said, "is intrepid.[61] How can one seek for truth and cherish love without intrepidity?"[62] Let us ponder these words, which are undoubtedly among the finest and most apposite in

---

[55] See above, pp. 142–4
[56] See above, pp. 111, 125
[57] See above, p. 116
[58] Reported by Lanza del Vasto, *Le Pèlerinage aux sources*, p. 146
[59] C. Drevet, *Pour connaître la pensée de Gandhi*, p. 67
[60] *Lettres à l'Ashram*, pp. 44–7
[61] Drevet, p. 101, note 2
[62] *Lettres à l'Ashram*, p. 103

human wisdom. He wrote to Nehru in 1933: "We wish to teach intrepidity to the masses."[63] Yes, to the masses. It is insufficient to hold that the strength required for gentleness is one of the properties of "dilection", flowing automatically from it. It is true that all the virtues, including strength, are implicitly contained in supernatural love. But in order that they may develop and attain their full scope, love must call out their appropriate actions along their own special lines. Our power to love awakens in response to divine love if we are open to it; in order that our love may be truly courageous, we find our own strength coming into play if we call on our faith or God's power for the tasks that he requires of us. Grace comes into it and an unconquerable strength manifests its unmistakable presence in the soul. It is an inner conviction which manifests itself outwardly in daring and intrepid action and it is basically a certainty in the unshakeable *faithfulness* of almighty God. The New Testament often reminds us of it, particularly in the Acts of the Apostles and the Pauline epistles, under the name of *Parrhesia* which should be familiar to all Christians.[64] In these texts we not only see the astonishing confidence and boldness of the apostles,[65] but they also instruct us as to the favourable conditions for the communication of divine strength.[66] Basically it is our purity of conscience which guarantees this perfect contact by virtue of which the power of God is communicated to us to our fullest

---

[63] Quoted by Drevet, p. 217

[64] The most necessary words of our Christian inheritance which are needed to express spiritual truths have been devalued, distorted in their meaning, and become susceptible to most banal interpretations. Short of using long circumlocutions, we can frequently see no other solution than to initiate the faithful to the meaning of some Greek words like *agape, parrhesia*, or Latin words like *dilectio* ("dilection" was used up to the seventeenth century in English, particularly for the love of God). Obsolete words could thus be brought back into currency; their very quaintness would be striking and once their meaning had been made clear, they might be useful to express certain important religious ideas. ("Parrhesia": "frankness or freedom of speech".)

[65] As in Acts 4: 13, 29, 31, 9: 28, 14: 2, 19: 8, 28: 31

[66] On the inner dispositions of a Christian, see what we have said in more general terms in Chap 4, pp. 115 ff.

capacity. What is required is "to hold the mystery of faith in a pure conscience"[67] and, as St John writes, "If our heart does not reprehend us, we have confidence towards God."[68] A good conscience is also a necessary condition for "dilection": "Charity is from a pure heart, and a good conscience, and an unfeigned faith."[69] The perfection of our contact with God within our innermost being in virtue of a pure conscience through faith and love, purges our holy "violence" from the harshness, tenseness, restlessness that the violence of the world arouses. A good conscience and "the brightness of eternal life"[70] exert their influence on the very source of spiritual strength. *Parrhesia* gives to our prayer an attitude of resoluteness in daring, which will make it like a command certain of being obeyed and which Christ has prescribed to us.[71] Our action, which is living prayer, receives its keenness and efficacy from it.[72] The soul experiences glory from it. It hopes against hope.[73] Its faith becomes similar to that of the father of believers "he was strengthened in faith, giving glory to God. Most fully knowing that whatsoever he has promised, he is also able to perform".[74] It constantly renews its strength in the certainty "that nothing can separate us from the love of Christ".[75] Purity of conscience, source of the fullest power, is like one of the poles of our action, while the state of the world is the other. The Providence of God always puts us in situations which, humanly speaking, are desperate. If they do not appear to us as such, it is because we do not look at them in depth or with divine insight. It is always "against all hope" that we hope. Jesus, who has set the scenes of the gospels as living parables, as rich in teaching as his words, has placed the prototype of all Christians, St Peter, in a situation in which we always find ourselves: he made him come to him by

---

[67] I Tim 3: 9, cf. I Tim 1: 19 "Having faith and a good conscience"
[68] I Jn 3: 21
[69] I Tim 1: 5
[70] Wis 7: 26
[71] Mt 7: 7 ff., 18: 19, 21: 21–22; Mk 11: 24; Jn 14: 13, 15: 7, 16: 24. Cf. Jas 1: 16–18.
[72] II Cor 1: 12
[73] Rom 4: 18
[74] Rom 4: 21. Cf. Heb 11: 19
[75] Rom 8: 38

walking on the waters.[76] Our life is always a walking on the waters. It is an impossibility, and as soon as we rely simply on common sense, which is too short-sighted for such an undertaking, we drown through lack of faith. "Why did you doubt?" Why indeed? Everything was going so well. We can only walk on the water as a result of faith in God as a response to his call. If Peter had not heard the word "come", it would have been foolhardy of him to leave the boat; he would have tempted God. But he did receive the call. Abraham heard a clear command to sacrifice his son; he could leave the responsibility to God. We are like Peter and his companions in the boat on the night of the storm, but Christ leaves us completely ignorant as to the outcome of our navigation.[77] If we are to hear God's call we must have in our hearts light and peace – and these come from a good conscience. To purify our action from violence as much as possible in a world of violence is indeed a perilous task; it is to walk upon a stormy sea. The *parrhesia* that is required presupposes a purity of heart in which the counsels of the Spirit of Jesus are recognized.

Here we link up once more with Gandhi, who never undertook anything without the promptings of his "little interior voice".[78] This was no suspect claim to inner light on his part; he was a realist and the success of his actions bears witness to this. We Christians are under the control of the laws of the Church to which we owe obedience, and this gives us prudence in the face of inspiration and the particular situation. They are brought to bear as we deliberate on how we can reasonably cope with a particular situation in the spirit of the gospel and yet remain faithful to the voice of conscience. They can never dispense us from taking an objective view of the situation, or from being responsive to such calls. We no doubt rarely benefit from the "power from above", because we have become used to seeking safety in conventional forms of obedience, thus dispensing ourselves from taking risks, which a more penetrating examination of the situation and unhesitating response to deeper inspiration might involve.

Purity of conscience, source of the greatest strength, is gentleness

---

[76] Mt 14: 28
[77] See above, pp. 87–88, 129
[78] See below, pp. 198, 208

itself and peace. That is where there develops "the hidden man of the heart, in the incorruptibility of a quiet and meek spirit".[79] The tendency of "dilection" is to gather within itself all the conflicting drives of our being. In other words, it seeks to give us our inner peace. "True peace," Pius XII reminded us,[80] "is not a repose similar to death, but rather the power and dynamism of life." The inner state of peace has a name in Christian tradition, *apatheia*,[81] which must not be translated as apathy! Neither is it a form of insensitivity or indifference, the horrible ideal of so many ancient philosophers and a form of self-deceit, since they no more succeeded in attaining it than the pharisees attained their "justice". We only claim to strive for the attainment of this blessed state. But we must strive for it, and it is a very serious matter that most spiritually-minded Christians today no longer even consider it a spiritual ideal. They aspire to a spiritual life while remaining enslaved to their passions. The word *apatheia* implies the quietening of the whole realm of the passions, and it is this which is most striking in those who have achieved it, by contrast with the normal behaviour of men. But considered positively it consists in the unfolding of the serene life of the evangelical beatitudes and particularly of the greatest of them: purity of heart and peace. St John Climacus puts them on the highest rung of his spiritual ladder; he calls them "heaven within the spirit".

Traditionally these two supreme beatitudes are considered to be the outcome of the two highest gifts of the Holy Spirit: "wisdom" and "understanding". One consists of a kind of acute sensitiveness to supernatural realities, and the other the savouring of them with which the Holy Spirit inspires our souls. Thus it is a perceptiveness and a savouring of the things of God that we hope

---

[79] I Pet 3: 4

[80] Easter Allocution, 1953

[81] On *apatheia*, see Hausherr in *Revue d'Ascétique et de Mystique*, 1934, pp. 47, 84–5; Bardy's article in *Dictionnaire de Spiritualité*; de la Briolle vol. 3 of *"Histoire de l'Eglise"* by Fliche & Martin, pp. 336–8; L. Bouyer in *L'Ascèse chrétienne et l'homme contemporain* (Cahiers de la Vie Spirituelle, Cerf, 1951) pp. 39–50, 43–4 (des Places), Introduction to the Works of Diadochus of Photike (Sources Chrétiennes, Cerf, 1956), pp. 14–15.

to attain by purity of heart and peace. This is an important test which is valid at all levels of spiritual progress. If we live according to the peace and purity of heart that is within us, we shall grow in these dispositions.

The other beatitudes have their part to play in *apatheia*. It may be useful to see how necessary they are to a soul that strives to purify itself from violence; gentleness and spiritual poverty are particularly relevant. So much so that meekness does not appear in St Matthew's list of the beatitudes, except as duplication of the beatitude of the poor in spirit. The man who is gentle, non-violent, must prepare himself for all deprivations and derelictions. He must humbly see himself as nothing before God and leave himself completely dependent upon God's good pleasure. He must be a "naked follower of the naked Christ".[82] He must "enrich the world by his poverty".[83] He needs the beatitude of tears; in other words he must be purified by a holy and sanctifying "sorrow according to God"[84] and experience a "continuous sorrow"[85] on account of the state of the world. His fundamental desire must grow to such an intensity that it becomes a hunger and a thirst which aims at nothing short of sanctity, such is this "holy violence", this burning zeal. Only a desire for sanctity can lead to choices which inevitably upset and overcome accepted standards. But this zeal for justice, to be truly Christian, must be merciful. It must be vitally alive in the souls of the gentle who are concerned with the misery of the world. While it refuses to exercise the violence of punishment since it may not anticipate God's judgement, it is nevertheless always tempted to set itself up as a severe judge of violent men. There is not only a great tension between the need for justice and the need for mercy, but also between two necessary but opposed forms of mercy: the one which is elicited by the misery caused by violence, and the other tinged with indignation, which considers violence itself as one of the most heartrending forms of misery. Peace according to God, far from

---

[82] This phrase is nowadays known for its occurrence in the *Imitation*, but is in fact much older. It is often found in St Jerome and was well known to medieval writers.

[83] II Cor 6: 10

[84] II Cor 7: 10

[85] Rom 9: 2

being a form of stagnation or evasion of the many struggles which make up the pattern of human existence, is conquering and creative. Christ blesses the peace-makers.[86] They are those who fight for interior unity[87] and for the progress of peace in the world.

Only God can give us this peace and he does not give it according to the fashion of the world.[88] It is promised to us in the midst of battles, contradictions and persecutions. "It is the Lord who is our peace",[89] it is for him "to give us everlasting peace in every place".[90] But equally it is for us to pray for it and to seek for it in conduct, which is in itself a prayer.

"Let your modesty be known to all men. The Lord is nigh. Be nothing solicitous: but in everything by prayer and supplication, with thanksgiving, let your petitions be made known to God. And the peace of God, which surpasseth all understanding, keep your hearts and minds in Christ Jesus."[91]

---

[86] Mt 5: 9
[87] Fr. Deman puts it well in *Construction de la Paix*, p. 5: "The only real peace is one which involves the whole of a man's soul".
[88] Jn 14: 27
[89] Eph 2: 14
[90] II Thess 3: 16
[91] Phil 4: 5–7

CHAPTER
SEVEN

A Pacified Psyche

CHRISTIAN GENTLENESS CAN BE ACQUIRED since it is as it were a fruit of dilection and spiritual strength. How will it grow? Evidently through behaviour which is constantly being renewed at its source: in a love of God which is applied to various duties and persons according to the designs of divine providence. But it will also be necessary for us to act in such a way that spiritual peace, for which we strive, will penetrate into the very depths of our being. It is doubtless equally important for growth in Christian gentleness, to pacify our senses, emotions and instincts, as well as to order our decisions and actions according to the teachings of the gospel. Lacking this elementary wisdom, many Christians remain worried, bitter, hard and violent.

We must therefore pay very particular attention to the psychological aspect of *apatheia*. Now it is, in fact, in the tradition of India, and more precisely in its revival by Gandhi, that we find the most explicit and helpful teaching. Let us quite simply profit from it in the same way as Catholic theologians like Augustine and Aquinas assimilated what was opportune in the old philosophers. We must be careful to dissociate this Indian teaching from its doctrinal setting and to reorder and inspire it within a Christian framework. We shall see how it is susceptible of undergoing this readaptation, and in the process our Christian outlook will rediscover with great clarity certain values, with which it should always have been familiar.

REVERENCE FOR LIFE AND UNIVERSAL "AHIMSA"

The teaching we are considering relates to what is known in India as *ahimsa*, which is the duty of sparing animal life, non-offensiveness, harmlessness towards all living beings. Properly understood, this quality can be taken as a disposition of the whole person, spiritual and voluntary as well as psychological, sentient and even subconscious. This comprehensiveness of *ahimsa* is explained by the unity of the human being, in whom one cannot make a clear demarcation between the psyche and the spirit. It is also explained by the astonishing flexibility of Indian thought. For Gandhi, *ahimsa* is certainly a spiritual virtue and it would seem to sum up for him all virtue.[1] As long as we keep an open mind and heart so that the various qualities of the soul interpenetrate, without which none has its own true nature, we can agree that by *ahimsa* we may designate the sentient and cognitive as well as the subconscious aspect of gentleness and peace.

This restricted use of the word seems to be in accordance with the ancient teaching of *yoga* from which the notion of *ahimsa* is derived. The great classic of yoga, Patanjali, enumerates this disposition, this manner of being, this behaviour amid the "restraints"

---

[1] See the conclusion of Gandhi's memoirs, *An Autobiography: The Story of my Experiments with Truth* (Beacon, 1957). In his conversation with Dr Thurman (reported in Harijan, 14 March, 1936) he said that "*Ahimsa* means *love in the sense of St Paul* and even more" – even more because it covers *all* creatures, not only human beings. Hence we see why Jean Herbert in his translation of Gandhi's Letters to his Ashram gives *amour* for *ahimsa*. Similarly Lanza del Vasto (*Le Pélerinage au Sources*, p. 142) at first identified *ahimsa* with charity. But later (*Nouvelles de l'Arche*, Oct., 1954) he corrected this to "respect and justice". This, we think, goes too far. *Ahimsa* in itself is anterior to any moral quality, even though it may become a kind of fulfilment, of universal respect and goodwill. We accept in preference the translation of Thérèse Brosse (*Approches de l'Inde*, Cahiers du Sud, 1949, p. 315).

which are prerequisite to all serious spiritual endeavour. These
have no moral value, providing rather a psychological technique
and a kind of mental hygiene. It is precisely from this point of
view that *ahimsa* is of concern to us in the promotion of gentleness; it will be the task of living charity to give it a Christian
character and supernatural value which it does not possess in itself.
Patanjali defines it thus: "*Ahimsa* means not to cause pain to any
creature, by any means or at any time."[2] Why this absolute
universality? It is here, at its very roots, that a Christian has to
bring a quite fundamental modification to what lies at the basis of
ahimsa. This modification is as easy as it is necessary. In India the
ascetic refrains from doing any harm to any living being, be they
pest or the smallest insects because of a tendency to fuse all
beings into one,[3] which can easily become a form of absolute
monism. Vivekananda, for instance, considered that in order to
become completely human, one must be able to think: "I am the
Universe, and this Universe is God, Existence, All."[4] We Christians must have, in the words of St Catherine, "a reverence for all
things" out of love and reverence for our heavenly Father who
created them. This disposition, involving no confusion between
Creator and creature, would be sufficient if seriously held, as was
perfectly exemplified in the life of St Francis of Assisi. The
trouble is that in most of us it is merely theoretical. It does not
result in joyous, spontaneous and effective feeling. Frequently it is
not even apparent at the conceptual level of ideas, words or intentions. Basically, it appears to us as a poetic fantasy, and we all
know that poetry is not to be taken seriously! To the eyes of the
modern Western world dominated by activity and utilitarianism
it shows a lack of common sense to take respect for creatures
seriously, spontaneously, because they "come from God" as
Thomas de Celano said. The loving outbursts of St Francis[5] for

---

[2] Mircea Eliade, *Yoga* (Routledge, 1958), p. 49. For Gandhi non-
violence arises out of *ahimsa*, an integral part of the passion to "protect
the cow". See C. Drevet, op. cit., p. 98; L. Corman, *La Non-Violence*,
p. 83; Lanzo del Vasto, *Vinôbâ*, p. 143.
[3] The doctrine of metempsychosis is only one form of it
[4] C. Drevet, op. cit., p. 84
[5] *Vita prima*, Chap. 29

all living things because they are God's creatures are considered rather embarrassing.

The Asiatic sense of the unity of all life easily leads to undifferentiated respect for human and animal life. "To identify oneself with every living thing!" – it is easy to see how such a principle can lead to the forbidding of the use of violence against any living thing whatsoever. Belief in reincarnation evidently contributes to it. It is hardly necessary to say that it is quite inadmissible for a Christian, who works out once and for all his salvation here below, in a body which will rise again on the last day. The human person is sacred and an animal is not a person. *Ahimsa* in India is sometimes inspired by a belief that there is only a single soul shared by all living things, or at least by men, and bodies are mere obstacles to its unification.[6]

It can therefore be seen how the Christian faith forbids *absolute* reverence for all life. Yet if we were logical in our faith and particularly if we had a right outlook on the conditions which favour the blossoming of divine love into the beatitudes, we should be able to reach a sort of attitude to life that would have a certain quality of universality. Let us put this into words – to abstain from any ill-will whatsoever even in thought, and still more from any evil act against any being whatsoever, whenever we can abstain without moral failure.[7]

The reason for this limiting clause is clear: there are many obligations in the complex structure of human life, differing according to changing conditions which are prior to the refusal to do harm. Our lordship over animals and plants, bestowed upon us by God at our creation,[8] carried out in the New Covenant by the uncomplicated simplicity with which Jesus made his apostles deal death to a shoal of fishes.[9] If some non-violent people wish to abstain from killing any animal life it is their business, as long as it does not involve any jettisoning of human values. They are

---

[6] Cf. Drevet, p. 108; Gandhi, *Lettres à l'Ashram*, p. 25

[7] Schweitzer once said: "Each time I do harm to any kind of living thing whatsoever, I must ask myself most carefully if this action is inevitable or not. I must never go beyond what is absolutely necessary even in apparently trivial things."

[8] Gen 1: 28–9

[9] Jn 21: 6

going too far if they wish to make it into a religious or philosophical obligation.

Why then does the universality of respect for life come about within the restrictions imposed by our human condition? For two reasons that have to be reflected in our conduct. We have given one already: the love and respect due to things as creatures of God. There have to be grave reasons for failing in this matter. We should strive to recapture a kind of wonder towards creation as part of the normal outlook of children of God. St Francis's attainment of it is an essential feature of holiness. One hears fine talk on the subject of "cosmic spirituality" teeming with theological and philosophical reflections on theories of the past, but it is quite a different matter to behave in a truly brotherly way towards animals and insects . . .

The second reason is psychological and reminds us of the concrete conditions of our nature in which our behaviour, as children of God, will have to take shape and bear fruit. It is that our goodwill must be integral as far as it possibly can, so that gradually our feelings, words, thoughts and even gestures will be affected by it. It will have in the end to permeate our instinctive life and, I would even say, our very nerves and glands, so that even our reflex actions shall be subject to the peaceful ordering of our souls.

Aquinas commented on the acts of compassion which were prescribed by the Old Law towards animals, as part of a general outlook of gentleness and kindliness which they inculcated and from which men benefited in their relationships.[10] Our relations with our neighbours are contaminated by projections of our bitterness and secret grievances, whose true causes are hidden from us, and which have an influence beyond our conscious awareness. Thus it is not sufficient to correct the clear pictures that appear

---

[10] *Sum. Theol.* Ia IIae qu. 102, art. 6, ad. 8; cf. ibid, ad. 1; art. 3, ad. 8. The objection that there are people who are kind to animals and cruel to human beings has to be faced. But such a fact does not militate against our thesis. It is not argued that kindness to animals leads to greater gentleness to human beings, but that respect for life must spring from a universal kindliness. It is only then that kindness to animals contributes to gentleness to human beings and increases it. It proceeds from an intention which goes beyond its particular manifestation to animals.

on our mental screens and in our actions and what proves on reflection to be obviously culpable: we have to strive to sublimate everything which is in the slightest way contaminated by ill-feeling. It is in fact useless for a Christian to refrain deliberately from unnecessary violence. He must strive to attain gentleness in his normal behaviour and never to will violence except with due deliberation when it is absolutely necessary.

Ahimsa is the most fundamental of the five restraints. The other four flow from it and are required for its perfection. They are: to refrain from lying, to curb all desire of theft, to curb sensuality, to be detached from possessions. The simple practise of these five restraints, if it is of a wise and vital kind, will get rid of much of the pent-up violence in the unconscious. They can become so effective that with them an ascetic could "meditate with impunity in a jungle: the attacks of wild animals against man being due to an atmosphere of fear, hatred and aggressiveness which habitually emanate from the latter".[11] It is when these unacknowledged and unconscious conflicts explode outwardly that wars are generated, which in their turn disturb men in the depths of their being.

Charity should, of course, be able to solve these interior conflicts. But they create unfavourable conditions for its operation, and, what is more important, it works on a different plane. In order to have its effect in the darkened soul it needs the help of *ahimsa*. The charity of so many desiccated intellectuals is manifestly unstable and lacking in substance. The same thing applies to so many anxious and superficial people. Charity will never give them deep peace because they imagine it will do its work in them by itself without their giving themselves assiduously to the "restraint" we have mentioned. It must be added that the term "restraint" can easily be misunderstood. Let us repeat once more – experience has taught us how much one has to insist on this – that one never achieves anything of value merely by self-restraint and compulsion. The negative aspect of all behaviour, which it

---

[11] Dr Thérèse Brosse, p. 16. Cf. *Le Yoga Darshana* quoted by Alain Daniélou in *Le Yoga*, p. 38: "No creatures are hostile towards a man in whom non-violence is deeply implanted." Vivekananda quoted by Maryse Choisy, *Yoga and Psychoanalysis*, p. 11: "If you harm no one for twelve years, even lions and tigers will lie down at your feet."

would be foolhardy to neglect, is nevertheless only beneficial if it is inspired by generous love.

The conditions favouring reverence for life and *ahimsa* vary greatly from person to person. Each one must discover, as he goes through life, in what circumstances he is particularly given to ill-will, and he will have to reinforce his love with greater lucidity and purpose in these directions. But there are certain great experiences which are common to all men and from which all can learn. It is with regard to these in particular, that we must now turn to the teaching of Gandhi: for he showed remarkable perspicacity about them, and had an acute sense of what impeded or helped a favourable growth of *ahimsa* and therefore of gentleness. He is also, without doubt, the greatest "experimenter" in this field.

OBSTACLES TO "AHIMSA"

Let us first merely mention the more obvious obstacles. They are very serious but they do not need underlining since their harmfulness is immediately apparent.

Any hard or haughty feeling, however momentary[12]

Lying

Hatred

Envy. This also seems obvious but we must lay stress on it. Our evil passions always exacerbate our frustrated desires. Resentment as shown by Nietzsche and analysed by Max Scheler, is like a corruption of envy.

We must generalize: *every single evil thought, however secretive*, harms others besides the person who conceives it. It not only lessens the power to love but it also has harmful repercussions, according to its precise nature. To many this traditional view will no doubt appear infantile, primitive, naïvely superstitious and unscientific. But there are many signs which oblige us to take it very seriously. "To keep to oneself what the world needs."[13] Any possession over and above what is necessary for our calling is a form of violence in a world sunk in the depths of misery. It is provocative of violence

---

[12] Gandhi's words, quoted by Drevet, op. cit., p. 142
[13] Gandhi, *Lettres à l'Ashram* (1937), p. 24

for its justification, its safeguarding, its display and its increase. It engenders that "carefulness" of which Christian tradition has recognized the gravity in Christ's parable of the lilies of the field and the birds of the air.[14] Two obstacles to *ahimsa* require our special attention: *fear* and *hastiness*. Christian spiritual writers hardly seem to be concerned with them. In fact, inner peace cannot be achieved without overcoming them.

"I see," said Gandhi, "how I can preach non-violence to those who can face death; to those who are afraid of it, I cannot."[15] "Desire for vengeance arises from a fear of an imagined or real evil."[16] To a Moslem leader in revolt against British rule he wrote:

"Have no fear. He who fears, hates: he who hates, kills. Break your sword and throw it away. So fear shall not touch you.[17] I have been delivered from fear and desire in such a way that I know the power of God."[18]

This must rank among one of the finest things that has ever been said by anybody. Gandhi does not claim that he has got rid of fear himself. We can only see the working of grace in such a liberation. But can we do nothing to call forth and promote this signal favour of grace?

The difficulty of what we attempt arises from the mystery of anxiety which lies at the root of our fears. Fear itself resides, as it were, at two levels. Take the example of Turenne who, we presume, was a balanced character. This brave man used to tremble when he went into battle and used to get hold of himself by saying: "You tremble, old carcass, but if you knew where I was taking you, you would tremble even more!" Thus the will can dominate fear, even when the body and the emotions are in its grip. Reason upholds, increases its lucidity; and judgement is so firm that it can lead us to behave as if we were not afraid. This is to vanquish fear, or rather, to put it more accurately in Gandhi's modest words, "not to be touched by it".

---

[14] Mt 6: 25 (see St Jerome's Commentary).
[15] *Lettres*, op. cit., p. 95
[16] ibid., p. 93
[17] Corman, op. cit., p. 42
[18] Drevet, op. cit., p. 129

The trouble is that fears of specific dangers are often infected by what Ribot called "a primitive, instinctive fear, anterior to any individual experience";[19] this is what anxiety consists in. What is it due to? When and how will it affect our judgement, inhibit our proper energy, paralyse our inspiration and inventiveness? When will it spark off the disordered aggressiveness which causes it? At times it rises up and causes confusion, at others it remains quiescent. One never knows what are the hidden springs that release it.

This is the great unknown, and to our way of thinking the frontier which inner gentleness cannot cross. To the extent which it is hard to discover, that anxiety is not sublimated, certain areas, as it were, of our interior being and behaviour will be insecure. The example of Turenne and of so many others shows that simple fear can be overcome, but it does happen that anxiety inhibits the will-power which could master it. One can do even better than control fear: one can, without relaxing the will which is threatened or the reason which is the guide, infuse these with a living faith in the "power of God". We believe that this is a disposition which gives the greatest likelihood of leading to liberation from fear. Thus the interior violence which was imposed by the will is resolved; there is no doubt that in this sublimation of fear under the threat of great dangers one can see the admirable effects of *parrhesia* and its necessity for the acquisition of *apatheia*.[20] But again we ask, how can anxiety be neutralized and overcome? It would be futile to pretend to answer this question, for every individual case is so different and mysterious. We must be deeply aware of the grave hazards of life. It is a great advantage to be on our guard against the compulsions of anxiety, in order to safeguard our inner peace in spite of them. And we may add that we are more likely to lessen anxiety and limit its evil effects if to the best of our ability, we lead a life of dilection with generosity and openness.

Haste is violence in the dimension of time. We have our own natural rhythms and we develop harmoniously and gently only if we conform to them. To rush them is to do ourselves great violence. We are thereby either troubled in that spiritual sphere in

---

[19] Quoted by J. Boutonier, *L'Angoisse*, 1945, p. 12
[20] Cf. pp. 158–160

which we rise above temporal limitations, or we become alienated from the better part of ourselves which become frenzied. We must of course be capable of occasional bursts of speed. But we must be careful to remain in control. Everyone must learn his potentialities in this respect. Undue haste is manifested in acts which are not rooted in the depths of our being; we do not give them time to come to maturity. Without this fullness they will be beneficial and fruitful neither to ourselves nor to others. They are torn from, rather than born of, us. Why this tearing? At times it is due to the prevailing atmosphere in which we live, at others to what St Francis of Sales called the "hastiness" caused by uneasy desires. Why this restlessness? Why this need to flee from giving oneself fully to present matters into a perpetual future, which in its turn never becomes a real present?

This again is anxiety seeping to the surface. It is at least easier to overcome "hastiness" than fear and anxiety. Even if our exterior life imposes too rapid a rhythm upon us, there are many actions in which we can get to grips with ourselves, by applying ourselves to doing them as perfectly as possible. We can invest them in a rare and objective way, with the energy which was dissipated in anxious aggressiveness, since it is so often fear that gives rise to the latter.

The problem is not so much that our rhythm should be more or less rapid, but that it should be such as to favour our inner composure, through which we are more spiritually *present* in our acts and can thus mobilize a fuller and less tense kind of energy. It is a great and traditional teaching that the chief characteristic of devoted zeal is *promptitudo*.[21] This does not mean speed, which is usually associated with the word "promptitude". What is meant here is the quality of a germ which develops by virtue of its inner principle of growth – in Latin *promere*. It is in connection with this need of organic growth, differing from person to person, that haste is or is not present, as a result of which harmful violence will or will not arise in the soul and in action. Tugging at ears of corn does not make them grow quicker. Living organisms must not be *forced*. This is an age when we are constantly being urged to precipitate action towards objectives which pull us out of time instead of

---

[21] IIa IIae qu. 84, art. 1

letting us move at our proper pace, and this is one of the fundamental reasons why it is so violent. Violence is inflicted upon
our inner life and we project it into our exterior behaviour and
against other persons. However, *ahimsa* is geared to "promptitude"
not to stagnation. We would compare it to the inner thrust of a
tree, which secretly loosens stones, if they impede its growth.

POSITIVE ASPECTS OF "AHIMSA"

Let us now see what experience teaches us with regard to the
things that favour *ahimsa*. Among the four other traditional
restraints are found: detachment from concern for the body and
poverty. Should we think of these as contributing to gentleness?
We shall see that they are, at any rate, favourable to its development if we look at them carefully. To the former Gandhi attributes
the requirement that "every creature should feel secure with
regard to us".[22] He who is totally dedicated to the truth must
pursue this detachment to the point of perfect chastity.[23] The latter
goes far beyond the sexual realm; it involves a control of all sense
organs. In this also our age is superficial and astonishingly un-
thinking: it hopes for spiritual progress from a chastity which
consists merely in abstinence from certain pleasures and affections.
But chastity is only fruitful if it is a purity of love which governs
our whole being. Otherwise it will be tense and peevish. It will
desiccate the heart, and far from making it gentle, it will make it
aggressive.

Fasting will also normally be required in achieving a balance,
which is indissolubly physical, mental and spiritual. Unfortunately
the West has generally lost its mystique and technique.[24]

Poverty, underneath its negative aspect, is also a positive
reality. It is a total discipline, by which the stability proper to a

---

[22] *Lettres*, op. cit., p. 94

[23] In sanscrit chastity is *brahmacharya*, which means a behaviour
consonant with a search for Brahma, Truth, and from this initial meaning follows the special meaning of "self-control". We must ignore the
incomplete definition of it as touching only sexual behaviour. (ibid.,
p. 131).

[24] See my *Cahier de la Vie Spirituelle* and my art. in *La Vie Spirituelle*,
Mar., 1956.

spiritual being is established free from earthly supports. It is a kind of temperance in respect of external goods. The evangelical mystique of poverty derives principally in a substitution of the command "Seek ye first the Kingdom of God"[25] for the classical commonsense formula "Let us live first!" (*Primo vivere*). It reverses the tendency of acquisitiveness, which is a principle of violence, into a tendency of withdrawal, which leads to giving. It is summed up in oblation. If this mystique of poverty does not merely consist in ideas, feelings and voluntary acts, but reigns in our interior life as a beatitude, it fosters the growth of gentleness. We have already noticed that in St Matthew the beatitude of the meek is in reality most probably a repetition of that of the poor. We should reflect upon this more frequently.

A footnote in a work of Olivier Lacombe draws our attention to the implications of this connection.[26] What it says in a few words deserves a whole book, and is particularly needed in the life of the West: "India declares that man can exert a true cosmic influence to the extent that he does not seek to constrain things from without", which is to do violence to them.

". . . but when he has renounced all external domination over them, and has become completely poor and without possessions, he becomes one with the being in depth of every creature and acts in it without acting on it."

This is gentleness, conceived and experienced at a singular depth, as a fruit of poverty, or in other words as a "dispossession" and a "possession of the earth".

Order, calm, the régime of a well-ordered life.[27] An entire bodily discipline. Each person and human community must have its way of achieving it. It will aim always at ensuring a "composure in the soul" and what we have called elsewhere "a vital relaxation".[28] As Westerners of the twentieth century, we live alternately in forced tension and flabby relaxation. Peace cannot be found in this way. Tension is a form of organic violence; it consists in a

---

[25] Mt 6: 33

[26] *Chemins de l'Inde et Philosophie chrétienne* (Alsatia, 1956), pp. 95–6.

[27] Drevet, op. cit., pp. 29, 124–5

[28] *La Vie Spirituelle*, Nov., 1955

nervous expenditure disproportionate with what is normally required for action. Spiritual balance and development, leading to progress in gentleness, presuppose physical behaviour which permits a recuperation of energy in proportion with its expenditure. It tends to ensure the bodily conditions which favour contemplation, as sport predisposes to action, and these are not the same thing.[29]

No doubt it would be advisable – without being too systematic – to find out which diet would be most appropriate. Even medicine might well substitute methods exempt from violence for present barbaric treatment.[30]

In general, *ahimsa* presupposes the closest possible harmony with the universe, by striving to respect its rhythms. It demands that we should use our ingenuity *to put ourselves in the position of other beings*. What this can achieve is exemplified in the experiences of Jacques, Bouillault who won the friendship of eagles and other wild animals and succeeded in getting a hen to snuggle down affectionately on the head of a fox. He tells us:[31]

> I have no mysterious "fluid"; quite simply, I have always tried *to put myself in the place of the animal* I studied, and first of all to see how it looks upon the world that surrounds it . . . The universe has a very different meaning for each one of them; it is not the same for the tortoise, the heron, the lizard, the eagle . . . To understand a given animal is to carefully reconstitute its universe, *its* way of living, in order to perceive as closely as possible the significance *to itself* of what it does and expresses.

No haste, slow gestures, clear words, looking them straight in the eye, signs of kindliness which animals can detect, infinite patience, forgiveness of injuries, soothing of the fears they experience and which make them aggressive.[32] Again and again it is a question of *fear*, but this time it is not a question of rising above

---

[29] Anyone who has kept the slightest degree of fitness should consult the little book by Dom Déchanet, *La Voie du Silence* (Desclée, 1957, 2nd ed).

[30] Something along these lines can be traced in Raymond Dextreit's *Comment guérir par les facteurs curatifs naturels* (Ed. *Vivre en harmonie*).

[31] *L'ami des aigles* (Julliard, 1956), p. 25

[32] Ibid., Bouillault, passim, especially pp. 35, 37, 38, 73, 82

one's own fear or dissolving it, but of appeasing the fear of other creatures.

The success of Jacques Bouillault has far-reaching implications: if only we behaved as he did to animals in education, human relations within communities, in politics . . .! We need to be concerned with our behaviour in small things and put great love into it. This is the secret of gentleness. If you feel yourself becoming impatient, relax your fingers, quieten your voice, look serene. For a long time Christianity assumed the heritage of thousands of years of human wisdom which was attentive to such attitudes. The liturgy, monastic observances, popular customs were a living wisdom in which there was a constant interpenetration of spiritual and bodily activities. The psyche suffers from their disjunction; it is fortified and purified by their harmony. Popular customs are now only artificially reconstituted folklore curiosities; and so for liturgical and monastic practices, they have become a matter of rationalization and dull conformity with the dead letter of the law. In truth, their virtue consists in the manner of their performance, in conformity with their nature, not mere *signs* addressed to reason alone, but living *symbols*; this virtue resides in the quality of the gestures, silence and chants. Only this quality ensures "the composure of the soul", a necessary condition of progress in gentleness. If these practices are not done *rightly* in a psychological climate favourable to the flowering of the inner realities they intend to convey, they will degenerate into a burdensome duty only too easily conducive to tension and therefore violence.

CHAPTER
EIGHT

Genuine and Sensible Love of
One's Enemies

WE MUST COMPLETE THIS STUDY OF THE
evangelization of the heart by a consideration of what Christ
demands of us with regard to our enemies. We have seen that
he knows perfectly well how "extraordinary" his demands are.[1]
We may well be surprised that St Jerome should find them so
natural: "Some one," he writes, "may say: I cannot fast. How
can he say: I cannot love? Someone may say: I cannot remain a
virgin, I cannot sell all my goods and give them to the poor.
But can anyone say: I cannot love my enemies?"[2]

This is truly astonishing. The love of enemies is the ultimate
of all Christian paradoxes. We shall try to see in the third part
of this work in what way it can be effective in action without being
unjust. But a spontaneous reaction of a genuine love in response to
the ill-will of others, straightaway manifests and achieves something within ourselves. How is this made possible? What kind of
love will it be? It is without doubt a paradoxical kind of love. If
we are misled by the word "love" into thinking that it must be

---

[1] See above, pp. 100, 104
[2] *Commentary* on Mt 5

identical in its expression and psychological attitude to the love of friends, we should be right in thinking it impossible or even vicious. The relationship of enmity is paradoxical, inverted and violent. Love is thwarted by it and it cannot side with it. But again we ask ourselves, what strange form will it take?

ENMITY AS UNNATURAL PROXIMITY

An enemy is one who hates me or does me harm. Let us exclude for the moment the case – which happens frequently in varying degrees and in more or less conscious forms – when I share in the responsibility for the opposition that keeps us apart. (For which I need to repent.) Let us simply consider the case of one who seems to be my enemy and without reason. Except out of perversity, or in virtue of a transcendent perfection for which, as we shall see, we are all bound to strive, I can neither feel nor express any kind of friendship towards him. What is most characteristic in friendship is the joy one experiences in living with a friend and the spontaneous sharing of all joys and pains. This certainly is not natural in relation to our enemies. For the love of charity, though it goes beyond nature, cannot go against it. The love of our enemy as an enemy would therefore be unnatural.[3] Modern psychology has taught us its true nature: namely, masochism. It is therefore not demanded of us in any way.

The love of enemies is possible and virtuous, as a case so to speak of reversal of the great law that has to govern all our earthly loves, the law of "proximity". Normally we love others according to their nearness to us and we owe them expressions of friendship in accordance with this.[4] The one to whom we give friendship is called, in fact, our neighbour.[5]

We have already used the analogy of a piece of woven material,

---

[3] *Sum. Theol.* IIa IIae, qu. 25, art. 8

[4] *Sum. Theol.* IIa IIae qu. 26, art. 6, 7, 8

[5] It might be objected that the parable of the Good Samaritan substitutes universality for the principle of proximity. Every man including an enemy is now a neighbour, but this parable adds a principle of gratuity to already established relations without destroying the old ones. The need of an unknown person is also a form of nearness, which creates an obligation.

or an electrical circuit for our different human relationships, to exemplify how they have to become conductors of the divine Agapè. They give it a different intensity according to the nature and degree of their proximity. We have a different love for our father, mother, friends and our feelings will not all be the same; we also love a wife, a son, workmates, someone who needs us, our country. Reciprocally, also, all forms of friendship and goodwill are improved by charity; by entering into them it gives them a supernatural quality. It is precisely because it enters into them that it affects them with many slight variations. It works in and through all our social structures. In this respect an enemy is quite the contrary of one who is near. His enmity creates the worst kind of remoteness; as far as he is concerned he makes it insuperable.

He breaks the current and puts himself outside the circuit through which charity normally flows. The injustice of his behaviour calls out hatred, a kind of hatred which is not directed against his person but against his conduct and the vices from which it proceeds.[6]

Friendship cannot be normal when justice is slighted. The restoration of justice is radically necessary for charity. This is how Joan of Arc fought against the English invaders, so that she could love them with a perfectly just love which was not sparked off by their unjust conquest: "I love them but in their own country." One of the paradoxes which the subverted condition of enmity involves, is that the first duty of love towards an enemy is to fight him – giving in to evil can never be justified. The whole question is to know how one can fight him. Since it essentially involves love, the spirit of Christianity will work precisely to replace the weapons of hatred with those of love. The Christian will have "to conquer evil by good".[7] This is the greatest of all battles.

Whatever form it may take, the attitude to our enemies must be purged of all unruly aggressiveness if it is to be virtuous and effective. Chrysippus is supposed to have cried to his slave: "How hard I would beat you if I were not angry!" When a staff officer

---

[6] According to the schoolman, the first – which is forbidden – is called "hatred of hostility", the second – which is necessary – "hatred of abomination". The unjust enemy is "abominable".

[7] Rom 12: 21

was once recommended to Joffre, he refused him saying: "That man cannot wage war, he has not achieved peace within himself." Enmity is horribly close to us. When someone hates us or harms us, it is an evil that touches us very deeply. The existence of an enemy is frequently the closest psychological presence that is experienced by man. It is capable of absorbing all his vital energies and of throwing him off balance. Neither indifference nor vague goodwill are possible towards an enemy.

In this predicament is it not unreal, yet quite usual, to say: the claim that an enemy has upon one's love is simply the fact that he is a man? It follows that we cannot "exclude him from the love we owe to all men". In fact such language, which seems rather feeble and negative, is indicative of something profound and dynamic. It is the cry of ordinary people during a war: "They are men like us." At heart such people are on the way to becoming like the good Samaritan towards an enemy if he appeared before them in flesh and blood and was in desperate need. There is also the opposite attitude. How difficult it often is to realize that the enemy is "a man like us" and to see that he is not excluded from our prayers. We must not be misled by certain phrases; they express something very close-knit, which cannot be straightened out in isolation. Through them charity may pass into men. But often only supernatural charity can lead us to establish any kind of bond with our enemies.

Is not this kind of charity too theoretical? Has it any human quality about it? "The only bond which links us to our enemies," says Aquinas, "is the bond of charity."[8] Has it therefore no natural quality at all? We must understand the real significance of the formula: "the universal intention of charity." It is not abstract. It means that we have to love all those whom God loves. We have to conform ourselves to this love; making it prevail in our hearts over the enmity which we deprecate in our enemies. We must preserve our vital awareness that our enemies are children of our heavenly Father. Our reprobation of their hatred, and the very war

---

[8] *De Caritate* qu. 1, art. 8. "Loving our enemies *in communi vel in communitate*" – not seeing them as individuals in the mass of human beings either from the point of view of loving them or rejecting them in themselves.

we have to wage against them, provides in a paradoxical but very real form, the human substance for our loving. This enmity, which we reject on our part, should also be rejected by them. It is perfectly possible for us to take a personal interest in them, by using a bit of imagination and visualizing what sort of persons they really are. St Francis of Assisi said that when we love an enemy, we think first and foremost of the harm that injustice is doing to his soul. Nothing contributes more to the reality of our love of the unfortunate man and it enables us to overcome our aggressiveness and to realize what that harm is through our understanding of his psychology.

To come back to ourselves. Let us think of a particular person who has injured us. Is it not true that we can identify ourselves with his own real interest, in such a way that the false interest he finds in opposing us may come to be seen by him as an injury he is inflicting upon himself? Is it not true that we can espouse the cause of what is best in an enemy and thus identify ourselves with his true self? Cannot we see that we can and must also achieve this in regard to our national or class enemies or any opponents of whatever kind? If we wish we can do this in such a way that we can understand them as groups of people whose history can be better known to us than that of many individuals with whom we have contact.

THE CHRISTIAN RENEWAL

In this effort of sympathy – in the literal sense of suffering what others suffer – we run the danger of sliding into a kind of moral smugness. Our pretension to wide sympathy can often lead us to make peremptory judgements which overlook the real plight of our enemies. Fundamentally our way of desiring their good can resemble the attitude manifested by inquisitors against heretics: they sincerely thought that they were purifying them by the ordeal of fire, or by committing them to hell if this was the place they were destined for. To take the side of our enemy in that which is best in him while we are fighting the evil part he is playing always means that we are also having a personal change of heart. This is the immense service that an enemy does for us.

The fight is always changing in character. It may be that we shall lay down our arms, that we feel obliged to turn them against ourselves. When one probes deep into the conflicts that afflict mankind, one generally sees that the side that has the better case often embitters the opposition by over-stressing its quite legitimate sense of the justice of it by refusing to recognize what is right on the part of the enemy. The spirit in which he thinks he carries on the fight is not really governing his heart. For instance in the 1914–1918 war the Allies "sincerely" believed they were fighting "a war of justice and right", but they proved in the peace treaty they imposed that they were only pursuing *their* justice and *their* right seen from far too narrow an angle. They set at naught such obvious rights – those of Austria and India for instance – so that they were certainly not serving the cause of justice of which they claimed to be the champions. The retribution for their injustice was not long in coming.

The perspective of even a few years thus enables us to reconsider our own case. We now understand how we sinned against our own principles in the wars we fought. We had not a sufficiently deep moral awareness of the cause we claimed to be defending because we had not a sufficiently realistic understanding of what it demanded. Our honour should have come from the service of a cause, instead of a cause serving our prestige. Reconciliation with our enemy was not our true aim, so that we could go beyond the grievances that brought about the conflict. Basically we were not prepared to be reconciled in the highest sense, with ourselves. We preferred to put on a façade of self-righteousness by clinging to a narrow application of the principles we invoked. Our attitude was pharisaical.

Past conflicts should give us misgivings about present ones. Enmity faces us with a challenge to refurbish our own principles; we need to rediscover the spirit that is supposed to animate them by exploding our bogus personalities and returning to our natural simplicity as children of God.

A DEEP PROXIMITY WITHIN ENMITY

Experience therefore teaches us that the close relationship existing between enemies is not entirely made up of violence and opposition. We can consider this in two ways.

First, as Fr Marie–Alain Couturier wrote[9] "believers and unbelievers, men of the right, left or extreme left, what opposes and divides us is not what is best in us". When we are able to have a genuine conversation, intelligent and confident, transcending the ditches and walls that divide us, we perceive that our prejudices and misunderstandings are not the sole causes of our conflicts. Let us not be naïve. We can perceive the pressures of passion, the interests and ideologies which divide us. All this is certainly real and relatively significant. But deeper still and more significant are the bonds of unity. I read for instance in an intimate diary of Fr Couturier (1948):

"They are communists for almost the same reasons as we are Christians and priests. They are not communists because of that dusty old genius who died a century ago[10] and whose economic predictions have been discredited by facts; they are communists because they have a certain idea of freedom and of its necessary conditions. We too are Christians because we believe in the dignity of man and his interior freedom, apart from the supernatural factors to which we attach an infinite value but of which we are in no sense the masters."

The exterior "I's" confront one another – those which, in the words of Marcel Proust,[11] "we manifest in our habits, social life and vices". These are our worst betrayers. Like good caricatures, terribly life-like, yet lying.

In each of us what is best is always prepared to be the friend of what is best in the other. It is thus that geniuses and simple people get on well together in spite of all barriers.[12] Could we not find our best friends among those against whom we fight?

Inversely how many of our so-called friends are but accomplices of our most sordid interests, our mean prejudices, evil inclinations, pride, ambition and hatreds? Our partners are so badly selected. Surely the real disputes are between the humble and the pharisees,

[9] Op. cit., p. 165
[10] Marx in fact died in 1883
[11] *Contre Sainte-Beuve*
[12] For instance, as Barrès says of Jaurès (quoted by Domenach in *Barrès par lui-même*, p. 171), "The leading men of all parties should think of themselves as kindred – even as allies".

between the merciful and the hardhearted, God and Mammon, the friends of God and those who cry out "Lord, Lord . . .", the child-like and the cunning. But this battle, the only really serious one, will never be organized into two camps: the party of the seed and the party of the tares.

Fr Sertillanges wrote a book fifty years ago on "our real ene-mies" . . . They are, he said, hatred, sham knowledge, false liberties, false equality, sensualism. In this respect Gandhi gave us the greatest example, in setting out "to deliver his people of evils of which the English were least though the most apparent"[13] putting "more passion into combating untouchability than British rule".[14] Are our struggles worth the harm they cause, when it is so much more urgent to fight "our true enemies" who score through all our victories? Is it not even more important to direct our energies to positive causes? In the last resort the words of Augustine are not only valid in the order of charity but on the human plane: "When you think you are hating your enemy, more often than not it is a brother you are hating and you are not aware of it."[15]

Death often needs to intervene for us to be aware of these things. The one who survives wonders "how could we have been so cruel to one another? We were made to understand and love one another and to do some great work together." But "what bonds are being woven between people whose knowledge of one another is limited to mutually inflicted wrongs".[16] While there is time, will they not break these bonds and try to get to know some-thing of one another beneath the harsh surface of their grievances?

I have mentioned a second kind of relation which establishes an affinity between enemies. It is no less deep or real. Everyone hates in the other a part of himself which he projects upon him. If he suffers from a certain defect, it is this very defect he will notice in the other, or which he will even gratuitously attribute to him and make him appear hateful. There is something still more

---

[13] Lanza del Vasto, *Pélerinage aux sources*, p. 144, and *Vinôbâ*, pp. 22, 25, 260.

[14] Drevet, op. cit., p. 95

[15] *Enarrat, super Ps.* 54, 11

[16] Dominique Arban, *Le Figaro Littéraire* (11 Dec 1954)

serious, yet this should be a true basis for reconciliation. Each one of us to some extent leaves "in the shadow" a whole part of himself, to which he does scant justice. An intellectual, for instance, neglects his sensitive and feeling side, which is somehow ill at ease within him. This fact is of such importance that Jung and Baudouin have made the "shadow" one of the elements which plays a significant part in the constitution of our personalities. When we dimly recognize our "shadow" in another, it may attract us, but what happens more frequently is that we feel ill at ease with it; then conflict arises. Jung finds a particular significance in the precept of Christ "Go and be reconciled to your brother": we must, he said, be reconciled to our inner brother, with our "shadow".[17] "What have you done to your brother?" – to your neglected and diminished "shadow"? It appears in another, and the shock of recognition creates enmity. What is required is that we should recognize that it needs to be complementary to our own integral fulfilment. The same thing is true for classes, nations and parties as for individuals. In France, for instance, the parties of the right betrayed a whole tradition of justice and generosity, when they saw the shadow of themselves which they had denied rise up in Zola and Péguy in the Dreyfus affair, in Jaurès, in Romain Rolland in Vaillant-Couturier; it outraged them. But now France and Germany are on better terms; as in the past, the French of *langue d'oïl* and *langue d'oc*. How many centuries shall we have to wait for white, yellow, and black people to agree to be friendly over the very things that now make them enemies?

In every respect, a dialectic of complementary realities, whose development should be inwardly pursued by every one in his own heart is allowed to degenerate into disastrous conflict as a result of various enmities. It is not in the least a question of muddling everything in confusion and compromise, but of bringing out in a balanced way the intrinsic value of all the elements involved. We should "distinguish in order to unite".[18] We should always

---

[17] C. Baudouin, *De l'instinct à l'esprit*, p. 271

[18] This is the very apt subtitle of J. Maritain's great work *Les degrés du savoir*; (*The Range of Reason*, Scribner, 1961). Abbé Pierre in his preface to Kaplan's *Tolstoi et Gandhi* says: "We must be bold to say over and over again that wars are not born out of differences between peoples, but of similarities and errors which they share."

appreciate differences. When one seeks for unanimity through uniformity, one arbitrarily pushes back into the shadow a whole part of the other or oneself, which has the right to be loved but which one condemns to hatred. A pretence is made of building a paradise of friendship, but it has hellish cornerstones. Uniformity is not necessary for charity. Let us love one another in a harmony which blends our differences. Let us therefore love one another *for being* different.

THE REALITY OF THE LOVE OF OUR ENEMIES

We sense already that such attitudes are possible with regard to our enemies, that they are a sign of true wisdom and can be genuine love. Evidently in order that they may be real, they will have to be inspired by "dilection". I hope that as this work proceeds the reader will be renewed in this dilection, and that he will be directing it more especially towards people who are hostile to him or towards common enemies – for instance, for the "average" Christian towards communism.

The important thing is to tend towards fulfilment. Enmity results from mutilations. It is always our deficiencies that make us fail. Peace will be found in the tranquillity of order. Why tranquillity? Because nothing will be lacking in it. Only a superior order can enable us to overcome particular rivalries. We shall love another in loving the same transcendent realities which fulfil us beyond our differences. An essential condition for this is that we should love, in an outstanding and unmistakable way, what the enemy is right in loving. He often remains perverse in his opposition because he believes he will not be able to share with us what is dear to him. Often in protecting ourselves against him, we seem to be at pains to give him the impression of depreciating what he is right in clinging to. Heresies, for instance, not only cause the dreadful evil of leading innumerable souls into error, they make the faithful react against what the heretics are right in asserting. This in fact upsets the general economy of belief and is the cause of many spiritual deviations. Great steps are being taken towards the reconciliation of Catholics and Protestants, because the former are now returning to biblical sources, which are quite rightly a source of life to the latter.

Thus it is a major duty for anyone who is a victim of enmity to do all in his power to accomplish prophetically in his own person the reconciliation to come, realizing in himself as far as he can the high synthesis which will ensure a fuller communion. This major duty must be seen in terms of particular duties of which people are not made sufficiently aware: be careful not to approach your enemy with an outward attitude which he has reason to hate, which is of such a nature as to deceive him about your spirit, interests and intentions.

Develop in yourself what I was delighted to hear Fr Sertillanges call "a taste for the enemy" (*goût de l'ennemi*). I cannot remember what conclusions he draws from this principle, but this taste would certainly encourage us just "to look in the same direction as our adversary, to see and judge what he sees",[19] put ourselves sympathetically on his side, and want to understand things as he understands them. The history of quarrels is that of the false interpretations of the thoughts of others.[20] This "taste for the enemy" has nothing perverted about it, since it consists in a love *of his qualities*. It is in this way that love for the immortal in him takes form; since this aspect of him is invisible, our love is in danger of being an illusion, and the hostility most manifest. Emphasize the element of truth to which the enemy clings. In doing this you will seem to be a traitor, but therein lies your great opportunity. If you are a servant of the truth, all truth will be your greatest ally in the heart of your enemy. It will be your ally in his conversion.

Limit enmity as much as possible. All friends of peace must be engaged upon this. For instance there is much to be done among the clergy to stop them thinking that unbelievers are in "bad faith", that heretics are unfavourably disposed towards us even in

---

[19] *Nos vrais ennemis*, p. 26. "Most people labour under illusions or half-truths and most of our hatreds come from obstinate isolation: we refuse to admit that the other man may have some right on his side; we shut our eyes to evident facts, calling evil a good thing which we do not find among our friends. Instead of building a bridge of enlightenment, we persist in digging trenches" (p. 27).

[20] This is especially true of the bitter quarrels among the servants of God ("How much bile enters into the souls of the devout?"). How often their disputes are marred by calumny! A chance example can be found in Martimort, *Le gallicanisme de Bossuet*, vol. 2, ch. 2.

matters which have nothing to do with revelation. In fact there is no milieu in which relations are not poisoned by judging persons in every respect from a partisan view of what is considered to be the "right" or "wrong" side, and one's outward behaviour follows from this judgement. But let us not be naïve either. We must also see the sectarianism of our adversaries and not only our own, know their manœuvres but always limit the evil to what seems indisputably so.

Let us multiply exchanges, and not be reluctant to have them or spoil them by malicious suggestions. Go even further: work as much as you can with your enemy. In particular, joint action in the relief of misery is the most efficacious way towards fruitful communion in God's eyes. When Christ commanded us to give his peace to everybody with whom we come into contact, he promised us that if we found no peace-lovers to receive it "it shall return to us".[21] When it seeks to touch the heart of an enemy, in the form of an intelligent, sorrowful and hopeful love which we bear him, and if this love is rebuffed, met with incomprehension and hatred, our peace is not disturbed provided that we had real integrity in our approach. But something has been consumed in us. The enemy "had not anything in" Christ[22] but alas, he has a hold upon us. Our action for peace is only valuable to the extent that our setbacks are redeemed by a diminution of the hold that the enemy has upon us.

The Christian paradox reaches its maximum intensity when peace can only be achieved through some form of war; when only violent means are to be found to save those values or the unfortunate and humble from an aggressor who threatens them. The paradox is then to go on loving the enemy in a real way while one resists him; most Christians do not even consider the possibility of simultaneous love of and resistance to the enemy. Would it not be crazy to say: "I love you while I strike you, plot against you and kill you"? It is better not to say it; how many of us could say it with real sincerity? Nevertheless it is true that on us is placed the obligation of loving him and fighting effectively against the evil he does, if violence seems the only way of defending the

---

[21] Lk 10: 5–6
[22] Jn 14: 30

truth. The real scandal is to take the abdication of love for granted. On the other hand there could also be scandal in refusing a necessary fight. Is there no way of avoiding either of these equally obnoxious alternatives? Only love can be sufficiently strong to be efficacious, as St Paul teaches us when he says that we should overcome evil by good.

"My religion," Gandhi said to the English, "forbids me to have any animosity against you . . . I only wish to win a victory over you by my suffering."[23] If our religion does not forbid us to have recourse to blows when they are necessary and unavoidable, it certainly does not authorize animosity. It does much more: it prescribes love. This can only be seriously achieved through the Cross, through sacrifice. "I only wish to win a victory by my suffering." Gandhi has translated into action, and with manifest success, the demands of a love which tolerates neither violence nor the triumph of injustice. A surprising way, but one which is quite normal and logical to anyone who has been caught up in the mystery of redemptive love.

-----

[23] Cf. Drevet, op. cit., p. 23

PART III

Non-violent Action

NON-VIOLENT ACTION

IN ORDER THAT THE GENTLENESS AND HOLY violence of Christ may grow in our hearts, we must strive as much as we can to spread the Kingdom of God, by the methods of the Kingdom of God. But what chance is there with human conditions as they are today and the resistance of the world to such a conception, that men will genuinely come to act without the wrong kind of violence? There is no easy answer to this question. At least one thing is certain and it has far-reaching consequences: the mystique and theory – not Gandhi's words, but ours – of the action which Gandhi practised seems to be essentially the purest application of the teaching of the gospel.

We have already indicated what is incompatible with Christian teaching in the beliefs of Gandhi.[1] We shall see that these do not in any way affect what is essential in his doctrine of action. Christian conscience approves of everything we shall select in it. The more one studies this great spiritual leader, the more one admires his understanding of certain basic truths of Christianity. His exceptional honesty and heroic generosity which are manifestly outstanding graces, enabled him to perceive these truths, as for instance the mystery of redemptive sacrifice, of the efficacy of our participation in this sacrifice for our brethren. He saw these truths with a clarity and depth worthy of the greatest saints. There were many factors which made it unthinkable that he should be interested in Christian dogmas.[2] What he knew of them seemed too

---

[1] See above pp. 163–4

[2] Among these were a quite undogmatic approach to moral and spiritual questions, a vague Indian syncretism, the influence of those through whom he came into contact with Christianity, notably Tolstoy

much involved in the "established order".[3] But his principles of action were most authentically those of the Sermon on the Mount.[4] This was not just a vague influence. As he was a realist of astonishing perspicacity in his understanding of men and concrete situations, he had in action the most acute evangelical sense of the "incarnation" with all that it implies of balance and humble submission to the inevitable and penetrating effectiveness. According to his apt expression he made "experiments with truth". The very obstinacy of his cult of the truth taught him the "beauty of compromise" without the slightest degree of compromise of the wrong sort. "The truth," he said, "has the hardness of a diamond and the tenderness of the flower of the peach tree."[5]

We will not recall his main achievements. They are so well known and it is quite easy to get information about his life.[6] Our

---

and Ruskin. He also had many contacts with liberal Protestants. An English Protestant missionary, Andrews, was close to him for a long time and edited his paper *Young India*. (Quoted by Muriel Lester in *Entertaining Gandhi*, 1932; p. 5 in Fr. ed.) He made close friends with certain protestant missionaries while he was in Africa; these were particularly evangelical and based their faith on personal religious experience of an illuminist kind. Gandhi said this had never happened to him. To these factors, which were decisive, one may add the influence of the colonialism of so many missionaries and the materialism of the West which was particularly flagrant during the 1914–1918 war.

---

[3] M. Lester, op. cit., p. 12 (Fr. ed.). (Corman, *Non-violence*, p. 111.)

[4] Gandhi came to know the Sermon on the Mount in South Africa in 1893. He himself said (as quoted by Corman, pp. 108–9): "It was the New Testament which really opened my eyes. When I read such passages as 'Not to resist evil but if one strike thee on thy right cheek, turn to him also the other', and 'Love your enemies . . . pray for them that persecute you that you may be the children of your Father who is in heaven', I was transported with joy. I found my ideas confirmed where I least expected it and Tolstoy's book *The Kingdom of God is Within You* gave them lasting shape."

[5] *An Autobiography*, op. cit., p. 185 (Fr. ed.)

[6] Gandhi's own *Autobiography* (op. cit.) has the incomparable value of authenticity and first-hand information, but it stops in 1921. The best French works on Gandhi are: Louis Corman, *Une école d'héroïsme ;*

task here is to draw out the main lessons of it. They stimulate our consciences since they are applicable to changing situations and so much in line with the teaching of the gospels. If we are to take a

---

les campagnes non-violentes de Gandhi (Stock, 1951) and C. Drevet, *Pour connaître la pensée de Gandhi* (Bordas, 1954). Nehru's memoirs (Fr. ed: *Ma Vie et mes Prisons*, Denoel) which end in 1941, are highly suggestive but look at the mystique of Gandhi from an external standpoint. (For a complete list of Gandhi's writings, see Brit. Museum Gen. Cat., vol. 162, under "Mohanadāsa".) Cf. also: *Non-violent resistance* (satyagrâha), ed. P. Kumarappa (1961) and *The Power of Non-Violence*, R. B. Gregg (F.O.R., N.Y., Clarke, 1961). The principal dates in Gandhi's life are:

Oct. 2nd, 1869: Born in the peninsula of Kattiavar in north-west India where his father was a Minister in the government. Married at fourteen, according to custom.

1888–1891: Studied law in London. Became a barrister.

1893: Went to Natal to plead the case of an Indian merchant. Experienced racial segregation and so stayed in South Africa to defend his compatriots and all the oppressed in general. Tried out *Satyagrâha*. Finally won recognition of the rights of Indians from General Smuts.

1915: Returned to India. Studied the conditions there for two years. From that time his aim was the independence of his country, but he saw that as the infallible and right outcome of the betterment of humanity in general, which was his real objective. He worked through politics (he was leader of Congress until 1935) and the Press (*Young India* and *Harijan*) but even more through education, social work (worked in the villages to inject life into them, campaigned to integrate the untouchables, to promote friendship between Muslims and Hindus) and religion (life in his Ashram at Sabarmati and then at Savagram, his fasts).

1921: First imprisonment after a strike and his fast.

1930: The "salt march" to promote the extraction of salt from the sea, since the government fixed the price too high. Imprisoned.

1931: Attended the Round Table Conference in London. On the way back spoke in Paris, Geneva and Lausanne.

1932: Returned to India and was put in prison.

1942: Imprisoned in the Aga Khan's palace.

1947: India given independence, but the country divided. Pakistan created. Terrible fighting between Muslims and Hindus.

30 January, 1948: Assassinated by a fanatical Hindu three days after his visit to a sacred Muslim shrine.

realistic view of the truth[7] we must be constantly rethinking our principles in terms of the ever-changing situations we have to meet. It is, in fact, by its struggle with intractable matter that the spirit progresses in its moral awareness of the principles that govern it. It only discovers the truth by living it.

Some major orientations emerge from clear and constant "experiments with truth". We shall examine them in detail in the two following chapters. They coincide in the most surprising way with the orientations which we discovered to be found in the gospels.[8] There are Christians who are quite rightly disturbed by contaminations which threaten the faith, and unfortunately there are others who dabble cheerfully with the prevalent atmosphere of vague and easy syncretism. They are inclined to give an equal value to different religions, they consider them to be imperfect expressions of a pure religion which they flatter themselves that they alone appreciate.[9] They declare that non-violence is above

---

[7] Traditional expression in Western Christianity freely used by Thomas Aquinas, as in *In Johann*; Ch. 3, 1.3, n. 7; *Summ. Th.* 1a Pars, qn. 17, art. 10 1a 2ae, qu., ql., art. 1.

[8] See above, Chap 4

[9] In the appendix to Mme Drevet's book already cited there is a striking refutation of this syncretism in the following passage, taken from a lecture on Gandhi by Fr Monchanin, who died young in 1957. He had founded an Ashram in India where he lived a life like that of the Hindu monks but under the Benedictine rule. [This is now being done by Bede Griffiths in South India – *publisher's note*.] He prepared the way for a reciprocal understanding of the western Christian and the Indian in the only viable way: the assimilation of Indian thought by the Christian conscience and the adoption of an Indian way of life (see Monchanin and Le Saulx, *Ermites de Saccidananda*, Casterman, 1956). This gives exceptional authority to his words: '*We must never water down our beliefs but live them to the full.* The Hindus must not hide aspects of Hinduism which seem repellent to the sensibilities of westerners nor complacently add Zarathustra, Buddha, Mohammed and Christ to the list of *avatars*. It is for them to develop to the full the implications of prayer and love found in the factors making up the spiritual experience of Hinduism, or at least those that seem such to me, an outsider, as I meditate on the most venerable writings and the most vital souls among them – that is to say the divine immanence. Muslims can hardly compare or equate the Mahatma with Mohammed,

all dogmas. How mistaken they are. Only supernatural realities
lie beyond dogmas, of which they are the formulation in rational
terms. Non-violence does not contradict them or transcend them.
So much so that Gandhi was able to gain the support of all the
various spiritual communities of India, particularly the Hindus
and Muslims (the latter are most exclusive), since non-violence
lies within them and overrides their differences. Gandhi made no

---

who to them is incomparable; they bear witness to the most direct
and clear-cut proclamation of the One. A few days ago I heard a Muslim
declare that Mahatma Gandhi was an *avatar*. I was deeply distressed
and Gandhi would have been too. I do not know whether he spoke
from cowardice, a desire for unity or under pressure. But he was denying his faith, verbally at any rate. He was denying himself and his
co-religionists.

Christians have no need to dissemble the face of Christ who is not
a mythical God but the Absolute who took on himself the nature of
all men in order to save all men. He made himself Becoming in order
to make divine the whole creation – a unique event. He is the Elder
Brother of the whole human race, *the unique Incarnation of all time,
of which the Only Church is his mystical body* and of which we are its
most unworthy members.

For a Christian it is not a question of proudly asserting rights or
forcible conversions by worldly devices or lures. God alone can turn
men's hearts. The Christian can only be a witness for he *is* never a
Christian but merely in process of becoming one.

For us God is neither impersonal nor one-personal. He is in his inner
self Three Persons. We reject all these systems – *Dvaita, Advaita,
Vishistadvaita*. We do not believe God is One in spite of but because
of his Trinity. He is Sat, He is Chit, He is Ananda, Being-Thought-
Beatitude in such a way that he constitutes three personal centres, each
polarized by the two others. "The Trinity is found in Unity without
being lessened and the Unity expands in the Trinity without addition."

That is why we are faced by more sovereign demands than our Hindu
or Moslem brothers. But are we to be reckoned defaulters because of
this? Muslim and Hindu friends, do you really think that we love you
less because we wish to show you ourselves as we truly are, without
obscurity? *We reject all forms of confusion.* The unity we desire will
not be won by force or trickery, by cowardice or abdication, but by
emulation in holiness, by *satyagraha*, by *ahimsa* as Gandhi taught
these.

compromises between different beliefs in his non-violence, since he would have claimed that it is superior to all and he taught in such a way that his method of non-violence could be accepted by all men who believe that the soul is immortal and that God is not just an idea, but the Living God.

CHAPTER NINE

The Mystique of Non-violent Action

FAITH IN GOD AND FAITH IN MAN

"The living God and the immortal soul", these are the two great realities; belief in them is the basic principle of non-violent action in this world of violence. It is a belief that is lived and involves a total self commitment; what we call a "mystique". For non-violent action presupposes a belief in "the strength of Truth", but this strength will only be a dream, a desire and finally a snare, if this truth is not all-powerful love, active and productive of grace and strength. Needless to say, certain unbelievers may have sufficient trust in the basic goodness of man to believe that this will prevail over selfish interests, wickedness and violence. Also that certain "unbelievers" of goodwill who believe in man, can pursue non-violent policies. But unconsciously their optimism implies a belief in God which alone can justify it, since only God can give it absolute value and bring about its eventual success. However this may be, we Christians cannot consider the matter in any other way than Gandhi: I mean that we attribute any virtue that non-violence may have to the God of love.[1]

---

[1] "In the long run non-violence cannot work in those who have not *a living faith in the God of love*" (*Harijan*, 5 September, 1936). "*It is*

The hero of non-violence must "become like a piece of clay in the hands of the divine Potter".[2] This is why he should lead a life of sacrifice, prayer and silence. He does nothing until "his small inner voice has spoken to him". If he allows his line of conduct to remain flexible beyond what is necessary for immediate action and at times changes his course,[3] it is not only due to his flexibility as a realist, attentive to unforeseen factors, but above all to a spiritual realization "that it belongs to God himself to conduct the battle for justice".[4] He attributes victory to God "an exacting master who constantly puts us to the test" but who, he adds, "has always brought me out of adversity". He verified for himself the great pauline dictum that strength is made perfect in infirmity.[5]

It is only when the combatant is totally helpless, when he reaches the very extremity of weakness and sees nothing but darkness around him, it is only then that God comes to his help. God gives his help when a man feels himself to be less than the dust under his feet. The help of God is only given to the weak and the forsaken.[6]

---

impossible to have a living faith in non-violence without a living faith in God. No man can practise non-violence without the power of God's grace. Unless he has it he cannot have courage to die without anguish, fear, revenge. And this comes from the belief that God is in every man's heart and that one should have no fear in God's presence. To know the omnipresence of God inspires man with reverence for life, even the life of those we call our enemies" (*Harijan*, 18 June, 1938).

[2] *Young India* (17 November, 1921)

[3] It is strange how irritated and even scandalized Nehru was by this. A first rate and most intimate co-worker, he lacked that vertical dimension of inspiration. The most inspired decisions of Gandhi seemed mad to him and likely to upset everything. After a short time, however, he agreed that they were realistic and opportune. See his memoirs (pp. 82–3, 91–5, 224–7 French ed.). It would be difficult to find a finer portrait of Gandhi than that given by Nehru (ibid., pp. 127–8), and some of his remarks call up the man exactly; e.g. "Frequently the unknown looked out at us from his eyes", and "he radiated light-heartedness' (ibid., pp. 222 & 364).

[4] *Young India* (2 February, 1925)

[5] See above, Chaps 4 and 6

[6] *Autobiography*, op. cit.

This religious mystique must also be indivisibly associated with a mystique of man. Gandhi declared that he could only find God in humanity. Apart from its apparent exclusiveness, does not this seem to be a faithful echo of a famous *agraphon* of Christ, which was handed down by Clement of Alexandria and Tertullian, "You see your brother? You have seen God".[7] In order to know God one has to be "purified by prayer and always be prepared to share the sufferings of men, whoever they may be. The condition for success lies in the use of strength of the soul"[8] – the only condition, Gandhi says here, and in a way it contains all the others – "is a recognition of the existence of the soul as distinct from the body and permanent. This recognition must not just be a simple intellectual idea, it must be a living faith".[9] Let us recall here what we said about the principle of heroism[10] which is required by the spirit. It is at this depth that Gandhi situates his mystique of non-violent action and thereby makes it into an heroic mystique: heroism is precisely a surpassing of man by himself, which is possible and necessary because he is a spiritual being.

The non-violent hero is not alone in surpassing himself; he believes that his violent opponent is also able to do this. His action has no meaning or efficacy unless it achieves this, as we shall soon see. Man's faith must go to these lengths. "It is an article of faith for the non-violent that *there is no man who has fallen so low that he cannot be redeemed by love*".[11]

There is no need to invite the reader to meditate on these words, neither is there any need for commentary; its plenitude will immediately be apparent to anyone who does not read them superficially but recognizes their power. Aldo Capitini asserted that the non-violent dares to act as he does because he believes that "God is being born" in consciences.[12]

---

[7] An *agraphon* is a saying attributed to Christ, not found in the gospels but coming to us from another source. What we have quoted is probably authentic, but the most authentic is St Paul's: "It is more blessed to give than to receive" (Acts 20: 35).

[8] *Harijan* (8 June, 1938)

[9] Quoted by Corman, *Campagnes non-violentes*, p. 136

[10] p. 149

[11] Cf. Corman, op. cit., p. 31

[12] *Danilo Dolci et la Révolution ouverte* (Desclée, 1957), p. 104

Finally, faith in the immortality of the soul must go to such lengths that the non-violent person believes "that death does not mean the end of a fight, but its culmination"; this is a reawakening among us of the faith of the martyrs.

> The body is only an instrument for self-expression, and he joyfully relinquishes his body when its existence becomes an obstacle which prevents the adversary from seeing the truth which the non-violent person is defending. He relinquishes his body, with an absolute faith that if anything can change the attitude of his opponent, it is the voluntary sacrifice of his body.[13]

Here we see the full meaning of the well-worn expression "to give one's life for something". In the same way Danilo Dolci, the Sicilian emulator of Gandhi, while he risked his life in terrible fasts to awaken people's consciences to injustices, proclaimed: "If I cannot awaken love by being alive, my dead body will provoke remorse."[14]

THE MYSTIQUE OF THE MEANS USED

To say that the end justifies the means is nonsensical. The means only lead to the end if they are of the same nature as the end. If means are used which are unworthy of the end, it is because the real end that is being pursued is in fact only roughly similar from a utilitarian and exterior point of view. From a spiritual point of view, it is the true end which is, in fact, being betrayed. The end is present in the mind that chooses the means and applies them: it determines the choice and its applications, and its moral value is communicated to the action that follows. According to Maritain's felicitous expression, the means are "in a sense the end in process of becoming".[15] There can be no question of reducing the end, as materialists do, to nothing else but a consequent *effect*, and to assert that it is nothing more than what the means make it. An end has

---

[13] Reproduced by J. Maritain in an appendix to his book *Du régime temporel et de la liberté*, 1933.

[14] Guy Ganachaud, *Les Bandits de Dieu* (Seuil, 1957), p. 43

[15] Maritain, *L'Homme et l'Etat*, p. 49

its own reality, which is anterior to the action, is more or less faintly present in the *intention* of the one who is acting. It finds its own consistency, as a result of its transcendence in relation to the activities that, to a greater or lesser extent, carry it out. But the end cannot be attained except through means which are adapted to it. Let us repeat – only peaceful means can achieve a true peace.[16] It may be that in most of the situations of the human race today it is not possible to achieve a condition worthy of the name of peace, without going through an intermediary stage of a so-called "order", which is but a state of false tranquillity obtained by violence. That, then, calls for a redoubling of peaceful heroic action in order to reduce the accumulated causes of violence which have resulted from anterior violence under the guise of peace.[17] Since neither the victors nor the losers will take an heroic line, violent situations can only evolve towards even greater violence. This is indeed what we are faced with in the modern world, where all believe that they want peace, but imagine that they can only obtain it by warlike means. "Who sows the wind, harvests the storm"[18] and Jesus himself said "All that take the sword, shall perish by the sword".[19] To put it in general terms, as Gandhi did, "There is as close a link between the means and the end as between the seed and the tree".[20]

The mystique of non-violence claims to break the fatal vicious circle of ever-increasing violence. *It puts peace into action.* Not in the illusory form of a merely theoretical "intention", which is

---

[16] See p. 56

[17] See the 1945 Christmas Message of Pius XII on the subject of peace won through violence. "Peace on earth? True peace? No – merely 'after the war', a melancholy and very significant phrase. Men are only just beginning to estimate what perspicacity, prudence, uprightness and goodwill are needed to bring the world out of devastation and physical and moral ruin, into justice, order and peace." And at Christmas 1948 he said: "May the United Nations become the pure and full expression of international solidarity in peace, wiping out by its institutions and decrees all vestiges of its origins in the solidarity of war."

[18] Hos 8: 7

[19] Mt 26: 52

[20] Corman, op. cit., p. 101

contradicted by means that bring it to nought, but in the form of a spiritual mastery overcoming the urges of instinct, substituting for the reflex action of counter-attack a fully conscious self-sacrifice calculated to arouse the consciences of the unjust. However carefully thought out and planned an attack may be, it remains on the level of primitive reaction. Because it is free and the very principle of freedom, the spirit is, or rather ought to be, averse to putting its ingenuity at the service of a sudden urge of the "flesh". I know it pretends to dominate it, but it frequently deceives itself; it disguises a movement of passion with rationalization. Even when it is in the service of a genuinely just cause and acts accordingly it remains in the same sphere as the disorder it seeks to repress. To assert its mastery to the full it must bear within itself in a prophetic state, the peace it is striving for, even during the time of conflict. It must uphold it against the assaults of injustice, and not weaken by adopting means which betray it. Such a mastery must necessarily be acquired at the price of a long and painful sacrifice which will have the appearance of surrender and defeat. We shall try to see how it is likely to achieve victory. From the point of view of the "mystique" of non-violence which we are considering now, we can understand the profound, even sublime, significance of Gandhi's words: "Violence is the law of the brute and non-violence the law of the spirit." Even if it is thought that his outlook is chimerical and that his non-violence is bound to fail, it must be acknowledged that it expresses in action the integrity and freedom which the spirit requires; and that its failure is due to the spirit's being kept in check in its present carnal condition. Whereas violence is quite clearly under the law of the flesh, even when it is commanded by a mind claiming to serve a just cause. We can also understand in what sense Gandhi was able to say: "The means are themselves an end." It is a matter of not putting off indefinitely the attainment of the end to hypothetical future, which recedes like the horizon as one advances; as life goes on, and it is always a battle, it is necessary to incarnate the end in the means themselves.

The really important thing is not the apparent success of one's life, but its quality. "To live in violence and war, is not to live."[21]

---

[21] Drevet, op. cit., p. 140

We must understand by this a life of complicity, for war and violence are an inevitable condition brought about by men's folly. The value of this life depends at every moment upon the active influence of this end: unalterable peace. It must will itself to be sufficiently strong to overcome not only inner turbulence, but also any forms of outward violence, by pacifying the hearts whence this proceeds. This is the supreme proof of man's nobility – the act by which the spirit asserts itself in breaking the vicious circle of disaster. Between the peace of God and the world's craving for this peace and the love which alone can obtain it, between the mystery of the God of love and the deep mystery of man's misery, a short circuit must flash, breaking into our way of living. The world in its present shape is a denial of peace and love. There must be men within it who polarize what is positive, and are all the more "charged" as the other pole is intensely negative. Gandhi expresses this by another image: "Even the toughest fibre must soften in the fire of love. If it does not melt, it is because the fire of love is not sufficiently strong."[22]

It is so essential to have this peaceful spirit in the world that Gandhi would only permit a non-violent action proportionate with the degree of peace that the mind had achieved. Hence his paradoxical words to Nehru: "If you have a sword in your heart, it is better to bring it out and use it."[23]

TWO PRINCIPLES OF "SATYAGRAHA"

In addition to the resistance by the violent person who counterattacks unjust violence, and still more, surrender by the loser who allows violence to take its course, it is imperative to have recourse to the only truly beneficial action, to a resistance and a revolt which changes the *heart* of the unjust person.

One must revolt and resist, for "if you act contrary to justice, and I know it and remain silent and let you do it, it is I who am

[22] *Lettres à l'Ashram*, p. 95

[23] Tibor Mende, *Conversations avec Nehru* (1956), p. 53. (Unfortunately very little in these conversations has any bearing on our subject. One feels that journalists are really not at home in the world of non-violence.)

unjust. But you and I are one. I cannot hurt you without wounding myself at the same time" and "every human action must be constructive and not destructive".[24]

Gandhi wrote to Nehru in 1933: "We seek to force no one, we seek to convert."[25] Just before he was assassinated, a bomb was thrown at him but missed him: "This is a brother," he said, "I have not succeeded in converting."[26] Revolt and resistance will have to be conducted in such a way that they clearly manifest "a determined will to agree".[27] "It is not a question of fighting in order to win a victory over the enemy, but to vanquish enmity and win peace."[28] Let us ponder over these words: overcome not the enemy but enmity. The two adversaries (one of which refuses to be an enemy) will both be victors in a peace worthy of the name, "the tranquillity of order" which will surpass both of them and to which both will conform, and in which they will find their mutual fulfilment.

"It is not the enemy you have to fight," to quote Gandhi again, "but the error of the enemy: the error which your neighbour makes when he comes to think that he is your enemy. Make yourself an ally of your enemy against his error."[29]

What action – words will be inadequate – will, of its nature, manifest the truth in the non-violent in a sufficiently convincing way for the unjust to experience a vital need to admit it and make it his own? In fact, the only way is for the adherent of non-violence to accept suffering when he could make the unjust suffer, and to do this in an action precisely chosen to manifest the truth he stands for and the injustice of the violent. The complexity of this action can thus be perceived, but we shall get a better idea of it in analysing its theory and practice.

It should not be confused with "non-resistance"; it is the very opposite – it is resistance. Gandhi sought a new word for it.

---

[24] Drevet, op. cit., p. 119
[25] ibid., p. 216
[26] ibid., p. 73
[27] A phrase used by Masson-Oursel in *Rythmes du Monde*, n. 2, p. 14.
[28] Quoted by M. Choisy in *Psyché* (1948), pp. 3–4
[29] M. Choisy, ibid.

During his first struggle in South Africa he coined the word *satyagraha*, which includes the idea of strength and of living truth. Experts translate it in many ways. "Strength of truth" is commonly used; Dr Corman says "steadfastness for truth".[30] Gandhi insists on "the indefectible grasp of truth"[31] and he adds: "it is also the power of love or the strength of the soul".[32] Mme C. Drevet speaks of "attachment to truth and the strength of soul which inspires truth", and Louis Massignon, "the civic claim of truth".[33] This latter formula emphasizes two points: first a concern which is essential for non-violence to be the opposite of consenting to evil or flight from it; and secondly, the civil character of the struggle which Gandhi called *satyagraha*, its intention to change the social order in an effective way.[34] Gandhi explained[35] that in order to practise *satyagraha* two principles have to be understood; they are "to adhere to the truth" and "to defend it to the utmost by voluntary suffering". "After all," he added, with child-like candour, "no one has ever disputed the necessity of defending the truth when it has been seen." He continued: "It is fairly easy to see that it is clumsy to try to force the adversary to accept it by using brute force." (It is indeed quite contrary to the nature of truth and the allegiance it deserves.)

"It is dishonourable," he went on, "to submit oneself to error because our arguments have not convinced; the only true and honourable conduct is not to submit even at the cost of life. Only then can the world be purged of error, if ever that can be entirely achieved. There can be no compromise with error when it injures life itself."

The connection between the two principles found in this text appears to lie profoundly in this fact: in this world of violence the mystique of truth is necessarily a mystique of sacrifice. "Abstract

---

[30] Op. cit., p. 13
[31] Memoirs of 1920, in Maritain, *Du régime temporel*, p. 258
[32] ibid.
[33] *Les Mardis de Dar-es-Salam* (1956), p. 7
[34] Gandhi explains another implication of "civil" – "When non-violent action infringes actual laws it is the opposite of ordinary transgression which is secret and tries to avoid the penalty." (From *Memoirs* quoted in note 31, p. 264.)
[35] Maritain, pp. 262–3

truth is only of value if it is incarnate in the lives of men who are ready to die for it."[36]

The wonderful thing about *satyagraha* is that this "mystique" has influenced the course of historical events with surprising effectiveness and completeness; it has demonstrated the power of evangelical gentleness in its most extreme form – in the love of enemies. St John has taught us: "Let us not love in word nor in tongue, but in deed and in truth."[37] The love of unjust enemies has been seen not only in isolated instances but in great movements of groups and crowds and even, in some measure, by vast masses. "To bear one another's burdens",[38] "to give one's life for our brethren",[39] this was seen to be practical on a national scale. Olivier Lacombe sees in this example "above all things an invitation to Christians to remember that the gospel works".[40]

[36] Corman, op. cit., p. 120

[37] I Jn 3: 18

[38] Gal 6: 2

[39] I Jn 3: 16

[40] *Conférences de Pax Christi* (1955), p. 56

CHAPTER
TEN

The Technique of Non-violent Action

Realism. THIS ACTION REQUIRES AS MUCH common sense as any practical action carried out with average intelligence. It requires the prudence and wisdom of the "sons of light".[1] Account has to be taken of human circumstances. In what case is resistance necessary? When is it possible? What objectives are worth pursuing and which should be abandoned because they will lead to violence? What is this particular enemy likely to understand? What spiritual means are at our disposal? In what way will this or that person react? It is instructive to observe in detail the work of analysis which Gandhi undertook, and in particular his concern for accurate sociological information.[2] His perception of the vital and symbolic objective to be attained was most admirable.

The Symbolic Objective. The is very important. The victims of injustice must be stirred to action about some objective they can achieve, which represents a real advantage for them, and in which

---

[1] Lk 16: 8

[2] Notably the inquiry carried out at Champaran, Corman, op. cit., p. 24. Cf. the excellent surveys carried out by Danilo Dolci.

they become aware of their right and their power, and which at the same time reveals to the aggressors themselves their flagrant injustice. It is thus that Gandhi led crowds of Indians on a march to the ocean to gather salt, which the British sold to them at exorbitant prices.[3] Danilo Dolci, who did not possess the means to construct a dam, which would have provided work for the destitute and enabled them to build a reservoir for the irrigation of unfertile land, organized an insurrection of unpaid work, a "reverse strike". He got these destitute men to rebuild a road which was becoming unusable as a result of administrative incompetence.[4] In this way, he forced public opinion to become conscious of the desperate misery of these destitute men and united the sharers of a common misery in constructive action. He thus rescued these men from their passivity and turned their wretched state into a means of redemption;[5] he revealed and released their latent energies.

Submission to Truth. The prudence of the non-violence leader must be of an exceptional kind to enable him to be a competent realist. Gandhi declared: "I must be capable of registering the slightest variation in the moral climate around me."[6] He must have such a comprehensive view of the truth that he is able to see a situation from his adversary's point of view.[7]

"The right for which the non-violent person initiates his campaign must be evident. If it is an illusion or a pretence, his efforts will come to naught through lack of grip, however great his courage. It is he who will have to recognize that he was in the wrong."[8] "National independence," declared Gandhi in 1935, "can be found only in the truth."[9]

The truth is "dictated by the interior voice".[10] One has to have

---

[3] Corman, op. cit., p. 122

[4] Danilo Dolci, *La révolution ouverte*, p. 99; Ganachaud, *Bandits de Dieu*, p. 71.

[5] A perceptive phrase, used by Carlo Levi in *Bandits de Dieu*, p. 12; cf. p. 66.

[6] *Young India* (16 Feb., 1922)

[7] Corman, op. cit., p. 122

[8] Lanza del Vasto, *Vinôbâ*, p. 71

[9] Drevet, op. cit., p. 138

[10] Corman, op. cit., pp. 15, 26, 51, etc.

sufficient inner quality to perceive it and follow it. "Before speaking about his interior voice, each person must become aware of his imperfections."

We have seen in Part II what inner reform is required for this submission to the truth. Gandhi made inner purification an aim even for a movement of the masses.[11] Each time the campaign threatened to degenerate, he interrupted its action, and he never made national independence an end in itself; he considered it would be an inevitable *result* of a growth of justice within the nation.

An effective love of the enemy. Resistance and revolt only begin when all means of conciliation have failed. The solution sought must be the most favourable for the adversary. It will inevitably be painful since he will have to abandon his unjust "rights". Everything has to be done throughout the struggle to make this as easy as possible. Gandhi wrote to the British in 1926: "I show you, as a friend, an honourable solution to a grave problem. The other solution, repression, is open to you. I warn you that it will not succeed."[12]

In 1942 he wrote: "My friendship requires that I should help the English to understand their error. They are on the brink of an abyss – about to fall into it. Even if they wish to cut off my hands my friendship requires that I should help them to get out of it."[13]

Naturally, such language cannot be taken seriously unless it corresponds to a real knowledge of both sides of the question. And it is not genuine unless the love of the enemy is real. We have much concrete evidence of the highly perceptive nature of Gandhi's love for the English. This love of the enemy is one of the causes of the positive character of non-violence.[14] It even goes so far as to give effective help to an enemy in trouble: Gandhi himself recruited soldiers for the English during the 1914 war.[15] Since enmity is not admissible but a persistence in desiring the well-being

---

[11] ibid., p. 46
[12] Drevet, p. 136
[13] ibid., p. 60, n. 1
[14] Corman, p. 14
[15] ibid., p. 21

of the adversary in fighting what is evil in him, loyalty can even
go so far as to warn him about one's own intentions. It will even
go so far as not to have any secret thought which one is not prepared to reveal to him and to give detailed information to his
spies.[16]

Religious respect for law. Just as the struggle becomes permissible
only if it proceeds from a genuine love for the adversary, in the
same way a revolt against unjust laws presupposes a religious
respect for any law worthy of the name.[17] Gandhi carried this to
such extremes that as a lawyer he was accused of failing in professional conduct. We do not know how deserved this was, but it
shows the bent of his character.

"It is ," he said, "only when one has been scrupulously obedient
to the laws of society that one is in a position to distinguish
between good and bad, just and unjust laws. It is only then that
one has the right to civil disobedience to certain laws in clearly
defined circumstances."[18] Catholic moral theology permits disobedience to unjust laws. For such disobedience to be legitimate,
the state of things must be manifestly unjust and oppressive and
every other means must have been attempted to obtain a reform of
the law. In the case of an armed insurrection, moralists require
a moral certainty that the damages resulting from the insurrection
will not be worse than the existing ones: this does not arise in the
case of non-violent revolt.

It would be strange to reproach Gandhi and his followers for
not shrinking from disobedience of the law: they only reached
that point when matters seemed desperate, in cases of manifest
injustice upheld by certain laws and made part of the established
order by the laws themselves – which drives men to violent revolt.[19]

---

[16] Corman, pp. 26–7, 104
[17] ibid., p. 106
[18] *Autobiography*, op. cit. (p. 605 in Fr. ed.)
[19] Such cases are unfortunately more frequent and more serious when
the world is in a state of flux, when laws are in many ways quite inadequate to the realities of the situation, or when legislators are too
preoccupied to reform them by politics which fill their thoughts, are confused and subject to violent prejudices, or when public organs are too
cumbersome to function properly. Jurists recognize this (see Lapratte,

Whereas what is peculiar to Gandhi is not disobedience but the avoidance of violence within it. It is a fact that religious opinion today approves of violent revolts (particularly if they succeed), whereas they are easily scandalized by revolts inspired by justice and love. Must love and justice therefore have no means of asserting themselves? In order to become effective must they adopt the very means they are challenging? Are outbursts of violence the only means of expression allowed to those who suffer unjustly from violence? Such questions certainly deserve to be considered.

Civil Disobedience. There is nothing more characteristic than Gandhi's concern for legality in the way he changed the whole attitude to civil disobedience both in its conception and expression. Before him it was taken for granted. It was considered merely as a poor alternative to violence. It was the weapon of those who were too weak to assert their claims by violent methods. The expression dates back to 1849 and was coined by Henry Thoreau.[20] The reality is much older. The exploited, whose labour was necessary for the prosperity of their oppressors, did not have to wait for Mirabeau in order to realize "that they only had to fold their arms in order to terrify". The effectiveness of this kind of passive resistance is

---

Les squatters et le droit, Alsatia, 1956). Moralists know very well that a law is not fit to be called a law when it ceases to be dictated by reason in accordance with things as they are. But even they perforce tend to rely on reforms which will in fact only come about if there is an outbreak of violence. Then they are drawn out of their passivity and approve. But they would disapprove non-violent actions the legality of which would be only too evident to anyone taking a realistic view of the "disorder" which is misnamed the "established order".

---

[20] Henry Thoreau (1817–1862), *Essay on Civil Disobedience.* He was an American writer of Emerson's school. Imprisoned for refusing to pay taxes to a government which upheld slavery and was carrying out a war to conquer Mexico, he published a justification in 1849: *Resistance to Civil Government* (to be found in the posthumous collection *Désobéir*, *tr.* L. Bazalgette, Rieder, 1921). His main work was *Walden, or Life in the Woods* (1854, *tr.* Fabulet). Emerson drew his portrait at the beginning of this work. Notes on him by Bazalgette in the intro. to *Désobéir*, who also wrote an accurate life of him in the form of a novel: *Henry Thoreau, sauvage* (Rieder, 1924).

assuredly of great significance: it forces men to see that violence is not needed for success. What is more, history gives us many instances in which violent revolt would certainly have been crushed, whereas organized disobedience forced the oppressor to give way.[21] La Boétie taught that the ruler only governs because of the "voluntary servitude" of his subjects. They have to learn to say "No" when he is unjust, and they will often succeed in forcing him to give way. But this pre-Gandhi form of civil disobedience has something violent about it. It *forces* the oppressor, through pressure brought to bear upon him. The word "forces" comes to mind spontaneously. Moreover, this conduct is *violent* because of the effect on those who suffer it, who are full of resentment and sometimes hatred. Their pent-up violence explodes when it finds an opportunity. Gandhi needed a new word to show that true non-violence, the work of truth and love, is not only opposed to "non-resistance" but also, as we have just seen, to this passionate kind of civil disobedience. *Satyagraha* describes his form of non-violence.[22] In spite of this precaution, it is still difficult for people to see the real difference. The cunning can never see anything but cunning in the action of those who are pure of heart; the violent believe that it is but a provisional disguise for violence.[23] The cunning and the violent make up the masses of mankind, and particularly its so-called "élites". Gandhi discovered that even those who were theoretically in favour of non-violence, could not take part in campaigns of civil disobedience without serious preparation.[24] In 1919 there was an outburst of violence among the masses of India, which the English punished by rigorous repression.[25] It was then that Gandhi accused himself of having committed "an error as large as the Himalayas", because he had believed that civil disobedience could take a non-violent form before the masses really understood its inner significance.[26] He therefore suddenly broke

---

[21] Several examples can be found in B. de Ligt: *Pour vaincre sans violence* and *La paix créatrice*.

[22] *Autobiography*, p. 406 (Fr. ed.)

[23] Corman, op. cit., p. 35

[24] *Autobiography*, p. 605 (Fr. ed.)

[25] Corman, op. cit., p. 35

[26] *Autobiography*, p. 605 (Fr. ed.)

off the action in order to "form a group of well-trained volunteers who had integrity and a clear understanding of the rigours of *satyagraha*. They in their turn could explain its nature to the people and keep them on the right road by constant supervision". Even with this group he had setbacks and found that it was a "difficult task to interest people in the peaceful aspect of *satyagraha*".[27] Thus civil disobedience, a fairly normal way of fighting for more or less interested ends and without the complete rejection of violence, when purified from all forms of violence came to be seen as a most difficult form of action. Gandhi distinguished it carefully from the stages that have to precede it, in which one limits oneself to non co-operation without positive disobedience.

Non co-operation and civil disobedience. These two degrees correspond to two stages of spiritual progress. To withdraw co-operation from "a government which refuses to repent of its injustices" requires interior purification; to disobey requires more: one must become sufficiently independent and be able to "govern oneself in every possible way".

Lanza del Vasto expresses the difference between them in these words:[28]

Non co-operation is a strike on the part of the citizen, who refuses all service to the state and at the same time rejects any benefits and honours from it. Civil servants and officers hand in their resignation. Public services are interrupted. Tribunals are replaced by arbitration. But the movement remains within the sphere of loyalty. *Non-violent resistance* is *disobedience* to a specific law, and in extreme cases, to all laws, decrees and regulations; through this disobedience the citizen deliberately draws punishment upon himself. The movement remains in the sphere of morality because it makes no attempt upon life, honour or other people's property, and is thus non-violent.

Followers of Gandhi consider that the alternation of these two methods is sufficient to overcome any kind of tyranny (and they have proved it) and that it is the only morally justifiable

[27] *Autobiography*, pp. 605–06 (Fr. ed.). See our comments on aggressiveness, pp. 60–66.
[28] *Vinôbâ*, p. 295, note 1

revolution, while it is the most effective in practice. That, in fact, it does not expose the people to premature and forced reforms, which would prove therefore false and deceptive. For it is only by earning them through voluntary discipline and the spirit of sacrifice that most people can obtain reforms. The conversion of men must precede the changing of systems.

In non co-operation itself, Gandhi theoretically outlines four stages, of which only the last one consists in refusal to pay taxes, which is in fact a form of civil disobedience. He will only countenance having recourse to this step after particularly burdensome actions have been carried out, like handing in one's resignation if one is a civil servant, or leaving the army or the police.

He sees two degrees in civil disobedience. The first is "defensive disobedience", which is an involuntary and reluctant disobedience to laws which are intrinsically bad and whose observance would be incompatible with self-respect or human dignity. Here are some examples of defensive civil disobedience: the formation of voluntary corps of *satyagrahis*, the convening of public meetings for peaceful purposes, the publication, in spite of contrary orders, of writings of a non-provocative nature.

The second degree is "aggressive and offensive civil disobedience", symbolical of a revolt against the state. It is disobedience to laws which may be just in themselves. He gives as an example refusal to pay taxes, and adds: "This offensive civil disobedience, either on the part of individuals or the masses, is a very dangerous weapon although it is the most effective of all the peaceful weapons at our disposal."[29]

The integrity of those who use it must be proportionate to this danger. It is scandalous to see it used by hotheads or violent people.

Although consisting in a revolt against laws which may be intrinsically just, disobedience may be morally justifiable, because every other means having been considered, it is the only non-violent way of combating an unjust government. The morality of such conduct is that of a "just war", with this surprising factor in its favour – that it does not involve violence and its evil consequences, and

---

[29] Corman, op. cit., pp. 114, 115

that it is directed towards true peace by peaceful means. We should always keep in mind the example of the liberation of India.

Spiritual development of action. Whatever may be the value of such considerations, it is far more important to consider the spiritual and psychological development of this type of activity.

It starts by stirring up the bad conscience of the adversary by shocking him. That puts him out of countenance. "I deceive the expectation of the tyrant so that he strikes the air, which takes him by surprise. He is even more surprised to come up against an inner resistance in me which eludes his grasp. At first this resistance will blind him, and only provoke him to greater anger against me, but later on it will force him to give way."[30]

General Smuts said to Gandhi: "I wish you would have recourse to violence like English strikers, for then we could get rid of the lot of you. But you don't even want to do harm to your adversaries."[31]

Nevertheless adversaries are subjected to unavoidable hardships as, for instance, in the case of a boycott. But they cannot fail to see that this is only the negative aspect which inevitably follows a positive action concerned with life and the most elementary human dignity; this was the case in the saving of the Indian countryside by the restoration of local craftsmanship, which had been ruined by the importation of English cotton goods.

In the same way, Gandhi's famous public fasts had the effect of hunger strikes and seemed forms of blackmail. If they are carefully examined, it will be noticed that they were never directed *against* anyone. This was so evident at the time that we were, at first, surprised by an answer he gave to a Protestant missionary. The latter objected: "Are not your fasts a form of blackmail?" "Yes," Gandhi answered, weighing every word, "the same kind of blackmail that Jesus exerts upon you from the Cross."[32]

One's surprise vanishes as soon as one reflects on these words. Gandhi seems to accept the word blackmail, but in order to reject what is normally implied by this word. For the supposed "blackmail" that Christ exerts upon us leaves us absolutely free, and is

---

[30] Drevet, p. 113

[31] Corman, p. 18

[32] Corman, p. 64

but an extension of his love. If we share in it, then this love acts in us as in him, but it compels us in no way from outside.

It will be noticed that the incorrect expression, a fast *against* this or that person or institution, was never used by Gandhi. Nevertheless since some of his closest followers, like Pyarelal, used it, it must be because he was not properly understood on this point. Yet he clearly explained what he was doing on each occasion. For instance, the great three weeks' fast of May 1933 signified in his words "a prayer from the bottom of my heart to purify myself and my followers in order to attain a greater devotion in the cause of the Untouchables".[33] The fast of September 1947, undertaken when civil war was threatening to spread throughout India and which effectively re-established order in Calcutta, was in no way "directed against Hindus in order to bring about a friendlier attitude towards Muslims". Gandhi declared: "Having exhausted all resources – in terms of human effort – and realized my utter helplessness, I rest my head upon God's bosom. This is the deep meaning and purpose of this fast."[34]

This is the true influence of his religious "mystique" upon his conduct.

THE POWER OF SUFFERING

The suffering which the unjust adversary inflicts upon the non-violent who resists him is decisive in the awakening of his conscience.[35] He complains – "Do you think that we don't feel it when thousands of your fellow countrymen suffer?" As if the one who complained was not himself responsible for these sufferings! "Do you think we have no heart?" To which Gandhi replied, "No! I don't think so, but I want you to experience this suffering,

---

[33] Corman, p. 77

[34] Corman, *Ecole d'héroisme*, p. 90. Cf the striking scruples shown by Gandhi about his fast during the 1918 strike; without intending to, there is no doubt that he did exert considerable pressure on the employers, *Autobiography*, pp. 555–6 (Fr. ed.).

[35] The words of an English officer are noteworthy, quoted in Corman, p. 129.

for it is precisely your hearts that I want to touch. When they have been sufficiently touched, we shall be able to negotiate."[36]

"Sufficiently touched" – what can this mean? It means that the adversary must get beyond the stage of sterile pity. He sees this as a sign of his kindly disposition, but it secretly enrages him against his victims. This unhealthy state of affairs will force him into the open, his sentimental compassion will give way to "understanding". "Only suffering opens a man's heart to deep understanding."[37] Much suffering is needed. Is it not astonishing that men cheerfully accept suffering in violent battles and are surprised when the same thing is asked of them in the cause of peace? With what bitter laughter we shall see at the Last Judgement the price that had to be paid for our so-called armed victories and defeats in terms of tears, blood, agony and death. What did they really achieve? Our tears will then be dried, but how we shall laugh! Men find it quite natural to throw themselves headlong into the most unequal struggles and to be massacred in vain, but they resent any sacrifices which are demanded in the cause of true freedom.

In 1920 Gandhi declared: "Before India can take her place in the world, we must be prepared to face with equanimity the assassination not just of a thousand men and women, but of several thousands. Let everyone consider hanging as a normal part of life."[38]

And why not? What is this in comparison with the hundreds of thousands of deaths that wars cost? What ruin they cause, and in what a state of demoralization they leave both winner and loser. And again, what are the *real* results? One of the greatest achievements, which is surely most urgently needed today, is for men to become morally aware of the heroism that is needed for peace.[39] It is high time we started working for it.

---

[36] Corman, p. 74
[37] Corman, p. 16
[38] Romain Rolland, *Mahatma Gandhi*, p. 62
[39] Pius XII, Christmas Message 1947: "Men who were whole-heartedly determined to win the war were ready for all sorts of sacrifices, even life itself. Whoever sincerely desires to work for peace must be ready for equally great sacrifices. Nothing is more costly to angry men than to give up reprisals and implacable resentment." We shall return to this from another standpoint in Chap. XII, pp. 244 ff.

Gandhi again gives us a decisive stimulus. Observers were astounded by the tragic heroism which he elicited from the crowds under the blows of the army and police.[40] In fact "the practice of non-violence requires the greatest courage, a boundless courage to stand up to every test,[41] including physical courage."[42] And the courage needed to see the action seems to fail under setbacks,[43] to face long delays. The first Indian campaign of Gandhi ended in 1922; twenty-five years of waiting were needed to see its fruits.

The Purification of the Non-violent. "To convince the oppressor through our purification by suffering".[44] In fact, while the oppressor becomes gradually conscious of the truth, the non-violent are themselves being purified by their witness. They attain to a spiritual level worthy of the dignity they claim. This great law was principally made evident in the suppression of the caste system of the pariahs. Gandhi imposed it on his compatriots as their first objective while they still took the caste system for granted and only thought of ridding themselves of the English.

"If the whole world regards us as lepers," he told them in 1921, "it is only what we deserve, since we treat a fifth of our compatriots as such . . . If India can regenerate itself in this respect, there is no power on earth which will be able to deny its right to independence."[45]

In more general terms: "Fulfil the constructive programme in its totality, and you will have total independence.[46] My aim is not simply to rid India of British domination: I want to liberate India absolutely from every kind of domination. Hence it follows that for me the movement for independence is a movement for personal self-purification."[47]

The Importance of Leaders. In this undertaking the importance

---

[40] Corman gives other instances: pp. 42–5, 55–6, 62–3
[41] ibid., pp. 96, 97
[42] ibid., p. 34
[43] ibid., pp. 52 and 78
[44] ibid., p. 34
[45] Corman, p. 59
[46] ibid., p. 108
[47] ibid., p. 32

of leaders and trained volunteers of integrity of all ranks is obviously of decisive importance.[48] They have to form a public conscience, and to enlighten it fully on the meaning of the movement and its methods. It mostly depends upon them to prevent the outbreak of violence, which is always ready to break out.[49]

In 1932 Gandhi was asked by Pierre Cérésole if non-violence had a chance of succeeding in the West. He had doubts particularly about the masses who seemed too alien to the spirit of non-violence. We always think that our élite (among whom we, of course, count ourselves) are capable of doing wonders. Gandhi answered,

> But are we quite sure the people aren't ready? Don't you rather think that you lack leaders? A leader must be a witness to God every minute of the twenty-four hours of the day. He must have complete self-mastery, be a stranger to anger and fear. You must forget yourselves, not let yourselves be overcome by the pleasures of the table or sex. Thus purified, you will have a power which is not yours – the power of God. Where does strength reside? A lad of fifteen could knock me down with a blow. I am nothing, but I have been delivered from desire and fear, so that I know the power of God.[50]

The Success of Non-Violence. Thus the second stage of the non-violent struggle is the cleansing sacrifice to which corresponds the awakening of the adversary's bad conscience, followed by a growth in true moral awareness. On this point we cannot do better than to quote some fine lines from Lanza del Vasto:

> The non-violent struggle will remove the veils of blindness one by one, those of hatred and anger, prejudice and contempt, suspicion and fear, human pride and obstinacy, mean calculation and narrow self-interest, whereas a violent struggle confounds all reason, confuses all grievances, thickens all veils, until the stronger puts the other man in the wrong. Confidence in the non-violence of man is expressed in this affirmation: that a man

---

[48] ibid., pp. 36, 69
[49] Corman, pp. 35, 46–7, 78, 80
[50] Drevet

who is forced to admit to himself that he is in the wrong, cannot continue the struggle.[51]

This victory has certain remarkable features. "The outcome of a non-violent 'war' is always a mutual agreement, never a *diktat*, still less a humiliation of the adversary."[52]

It is necessarily a compromise, but one in which the essential goal is achieved: the adversary becomes an ally. "The outcome of a non-violent campaign can only be considered worthy if it leaves both combatants stronger and more vital than they were at the start."[53]

Let us conclude, by emphasizing the deep psychological value of such behaviour; Maryse Choisy expresses it thus:[54]

The whole dynamics of non-violence comes from the fact that it succeeds in totally dissipating the unconscious feeling of guilt in the non-violent, while it simultaneously actualizes a proportionate sense of guilt in the adversary. It is the guilty conscience that makes him vulnerable. But to the extent that the non-violent is prompted by love, he not only convinces his opponent of his guilt but also helps him to accept it. It can no longer be projected into a form of paranoia. On the contrary, it inhibits the aggressive urge. Because, at the very moment of its discovery, the adversary feels himself to be forgiven by the non-violent. Thus in this interior dialogue, there is a threefold dialectical movement of contrary relations: the non-violent prevails; the violent is touched, and the non-violent is lifted up with him. This is what this "discovery of genius" consists in.[55]

---

[51] *Vinôbâ*, p. 70

[52] Corman, p. 16

[53] ibid., p. 28

[54] In *Psyché* (1948), p. 11. (Reprinted in *Yogas et Psychanalyse*, p. 240.)

[55] The expression "discovery of genius" may be misleading. We are so utilitarian that we are in danger of seeing non-violence simply as a clever tactical move. It is to be hoped that the "mystique" described in Chap. IX, with all the living faith in God and in the immortality of man which it demands, will put into its proper perspective the aspect of psychological "technique", with all that this implies of opportunity, cleverness, good luck and genius.

CHAPTER
ELEVEN

Difficulties

WHAT PERPLEXITIES THIS "DISCOVERY OF genius" brings with it! Before considering these, we must make a few preliminary remarks.

First of all, we should not be surprised at our perplexity; it should not lessen our self-assurance. The question of what life is or may be is always perplexing. It is the property of life that it is always new. It always seems to produce *more* out of *less*. This is precisely what is ignored – and hindered – when we reduce it to terms of visible results. Life discovers itself. "What will this child become? Can a tree come out of a small seed?" It is for us to become the seed, the leaven, the fire. It is a delusion to disregard prophets because they are not able to give precise predictions about the future. What they are qualified to do is to give directives as to the way in which it has to be moulded. At the most, if they are politically competent, they can, like Gandhi, indicate objectives more or less at hand and how to reach them. But even such rare kinds of prophets are themselves obliged to change their plans as the action unfolds and they do not fully reach their objectives. What forms can non-violence take, and to what extent can it succeed? Practising it is the only way of discovering what it can achieve. It is a question of keeping at it and trying different methods again and again. Man has a strange craving for security, yet his human condition involves many hazards and risks. He thinks he will find it by violent methods. Yet it should not need much reflection to realize that there are far more grounds for misgivings about their use than there should be about the heroism required for non-violent action.[1]

No method is absolutely certain. "We have to work all our life in the distress of our time," Charles de Foucauld used to say. "Difficulties are not storms which we only have to wait to see pass by before getting down to work in fine weather; no, they are the normal state of things; in order to achieve something worthwhile we must expect to be involved in the distress of our age during our whole life."[2]

Our perplexities with regard to non-violence are, at their most acute, purely and simply what we feel about the future in spiritual terms. This is always in a critical state. It has always been easier to kill than to live. The genius or the saint is easily overcome by a little piece of sharp metal applied at the right spot. When the body is locked up behind iron bars, it is vain for the spirit to work out heroic schemes. Modern psychological techniques find it fairly easy to undermine the springs of genius and heroism. Seen in this light, it would seem that the powers of death have it all their own way. But is this not due to the fact that the forces of life are not taking advantage of times of respite, to mobilize the spiritual powers of the world? They have not sufficient faith in their power to do so: at times they believe too easily, as if success were certain, at other times they regard themselves as beaten from the start. In fact they must work you to a pitch of heroism; everything that perplexes us demands this from us.

THE AUTHENTICITY OF NON-VIOLENCE

The non-violence of Gandhi brings to mind a saying from Kierkegaard's *Journals*: "A reminder of these categories of Christian living which demand a maximum of effort from us is like a flight of migratory birds over a lot of tame birds."

---

[1] Cf. Chap. I above
[2] Quoted by Mgr Mercier in the bulletin of the Assoc. Charles de Foucauld, *Jésus Amour* (1956), No. 104, p. 42.

There can be no true life without these far-reaching flights; but how often do we, farmyard birds that we are, rise above earthly levels? Kierkegaard added: "My task is to raise the price of things, and if possible to whisper to each one privately what might be expected of him." Everybody should be doing this to himself.

Any non-violent action, if only slightly vigorous and sustained, presupposes a fairly high level of spiritual development. This type of action does of course contribute to such a development. Those who dare, however, suddenly to initiate the process, will find that with God's grace it develops progressively with their own spiritual maturity and strength. There is every chance that they will make the grade, since as they become increasingly aware of the unjust situation in which they find themselves, they do not give way to resentment, but rather turn this resentment into loving concern for the unjust. This is the very heart and soul of non-violence, which, while it takes a fully realistic view of the facts, is nevertheless committed to truly peaceful behaviour. This commitment involves them in a gradual transformation by the truth adhered to, in the light of the first principle of *satyagraha*, as well as a voluntary acceptance of suffering according to its second principle.

With respect to spiritual and moral attainment, a distinction must, of course, be made between what is to be expected of leaders and followers. All must be initially determined to go as far as they are able according to their lights; which is the root principle of heroism. But it must be remembered that the moral awareness of the Indian masses led by Gandhi or of Danilo Dolci's followers, may in fact be quite rudimentary. Great generosity in gentleness can in fact coexist with the most inveterate wild instincts. When Dolci led his poor followers into action, he had to give them strict instructions not to carry knives. We frequently fail to recognize man's potentiality under grace to take sudden leaps forward from great depths to a certain level and to remain there, provided good leadership is there to give him confidence. St Paul gave as a programme of action to certain converts who previously *lived by stealing*, to work so that they "might have something to give to him that suffereth need".[3] He expected no less immediately.

None the less, much non-violent literature often makes us feel

---

[3] Eph 4: 28

as uneasy as the naïvely optimistic approaches of some Protestant sects. Our over-simplified theoretical idealism and sentimental hopes take little account of reality with its oppositions and bitter conflicts. Our perplexities in this respect will be solved to the extent that leaders are found who are true realists. If they have an instinct for what is possible and give substance to dreams in opportune action, then the wild and erratic hopes of simple people could become a great force.

Unfortunately the two principles of *satyagraha* presuppose a faith in the might of truth and the power of sacrifice, with which Gandhi thought Europe might be insufficiently endowed.

"You cannot move an inch," he said speaking about Europeans, "unless you have faith in yourselves." Nevertheless he added, "only non-violence can save Europe".[4]

In fact, we can hardly detect among our European élites, such as they are, the courage and disinterestedness which would proclaim above all their differences, faith in a certain ideal, such as for instance a rejection of atomic weapons or opposition to torture. This seems to be a major obstacle in our countries. Certain leaders might rise up, the masses might make a generous effort, but trained élites would be lacking to spread the ideals of *satyagraha*. Our so-called élites are too agitated about trivial and conflicting ideas, too much at the mercy of their passions and their little feuds. One cannot imagine them allowing new men to rise from the masses to give the lead, they are too anxious to keep the big organizations going, the press, civil service, big business, education etc. – all these things which stifle originality and the life of the spirit. There is nothing more hostile to prophecy than their inertia, and non-violence is a prophetic action. It is they who throw a Danilo Dolci into prison.

What seems most lacking everywhere in our Western world is a disinterested zeal for great human issues. There may be sudden bursts of generosity, as in March 1954 in France in response to the appeals of the Abbé Pierre for the homeless. But the backing for even a praiseworthy effort of this kind falls far short of the real need.

The outlook of materialism, with its short-sighted and selfish

---

[4] M. Choisy, *Psyché* (Jan., 1948)

aims, is what is most unfavourable to non-violent action. How can one make it accept the possibility of finding a solution, apart from violent struggle or cowardly surrender? Men only consider these alternatives. If one preaches non-violence to them, will it not seem like asking them to give up, under a pharisaical veil of noble intentions?

All along the line of failure that we have traced so far we see the ambiguity of non-violence.[5] We must take this into account. We must be particularly on our guard against pretensions to absolute integrity. When a feeling for the absolute makes one overlook certain human realities, as, for instance, one's homeland (which is accused of being an obstacle to universal love and looked upon as necessarily bellicose and selfish) it is in great danger of becoming more emotional than spiritual in outlook. Unruly emotions demand everything or nothing, and show a bitter and deceptive partiality. The spirit respects the whole truth, all the relations that hold things together. It is much easier to go to extremes – so many "purists" have no respect for integrity. The non-violent are an easy prey to pharisaism. They pretend to be governed by the compelling power of truth which the statisticians ignore; this can easily lead to deceptively fine ideals, flattering in nature but ineffectual because they have no real grip on reality. There is a certain rejection of the sordid world which is particularly puzzling – namely the rejection of modern technical progress. On the one hand it is difficult to deny that it is essentially violent and productive of the worst kinds of violence.[6] Yet on the other hand, it is foolish to reject it outright. We are not only unable to stop technical progress but the rejection of something which is so much a part of the structure of truth in our present world is to invalidate our experiments with truth from the outset. The urgent task is to seek how this formidable process can be directed to man's well-being, or at best how his soul, freedom and love can adjust to it. In order to achieve this, it may be a good thing for some individuals to withdraw as much as possible from our mechanically-oriented civilization in order to live as closely as possible by certain laws of wisdom. But such a withdrawal must be a preparation for a more fruitful dialogue with

---

[5] Chap. 1, pp. 60 ff.
[6] Cf. pp. 67 ff.

the masses of their brethren who are enmeshed in new social conditions. To make it a principle to reject these conditions is to refuse any communication with others. If non-violence required such a withdrawal, it would be nothing more than an aesthetic attitude, a romantic attempt to recreate the past by means of archaeology or folklore.

Gandhi was an experimenter. How did he evolve? His campaign on behalf of the spinning-wheel and local craftsmanship in general was certainly more than a useful opportunity given to many Indians during the thirty years that preceded independence. It had and it retains a deep human significance. But was it exclusive? We can leave this for competent experts in his teaching to discuss.

As an expression of faith, a break from "established disorder", non-violence is necessarily on the road to martyrdom. Each time this idea has loomed in our minds we have hesitated to put it into words; some people are too eager to seek martyrdom for themselves or for others. If martyrdom in one form or other is to be the lot of the non-violent, then it must not come as a sanction of his irresponsibility, but be patently inflicted by the injustice he challenges. Just as he has to fight for a solution with which an adversary of good faith can agree, in the same way he must point to a path by which all can reach victory, and use resources proportionate to the forces at his disposal. Purity on earth must be clothed in real flesh and blood. "Feeble thinking," in E. Mounier's[7] admirable words, "likes to justify its withdrawals by a flattering concern not to sully the purity of the spirit by the sordid compromises of life; as if for an actual incarnate spirit purity did not first and foremost consist in its acceptance of the job in hand and the means that are within its reach." Gandhi has shown how a non-violent person who is primarily concerned with the absolute is not bound to ignore the real world, because it is full of injustice.

No doubt the deepest reason why non-violence must be particularly moderate in action is because it has as its basic principle a benevolent understanding of the unjust enemy. It must therefore be prepared to accept many uncertainties and misunderstandings. It is easy to pretend to understand the other side. We know from experience that it is often those who pretend to have a sympathetic

---

[7] *Traité du Caractère*, p. 686

understanding of us who know the least about what we really have at heart; and that when somebody happens to open their hearts to us and enables us to see things from within, things appear quite different from what we had imagined. What kind of value can therefore be given to the knowledge that a nation claims to have of its oppressor, or any victim of those who make him suffer?

This is certainly a great difficulty. But it must be a spur to making greater efforts towards objective understanding of others; violence is an obstacle to this, whereas non-violence fosters it. The greater the difficulty experienced in seeing the truth from the other person's point of view, the greater the effort that has to be made. Violence takes for granted and reinforces the entanglements of deadly reciprocal misunderstandings that are implicit in human relations. What needs to be done is precisely to disentangle what we can and to substitute, where possible, a fresh, clear pattern of relationships.

The clarity and smoothness of such communication will at best be so approximate that we can only work towards it. The non-violent can never afford to be proud of their achievements.

DANGERS OF BETRAYAL

It matters little in the last resort if non-violence is misunderstood, if it is mistaken for hypocrisy or moral blackmail; this is inevitable. We are of course assuming that the action of the non-violent is just. It is impossible to stand out against injustice in any way whatever without giving the impression of being unfair to the unjust in the eyes of some people. They are mistaken and it is unfortunate. The "violence" the unjust complain about is really a foretaste of the repentance they will eventually have to be brought to accept.

On the other hand there are two real dangers of betrayal of the ideal of non-violence.

The fight against unjust violence threatens to draw the non-violent into the trap of violence. Injustice leads to ever-increasingly explosive attitudes of inner resentment in the oppressed. Gandhi was always very conscious of this danger; it worried him greatly.

"Our non-violence seems due to our powerlessness: as if we were nursing in our hearts a desire for vengeance when the opportunity came. Can voluntary non-violence arise out of the enforced non-violence of the weak? Is what I am trying to do a vain attempt?"[8]

This anxiety can only be got rid of by the heroism and realism of leaders. This has been and always will be the answer. Non-violent resisters can never be too prepared, their spiritual discipline can never be too strict, and every collective action presupposes good organization and trained men of action. Non-violence will then be able to preserve its integrity in varying psychological and practical situations.

A sense of timing is thus essential. Non-violence can claim to be effective only within predetermined limits and along specific lines. Undeniably there is always the danger of being impelled outside these. This is not fatal, for every human action has its risks. However, non-violence in action corresponds so closely to the spirit of the gospels, and is so necessary to mankind in its desperate plight, that it must run these risks.

The major objection is obviously the possibility that it will give free scope to unjust violence where just violence might have prevailed. However much the non-violent may claim to resist evil, do they not in fact give it a fatal advantage? The answer is always to be found in making a correct assessment of each situation. One of the essential principles of the theory is never to act when there is no possibility of a positive result; all the more reason to be on one's guard against playing the game of power politics. A good appreciation of the risks involved is extremely difficult. The violent are of course faced with the same anxiety: they know that if they sow the wind they must also be prepared to reap the storm.

A true appreciation of the human values that need defending and a sense of their vulnerability in a concrete situation are essential. Pius XII reminded us that "there are certain values in human society which are of such importance that their defence against an unjust aggressor is undoubtedly fully justified. Their defence is equally incumbent upon the solidarity of nations who have a duty not to abandon a people which is the victim of aggression".[9]

One cannot over-emphasize the sanctity of natural values which, though relative, are nevertheless, in the words of Congar, "worthy

---

[8] Romain Rolland, *Mahatma Gandhi*, p. 157
[9] Christmas Message, 1948

of respect for what they are in themselves". In opposition to the views of certain conscientious objectors, the latter wrote: "The intermediary order of secular realities, the nature of things which lies between the Christian mystique of charity and the realm of concrete action in the world, must not be left out of the right ordering of things."[10]

As an eminent theologian, Fr Congar thus goes beyond the objectors' own position, discerning and indicating the precise point which the majority of the non-violent do not seem to take sufficiently into account. For instance, I have heard one of them, a devout Christian, declare, "People have recourse to violence through lack of faith: it is as if one imagined, so to speak, that 'a part of God' needed propping up by a country and if that country were crushed, God would be partially annihilated. But God has no need of us: it is we on the contrary who have to remain faithful to Him to the point of sacrifice, and who can then hope for His help."

A return to reliance upon God's power is, as we have insisted, essential, and it leads to a necessary tendency to abstain from violence in every possible way. But considering the actual condition of mankind, it cannot underestimate the importance of natural realities. The false picture of a "part of God" upheld by a country and collapsing with its defeat, must not put us off or affect our appreciation of the reality of which this is but a caricature; the values upheld by a country give glory to God in so far as they are authentic in human terms, they *need men* to sponsor and defend them. It is this humble deployment of human means which calls forth God's help and which must strive for integrity in order to give a worthy basis for its cooperation. Without this human contribution, we tempt God. But what is this integrity? Here we are thrown back into the perplexities of each concrete situation, among them the maturity of the conscience involved. To what extent does the safeguarding of human values allow us to abstain from violence, an abstention which is counselled by Christ and which is therefore God's will for us when it is rightly applied? This correct application must be found by us, whatever the cost, but we are left to our own counsel under God's guidance to solve the dreadful perplexities of human situations.

---

[10] Y. Congar in a leaflet ed. by Equipes Enseignantes, Paris, 1953

We stand perplexed between the dangers of two opposing deviations: the temerity which tempts God by a disincarnate supernaturalism (or idealism); and the contempt of recourse to God which rejects his help in a short-sighted "realism", giving way purely and simply to the suggestions of the "elements" of this world and the promptings of "flesh and blood". Such is the diversity of human conditions and moral awareness that the right course of action will have to be chosen, according to the situation, somewhere between two conflicting extremes. At one extreme most people are incapable of upholding spiritual values if the normal conditions for their practice have disappeared; they therefore have no other means of preserving their right to existence than to die in violent resistance, without any human hope of success. At the other extreme, we find certain people of great spiritual quality, like Gandhi, who, during the Second World War faced possible Japanese occupation of his country. Such people consider it their duty to inspire a non-violent resistance which, while it may give the appearance of a cowardly defeatism, will in the long run ensure the victory of truth after a temporary setback. Both these courses of action are heroic, the first according to the most noble standards of human tradition, the second according to an ideal which man must realize. For if we reflect, it will no doubt become clear to us that our choices depend on the material factors in the situations, but that they are governed – probably to a greater extent – by the inner quality of our moral strength. In addition to the violent hero's basic requirements of physical courage and passionate determination, the non-violent hero needs effective and creative conviction. He must have that "strength of truth" whose nature we have already considered.[11] The non-violent hero must be so possessed by truth that he can not only convey it to others in a given situation but also sustain it through dark periods with enduring patience and perseverance.

CONDITIONS IN THE MODERN WORLD

What room is there left for non-violence in the world as we see it developing today? It is only effective if it touches the consciences of

---

[11] pp. 115–7

the unjust. But consciences are now obscured by such violent passions, and when these are subdued, what can be achieved against the pressure of vast impersonal forces?

Consider for instance the fury provoked in France among the upholders of public order by the denunciation of the use of torture by Frenchmen, or the accumulation of anger among coloured people against Europe, or the vast masses of Asia, or the intractability of Islam . . . Can any caught up in such mighty pressures listen to the sweet voice of reason, even when their best interest is at stake? Still less can one look for a disinterested sense of justice in such situations. As the consciences of men are awakening on all sides, as spiritual families are linking up above the barriers of nations, classes, parties, the hazy conscience of the masses and the still more clouded consciences of the highly intelligent, the "illuminati", the so-called élites, all seem incapable of affirming anything more than their own prejudices. How can one therefore hope to touch consciences? Is not one merely exacerbating ideological passions, like the cult of the State, chauvinism or the mystique of class warfare?

What is the point of trying to reach the consciences of people blinded by prejudices and passion? What can individuals do even if their consciences have been enlightened and corrected? Fate holds all in its vice-like grip, who can hope to escape it? Human organizations are now beyond man's control. The social man of our emerging world is so subjected to the elements of this world, that whatever inner freedom he may have – unless it is completely stifled – he has no choice but to submit to the inescapable pressure of these elements. All he can do is to make a few feeble protests before submitting.

It is useless to go on reflecting along these lines; one always reaches the same point, whatever the line of approach. The political, social and economic structures are in control with all their technical apparatus. If they break, go wrong or change their direction, it will not be due to an awakening of consciences but to the pressure of mass movements, governed by blind and insane greed or by violent upsurges of the will to power.

The destiny of the world is at the mercy of two forms of materialism. One speaks the language of the spirit, and even at times pretends to stand for "Christian civilization",[12] while the other is overtly materialistic. Since the first contains contradictions even greater than the latter, it is to be feared that the latter will always have the advantage. All the more because Marxist materialism appears as a means of salvation to the great majority of men: to underprivileged classes and nations. The inner contradiction of any form of materialism is that it treats the destiny of men as if the spirit within them is a mere by-product of matter, whereas it is in fact the origin and agent of this destiny in so far as this is *human*. To this common contradiction, a materialism which pretends to recognize the rights of the spirit is doubly deceptive. It gives lip service to these but at the same time refuses to conform to its laws. There is no need for a war of extermination (which seems improbable in any case) for such materialism to extinguish the feeble spiritual inclinations of its adversary. All that is required is that the multiple combinations of the "elements of this world" should be victorious through a vague dialectic, driving out injustice by violence and inevitably increasing violence by so doing. The terrible logic of events seems to indicate that the world will have to go through a very long period of darkness before materialism comes to see its own contradiction as a result of being repeatedly confirmed in its false security by what it persists in interpreting to itself as a victory.

---

[12] In his Christmas Messages of 1941, 1955 and 1943 respectively, Pius XII said of the real materialism of so-called Christian civilization: "A mask of dead Christianity, lacking in the spirit of Christ" . . . "We call on Christians of the industrial era not to be content with anti-communism based on the defence of an empty liberty" . . . "A civilization in which more and more striking technical progress is accompanied by an ever-increasing decline in the spiritual and moral spheres."

CHAPTER TWELVE

Certainties

THE DEEP MEANING OF HISTORY

Thus the great factors that determine the course of events become increasingly cruel to man. Yet in some cases moral awareness has become increasingly perceptive of what man has to become in the world as it is; it has become stricter in rejecting what betrays this and more generous in fighting to accomplish it. This threefold progress is not always simultaneous, for it is not always the same men who are capable of its achievement in every direction. What matters is that in one of its three forms, and wherever possible conjointly, this increase in moral awareness should not remain merely theoretical, but should become effective in a renewal of hearts and in an integrity which expresses itself in significant action. It was clearly manifested in Gandhi and so many others inspired by his example.

"How can there be a progress of moral awareness in relation to the gospels?" is an objection we must be prepared for from many Christians. What comes first in relation to the gospels is an effective renewal of people's lives. St Francis of Sales compared it to a musical score that had to be sung: the song of a holy life. We shall never come to the end of understanding the genius of this music, nor of conformity to it, nor of making it heard throughout the world. It is precisely in our present age, when one begins to wonder whether the smothering of the spirit and its free expression

234 Non-violence and the Christian Conscience

are not leading to the disappearance of faith from the world[1] and the extinction of charity,[2] that one witnesses the emergence of people who, inspired by this same faith and charity, far from being despondent insist on going much farther than in the past in the pursuit of peace. These men refuse to believe that their lives are in full conformity with the gospels unless they reject certain forms of violence which still seem necessary and legitimate to others. Thus we find a dramatic increase in the ever recurring tension between the spirit of the gospel, which lives in the hearts of men of goodwill, and the temporal conditions in which it has to be applied.

A prime certainty, which was considered in the first part of this work, is that the teaching of the gospel demands an indefinite progress in the pursuit of peace and gentleness (without of course ignoring the claims of justice). Peace and gentleness are at the very heart of any action in harmony with the gospels: in the heart of Christ, and on earth in the hearts of God's children.[3] Whatever may be the course of history, and however heartrending it may appear to our limited vision, we are nevertheless certain of giving this history its eternal and salvific meaning, in as much as we work in it a work of peace and gentleness within the limits of justice. The duty of every Christian is to use all in his power to direct it along this way.

How are we to direct its course? How are we to infuse as much as possible the spirit of evangelical gentleness into public morals and institutions? As Christians we cannot be too concerned about the double risk of either escaping into "pure spirituality" or of capitulating to the outlook of the "realists" – two extreme views which have much common ground. Their danger leads us to insist on the importance of a *feeling for concrete situations* which must always guide the non-violent in their actions. It has been said that this requires a kind of flair for what is opportune. But it is perhaps even more a flair for discerning the deep significance

---

[1] Lk 18: 8

[2] Mt 24: 12

[3] Mt 5: 4, 9. We allude here to the beatitudes concerning the gentle and the peacemakers – "They shall be called 'the children of God'" and "They shall possess the land".

of contemporary events. History does not take shape on the surface, or simply in the hearts of those whose lives are inspired by charity and the beatitudes. There are two ways of being false prophets: on the one hand there are the superficial men who claim to detect certain definite patterns in transient phenomena, and on the other hand there are the presumptuous spiritual people who claim to judge what is going on from their ivory towers. An evangelical sense is not sufficient for the true man of action, for he needs to be deeply aware of every level of contemporary reality. He needs to be competent in human affairs but in a far more perceptive way than the oversimplifications of the press and other opportunists. The sponsoring of non-violent action requires a kind of prophetic competence in order to detect in the depths of the present, in which the future is being prepared, the elements of a situation that needs to be reformed and which can form the basis of a just new order.

It will be objected that non-violence only succeeds along the lines that history is in any case developing. This view would be an unfair generalization of a minimal, and rather gratuitous, interpretation of the action of Gandhi. The liberation of India which was delayed for thirty years after the start of his campaign, was, it is argued, in fact due to the weakening of England and the end of the colonialist era. It was England's political wisdom which saw that the time had come for friendly withdrawal. Could it therefore be maintained that this withdrawal was a proof of the power of *satyagraha* and of its effective influence upon the course of history by the mere power of Truth? One could go on arguing about this till the Last Judgement. But granted a minimal interpretation of the facts, it would not follow that the significance of non-violence can be explained in purely historical terms. On the contrary, it is non-violence which gives history its significance.

Historical events take on quite a different significance from what would otherwise have been the case had they simply been determined by the interplay of purely material forces, and particularly if they had been achieved at the price of violence. India entered into history as a sovereign nation, more as a result of self-conquest through non-violence over the temptations to brutal revolt, than as a result of victory over its oppressors. This is incommensurable and this is what is important, humanly speaking. We feel it all the more as with deep distress we wonder whether this nation is not now going the same way as the rest . . .

If one were in fact forced to recognize that violence only succeeds when situations are already ripe, then at least it has the success of achieving it without the usual recourse to cruel excesses. Why is not this example followed in so many similar situations? What is the use of Gandhi's splendid example if we go on trying to achieve through killing and implacable hatreds what could be achieved by peaceful means?

If this victory is judged to be only partial, remember that this is true of all human achievements. It is true that the liberation of India through *satyagraha* has left India in a state of division. Gandhi suffered cruelly on account of this setback. While the crowd celebrated independence with delirious enthusiasm, he could only weep over the "vivisection" of his country, and he saw only too clearly that the people had not reached that degree of human worth which, according to him, alone made it worthy of independence. Failure in the midst of success is the inevitable lot of our fallen human condition, and that is the Cross. The results of violent action should be far more strictly called in question.

We must not allow ourselves to be intimidated by an over-materialistic interpretation of historical success; let us not take too crude a view of history. Marxists, capitalists, imperialists and all types of "realists" will always take a dim view of any results which do not include the forms of injustice which are inherent in their own systems. Christians and all who are concerned about human values, look at events with an eye to finding out whether they are acts of love, whether in their effects they increase or impede the development of love. History will never give us a record of the humble power of love, which constantly strives to repair the ruins caused by violence. Is the balance sheet of history decisive finally? Humanly speaking it is not certain, but if it is, it will give credit rather to force than to the hidden power of love. It is strange that it should be so hesitant in manifesting what it can achieve for the public good. Why do we not succeed in making its influence felt in those directions where, as Danilo Dolci so forcibly puts it, "death infiltrates itself most"?[4]

---

[4] Ganachaud, *Bandits de Dieu* (Seuil, 1957), p. 121

Are we expecting too much altruism, reaching too far beyond the bounds of our immediate experience? No doubt it is because profound insight into the miseries of mankind undoubtedly reveals that these are always caused by vast combinations of collective (and unconscious) selfishness. If generosity concentrates its efforts upon precise issues where action can achieve results, it would be revolutionary. "Established disorder" needs to be condemned and fought against. However, up till now the unprivileged have only known either resignation or violent result. The writer Alain once said: "Peace has never been tried", and Gandhi cried out, "Let us invent a new kind of history".[5] With regard to the revolutions which confine themselves to violent insurrections against violent abuses, Aldo Capitini[6] advocated what he called "open revolution", that is, revolution inspired by love which opens the way to better human conditions. However perplexed we may be about the implications of such a course of action, we must realize that we have to do everything in our power for its success. The spirit of the gospel and mere humanity are not alone in demanding it; the underlying sense of history leads to the same conclusion.

For the tragic situation of the world is such that mankind will not avoid the most appalling disasters in which all that gives life its value will disappear for centuries, if men continue to try to settle their conflicts by violence. We are not simply thinking of atomic bombs, bacteriological or chemical warfare which they may inflict on each other, although human folly is great enough that their possible use cannot be ruled out. But it seems to us more probable now that these weapons will not be used, any more than poison gas was used in the last war. We are not even thinking of the antagonism of the two blocks, which certainly threatens untold misery and poisons all relationships, but is, in fact, only an episode in the ever varying, ever spurious tensions which already exist between the various forms of materialism. What is infinitely more serious, and the worst of the evils and dangers of today, is the enormity of human misery and its increase, which is unavoidable without a brand of heroism that no one seems prepared for.

[5] Text published in *Nouvelles de l'Arche*
[6] In the miscellancy *Danilo Dolci au la Révolution ouverte* (Desclée, 1957).

This is the reality in the light of which all our human problems need to be considered:

"The world," wrote the Abbé Pierre, "is truly at war, the war for bread, home, work, education and social services."[7] Poverty and distress are now on such a vast scale that it is no longer possible "to subsist, unless those who claim to be civilized decree a real mobilization, comparable to what happens when an enemy violates our frontiers or some national catastrophe results from some natural disaster".[8] One person in three is hungry, two out of three are in a state of health comparable to that of people in concentration camps during the war, about a thousand million are homeless.[9] These facts are just some among many which make no difference to our lives. If we could only seriously visualize all that these figures imply from the point of view of the millions who suffer, the anger that is stirred up in them now that they no longer look upon these miseries as natural disasters but see them as an injustice, the despair that stifles their very desires . . . It should be obvious that the main task of our generation is to attempt to ensure a better human life for them; they are suffering from *violence*. In reality this is what all the violence of the world leads to. This is paving the way to unprecedented forms of violence which will be sparked off by the states that are oblivious of the nature of the terrible forces they are dealing with in terms of the politics of another age. A mere plaything of the elements of this world, man is most likely to be crushed in the most appalling tragedy of history. One may well wonder whether there is still time to avoid it. If on the other hand he wishes to make history, then he will have to conquer the terrible tragedy of human misery, and his genius and heroism must be on the same scale as the tasks that he now faces.

THE RELATIVE AND ABSOLUTE ASPECTS OF VIOLENCE

Set against this tragic background, there appear both the relative nature of non-violence and the necessity for it as the absolute

---

[7] *Documents de l'I.R.A.M.M.* (March 1956), p. 4. (Institut de Recherches et d'Action sur la Misère du Monde.)

[8] ibid., p. 7

[9] Abbé Pierre, *Vers l'Homme*

from which it proceeds. Love must lie at its roots, but one of the most essential features of this love is to reduce violence as much as possible in the means used.

If non-violence is conceived in a negative way, as its name unfortunately suggests, it ought to be quite obvious that it can never be taken as an end in itself, or be one's principal concern. We speak in the conditional tense because unfortunately there are, in fact, many among the non-violent who are obsessed by a negative approach. In its extreme form there are certain conscientious objectors whose whole moral approach is dominated by a rigorist interpretation of the precept: "Thou shalt not kill", and in countries where conscientious objection is not recognized bý law, they are precluded from doing any fruitful work since they are sent to prison.[10] When non-violence is taken quite literally through sentimentally or abstract theorizing, it gets bogged down in side issues. It becomes a bogus kind of religion. It is then derisory when seen against the background of the world's misery. But we are concerned with non-violence as Gandhi conceived it. Is it really too late to designate it by a word which would express its positive character: "the strength of Truth"? This name would make us face squarely the real issue which is rightly perplexing; can we seriously dare to think that the truth is in itself powerful enough to triumph over all forms of injustice if its messengers have sufficient courage and integrity? That it is invisibly triumphant is quite certain, provided that its visible defects are not due to a facile kind of idealism and lack of awareness of life's contradictions. Can we claim to remedy so many ills – notably poverty, the greatest of all – by mere persuasion without any form of violence or compulsion? It is quite certain that wars, revolutions, the mere threat of subjection and other sanctions only make things worse; however, it is no less certain that a vast campaign inspired by love and justice

---

[10] It is shameful that certain countries have refused to give a legal status to conscientious objection. Even if one thinks that objectors are mistaken, they have something to contribute, for if their convictions are sincere, they stand for generosity and strength, which it is shocking to misconstrue and suppress, and which could easily be used for the common good. They could be made to do non-military work of a useful kind and which could be longer than and as responsible a burden as military service.

in the world as we find it, would run up against formidable collective selfishness. Could these be overcome without violence? A bitter ransom has to be paid for man's fallen condition. Violence should be strictly curbed and only exercised within an action which is obviously inspired by justice and peace.

In other words we must discover whether the strength that we hope to receive from truth can flow from abstract principles; in this case it would be ineffective and false in spite of its name and claims. For truth is only faithful to itself in its applications to the world, if it recognizes the factors presented by the world. We have already seen more than enough causes from which violence inevitably ensues.

Thus the deeper significance of Gandhi's saying becomes more manifest, "Action taught me the beauty of compromise".[11] This merely seems to express an acceptance of partial gains – "one step at a time" was another of the Mahatma's sayings. But this in itself has much relevance to a philosophy of action. For to accept a partial success of justice is to consent at least provisionally to a certain measure of injustice, which implies *violence*. The important thing is not to confuse *compromise* with *complicity*. The latter makes a pact with evil, whereas the former simply endures the unavoidable. This is a distinction which is very difficult to apply in practice. The obvious danger is to betray the ultimate aim under the pressure existing conditions bring to bear upon concrete action. The greater the perceptiveness with regard to what is possible and technically feasible, the more necessary it is to be guided by absolute principles. Justice and love entail absolute demands, whereas non-violence can only be relative in a world of violence. This relativity not only implies that there will always have to be a limit to the integrity of any given action, but that it will also have to include some measure of violence. What is vital is that this violence should be truly and unavoidably required by a love which would fail in its obligations if it did not have recourse to it.

Non-violence should never be systematic. Quite simply, if the strength of truth abstains from violence it is not because that is its plan: we must not think of this abstention as its intention.

---

[11] *Autobiography*, p. 185 (Fr. ed.)

The aim that one is striving for should always be the good of men, and this good seen in its totality requires that *as little violence as possible* is exercised in the means used for its attainment. For this true and lasting good presupposes the free cooperation of the persons one hopes will benefit from it. The action must therefore be conducted in such a way as to elicit their free cooperation, instead of trying to compel or basely seduce them. Therefore, if this realism has true integrity, aiming at more than immediate results too narrowly conceived and thereby more productive of evil than good, it will inevitably purify itself as much as possible from violence. It can never, then, have a fixed standard or take a definite form. The strength of truth must constantly discover new methods of approach.

This necessity is most striking in relation to the misery in the world. "The revolt of under-developed people," remarked Fr Lebret,[12] "rather than being a form of envy with regard to the rich, is an unconscious reaction of the unloved against those who should have loved them."

Everything will be useless or indeed harmful which does not provide a remedy for this fundamental evil. It is only too obvious that "charity", in the devalued and distorted sense that this noble word has come to have, cannot be adequate. It should also be obvious that the competition among the big powers to offer "protection" to the developing countries, as much as the resentful outbursts of these wretched people, will only make matters worse for them. Distress calls for disinterested friendship. The distress is so great that it demands sacrifice from all those who care about human values in the world.

Here is a knotty question which has to be faced but from which every type of Machiavellian disputant should be excluded, as well as unreal idealists and the weak hearted who are prepared to wash their hands of it all. It is very complex and we must strive to throw some light upon it. It arises between men who are both truly concerned about reality and in demanding justice. It is an ever-recurring problem. The great majority of men of goodwill can see no other alternative than the sword, which they maintain should

[12] "Le Tour du monde en seize questions", *Informations catholiques internationales* (Jan 1, 1957), p. 15.

be used with as much and if possible with greater violence than it is by the unjust, in order to assert the claims of justice. There is, however, an increasing minority of men who wish to clear a way in the jungle of this world for justice by the sheer force of love and truth. What may throw some light on this problem is to grasp the nature of the opposition which exists between two different conceptions of violence.

The first maintain that it is possible to exercise some control over violence, to have recourse to it only to the extent that it is required by a justice that common sense recognizes, and to control its evil effects. The proponents of this view are right in theory – we have already maintained the same position: that violence is good or bad according to the use we make of it (the extent to which it is used being taken for granted). The decisions of moral theologians on a "just war"[13] have a certain theoretical force. But unfortunately violence in fact eludes the expectations and control of those who have recourse to it. It always eludes this control in an unexpected manner, following the anarchical "faults" in man's fallen nature and the disorders of his achievements. It does this in the most terrifying way. In particular, war, rather than being an ordered sequence of human acts, is an unleashing of frenzied passion, of vast anonymous and blind forces which it is impossible to evaluate or even identify adequately – economic, social, ethnic forces . . . It is a "chaotic explosion . . ., historical madness, unjustified and unjustifiable".[14] This is only too obvious in its development and in its consequences, but it is already to a very great extent in its inception, whatever the recognizable responsibilities of particular men may be. It is as unreal to moralize about it[15] as it would be to legislate about tornados, or the economic crises of capitalism. It is more profitable to work during so-called periods of peace for less injustice in the world. On the other hand the non-violent underestimate the extent of violence within man, how

---

[13] Mgr Bruno de Solages, *La Théorie de la juste guerre*; and see below pp. 252–3.

[14] Paul Ricœur, *État et violence*, pp. 13–14 (Geneva, 1957)

[15] J. Verhaegen, "Les impasses due Droit international pénal", *Revue de droit pénal et de criminologie* (Oct., 1957), Brussels. This is a very important article.

inescapable it is in its ramifications and its influence upon morals, institutions, as well as its in-built power in technical organizations. They only see its superficial accidental expressions. Its outbreaks seem scandalous to them because it is so contrary to the most basic requirements of humanity. They also place too much confidence in man's power to control violence; they rely on man's inner spiritual power over the violence of others. This mistake is no doubt more praiseworthy. Hitherto there has been too little faith in the power of truth and love; it is good when love is bold and it is of the nature of great love to include even a certain measure of folly. However, the strength of truth will be discredited and its cause compromised if this folly is not simply an expression of the breaking in of the spirit, but rather a failure of the spirit in the face of reality when it comes to acting in the concrete. The spirit must be strong enough to dare to face dreadful truths.

The excess of violence is becoming so formidable in the world today that both sides ought to recognize it. But genuine recognition means that the first mentioned group must immediately reject the fiction that recourse to violence can still be considered normal as it once was. It means seeing it as Christ did, that is, as we said previously, "as a pitiful ransom paid to man's fallen condition". This ransom is of course inescapable but we should restrict it as much as possible. This same recognition forbids, except in certain cases, that the non-violent should be too absolute in their claims. We said "except in certain cases", for there is need for some to act abruptly. Some people have a vocation for this. This vocation is in line with the absolute nature of truth and love, the incompatibility of God's word, or simply of the spirit and the violence which is rampant in the world today. Since such men must be capable of giving a witness of complete integrity, there will be very few of them; this integrity presupposes a very rare degree of intelligence and character, as well as a legitimate exemption from common duties towards their neighbours who are forcibly implicated in their endeavour.

We can neither admit the current condonation of violence, or believe in a significant change of the violence of the world into justice, love, gentleness and peace. There must be a final break with the first and any morality which pretends to justify it can be nothing more than an academic game of self-deception and hypocrisy. The other is an illusion which threatens to discourage many generous people from working effectively for the good of mankind. Reflection on the state of the world and the prospects of mankind forces us to take the same view as arose from proper understanding of the demands of the gospel: that of a beam of light and fervour which penetrates right into the cold darkness of the world. To receive and transmit this light requires absolute purity. One has to be all the more uncompromising, because the forces of darkness are not simply passive but most active, as St John perceived. But action springing from a source of absolute integrity will have to be conditioned in the concrete by an understanding of the realities of each situation.

DEVELOPMENT OF CONSCIENCE

We shall now indicate by way of example some of the principles of action which should be apparent to those of a more highly evolved, mature conscience. They will be surprised that these were not effectively carried out in the past in private, economic and political life. Let us weigh them seriously, though here we shall simply enumerate them:

> To guarantee first of all for the dispossessed a certain minimum below which life ceases to be human.[16]
> To put the good of men before profits in the field of economics.[17]

---

[16] The keynote of Abbé Pierre's policy: "Serve first those who suffer most." Roger Dauphin (*Faim et Soif*, no. 20) says: "In a society where the proper hierarchical order ranks from the top downwards, it can never be possible to serve everybody. On the other hand, if at the outset the minimum necessary for human life and the realization of a human destiny is assured to every working family, there will always be enough for the needs of all."
Danilo Dolci says: "First we must give tenderness and care to the humblest" (*Danilo Dolci et la Révolution ouverte*, p. 106).
"Start off by providing security for the weakest" (G. Ganachaud, *Bandits de Dieu*, p. 158).
[17] Cf. the efforts of L. J. Lebret and of *Économie et Humanisme*. See also F. Perroux, "Note sur les coûts de l'homme", *Économie Appliquée* 1952 and "De l'avarice des nations à une économie du genre humain", *La Vie Intellectuelle* (Nov., 1952).

To see things from the standpoint of others in order to appreciate what is suitable for them.[18]

Contrary to Goethe's cynical saying, to run the risk of disorder rather than injustice and to accept at any cost as absolute any claims which guarantee respect of the human person (thus to reject torture,[19] whatever may be the consequences for oneself and for others).

Anyone who does not merely want to quibble over words will immediately realize that these principles of action are only the down to earth, realistic application of the guiding principles of the gospel, and that taken together they provide an answer to the real needs of our age. Once this has been appreciated, these principles cannot be eluded; they must be professed openly if one is to be part of the movement of *Agapè*, which we considered in the first and second parts of this book. But as soon as an endeavour is made to conform to them it will be discovered that they require heroism; an examination of any general or particular situation in the world will show that this is so. We must make a thorough examination of the factors which govern the life of a nation, a social class, a commercial enterprise, a family or any human grouping, and even of the individual human person; we must go beyond superficial data, to the material and psychological factors which produce prosperity or misery. A realistic view of misery will lead us to rediscover that one or another of these principles is what is needed. And not only for the under-privileged. Since we are members one of another, they are necessary for all of us.

A concrete example was given by Fr Lebret who, by trying to understand the plight of a group of fishermen in St Malo, was led

---

[18] As we consider the world's problems, which seem to come up at one and strike one in the face, what stands out is the complete disregard of the duty of putting ourselves in other people's shoes. Thus the great mass of ordinary people seems to have suffered equally from the worst social injustices and from the most well-intentioned paternalism. What colonial peoples and subject races have resented most bitterly is not so much that they have been exploited, as that they have not been recognized and understood.

[19] Pierre-Henri Simon, *Contre la torture* (Seuil, 1957); Joseph Viala-toux, *La Répression et la torture* (Ed. Ouvrières, 1957).

step by step to see and apply these principles.[20] The "realists" bent on vulgar profit are not only "insensate" in the biblical sense of the word – that is to say men without a sense for God or spiritual realities – they are stupid from a human point of view, or merely short-sighted. In the words of Fr Teilhard de Chardin: "In order to ensure mere survival (*survivre*) men must live at a higher level (*supervivre*)". And as Pius XII warned us: "He who wishes to earn peace, must be prepared for no lesser sacrifices than are required for war."[21] This is a frightening thing to say if one reflects on its full implications. No less admirable and disturbing are the words of Cardinal Faulhaber: "*Vox temporis, vox Dei.*"

It is self-evident that today the mental outlook of the majority of people completely contradicts the requirements of the gospel as well as the needs of our time. A single observation will bring this home to us: "The world is able to spend billions of dollars on 'defence' and only a fraction on human, brotherly aid."[22]

Furthermore this assistance is not very brotherly since the powers who agree to provide it turn it into a means of political propaganda. Progress in the development of conscience and moral awareness is therefore most painful, for as its demands become more and more urgent, its commitments must take into account the possibilities of derision and cynicism which the understanding and cooperation of the masses and the so-called "élites" permit. The half-hearted pursuit of peace on a world scale is the fault of governments, of strange amalgams of great masses of selfishness, hypocritical ideologies[23] and the blind passions of their people.

---

[20] See articles in *La Vie Intellectuelle*, Jan. and Feb., 1933, also *Economie et Humanisme*, 1957, No. 106, pp. 456–9 for the more general problems of economics.

[21] Christmas, 1947

[22] Fr Lebret, *Faim et Soif*, No. 20

[23] In many statesmen these may well not be consciously hypocritical; most of them are genuinely convinced that they act out of sincere motives. It is the system of which they are the tools which is hypocritical. Sometimes at the end of their lives they become aware of this, e.g. Clemenceau in *Au soir de la pensée*, where he said: "The fact is that we have always been dominated by interested oligarchies tricked

Even among the élites we are forced to admit that generosity and intelligence do not go together. How is it that eminent men in the highest positions do not join together regardless of frontiers and other considerations, in joint action for the awakening of moral awareness – even perhaps going to the extent of non cooperation, and where necessary, civil disobedience?

Much needs to be done before the principles we have enumerated become vital convictions, so that they may be translated into decisions and conduct in the various spheres of influence where men of goodwill can be effective. A multiple task needs to be undertaken:

> To substitute among Christians a true sense of evangelical obligation in place of the ready-made and generally accepted moral outlook, which is in fact simply devised to provide a sop to people's consciences.
> To restore effectively the primacy of love.
> To demonstrate that these principles are the law of life of the New Testament in necessary and authentic action.
> To give these principles a human content by revealing their implications and consequences.
> To show up the injustice of the tenets of established disorder in the light of these principles.
> To prepare people for necessary refusals.

If men's consciences were governed by such principles they would soon reveal what forms of non-violence should be taken. This would emerge spontaneously without being sought, as an outcome of certain vital principles. This is preferable to preaching directly about it, for this often spoils everything. Nevertheless, account must be taken of what has already been thought and achieved; the part non-violence has played in the past in the thought and lives of men contributes to the awakening of consciences today. We look to historians to bring these facts to light, who will enable us to see in depth their significance for mankind. Too little is known about such achievements, from the outstanding actions of a William Penn or a Gandhi, to the humble acts of everyday life. We need anthologies of non-violence prepared with

---

out as ideologies. And the story of democratic oligarchies is not very different. In the two thousand years since Aristotle things have changed very little as far as I can see."

rigorous criticism, for it is only too obvious how much this realm of behaviour lends itself to aberrations and illusions.

The three chief spheres in which such an inquiry should be pursued for its true understanding are theology, depth psychology and political science. Initiation into the "mystique" of non-violence, its psychology and theory, will need to be all the more thorough in order to build on secure foundations.

The problem can be approached from different angles. We have already said[24] how humanists can cooperate with Christians in this sphere. Certain anxious "realists" are turning to non-violence in their despair, as a last resort to stem the flood of misery; they are in grave danger of seriously misusing it unless there is an awakening conscience and a dramatic conversion on their part. It is of course all to the good if they finally come to see that violence leads to disaster, but if they simply cling to this negative outlook and if non-violence is for them a mere makeshift, it will simply serve as a disguise for their despair. If the strength of truth and love is reduced to mere slick technique, it will soon degenerate. It can only acquire real efficacy by a kind of "excess", inspired and caught up in a current of life that springs from the living God. Then in the admirable words of Aldo Capitini,[25] "God is being born within it". This gives it the prophetic and creative quality it needs to have. Let "realists" become aware of their folly and it may only mean that they enter a sphere where action is purged of violence, but they must do so effectively. Such behaviour is worthwhile and efficacious only if it is carried out to an heroic and prophetic degree. In this world it is simply the echo of a victory which is not of this world. Faith awakens and begins to stir. A prophetic attitude only succeeds partially in this world to the extent that it clings to a timeless vision. If it gets to grips at any point with the intricacies of the elements of this world, it will destroy it.

THE DEVELOPMENT OF CONSCIENCE IN RELATION TO WAR

The certainties that have now been reached in man's moral

---

[24] See above, pp. 148, 197
[25] *Danilo Dolci et La Révolution Ouverte* (Desclée, 1957), p. 104

awareness have never put him in a greater state of perplexity than with regard to war.

In formulating these certainties, Pius XII spoke not only in the name of Christ but assuredly on behalf of any man of goodwill who has reached maturity of conscience in the mid-twentieth century:

The theory of war as an adequate and fitting method of solving international conflicts is now superseded. If ever a generation has welcomed from the bottom of its heart the cry "War on war" it is the present one. The deepest wish of anyone with a grain of humanity in him must be to shut the door on it for ever.[26] When the instruments of war "become uncontrollable by men" and result simply in "annihilation of all human life within its sphere", they just cannot be used even under pretext of "defence against injustice and the necessary safeguarding of rightful possessions". "Their use must be rejected as immoral."[27]

Defence against injustice of any kind is not justification for the use of the violence which is war. Even when the damage it causes is not comparable with that caused by injustice which is tolerated, we are under an obligation to suffer that injustice.[28]

Those who cry that we must prepare for war in order to ensure peace are endangering peace.[29] Peace cannot consist in a costly exasperating relationship of mutual fear.[30]

The "curse of our age"[31] is the fear of the possibility of total war and demands a whole complex collection of measures; agreements to work for total disarmament "that is to say simultaneous and reciprocal reduction of arms",[32] which is nevertheless a not very sound guarantee of lasting peace, unless it goes with the abolition of hatred, greed and inordinate desire

---

[26] Christmas 1944. Pius XII said to Cardinal Innitzer: "The Pope is opposed to all wars, including those aimed at eliminating the communist danger" (reported in the article "Guerre", encyclopedia *Catholicisme*, col. 352).

[27] 30 September, 1954

[28] 19 October, 1953

[29] Christmas, 1948

[30] Easter, 1954

[31] Christmas, 1947; cf. Christmas, 1954

[32] Christmas, 1951

for prestige;[33] measures of preventive pacification to eliminate or mitigate antagonisms between nations; guarantee against the setting up of totalitarian governments of "nationalist states which produce the germs of rivalry and are sources of discord".[34]

A widespread awakening of men's consciences is essential in the light of the incalculable extent which modern warfare may reach. But this same disproportion causes bewilderment in deciding what particular courses of action should be taken, just as the needle of a compass goes wild if it goes too near the pole, or an over-loaded circuit blows the fuses. As a crowning misfortune, this disproportion not only affects the actual operations of war, it also applies to the forces in conflict in a "cold war". It goes without saying that all men of goodwill should work for peace, but humanly speaking what do they amount to and what can they achieve in the face of so much greed, hatred and fear? Already in the political field, of which Clausewitz said war "is but a continuation by other methods", as politics acquire the same "total" character as war threatens to do, man is superseded. It is astonishing that so many men of intelligence have not grasped this fact and do not see the moral consequences that ensue. These are the consequences as we see them:

In the first place, there should be a repudiation in principle of total war, whether it be "cold" or "hot". Any man of goodwill, and still more any Christian, should combat the "crusade" or "holy war" mentality, the bogus pretence of a "sacred duty" to "defend" a so-called "Christian civilization" by means that contradict it: namely by weapons of hatred. But still more basically, he must reject any form of "mystique" of war – whether civil or international – as a fight between good and evil, justice and right against injustice. "Who has the right to think he is without fault?" as Pius XII exclaimed during the last war.[35] Whether wars are total or not in the use of means, they are now total in principle as soon as the passionate outbursts of a fallen world pretend to find their

---

[33] ibid.
[34] Christmas, 1954
[35] Christmas, 1943

justification in an appeal to a moral absolute. An evident sign of this sin against the Spirit is found in the cruelty of ideological wars. As Pascal said: "One never does evil so wholeheartedly and cheerfully as when one does it from conscientious motives." *It is imperative that this repudiation should become absolutely clear on the part of Christians.*

Must every Christian therefore become a conscientious objector? *Logic* would seem to demand it with regard to a truly "total" war, even one which was only ideologically so. For a repudiation in principle would *logically* seem to require a refusal in practice. A total war is indeed such a scandal to the human spirit and to supernatural faith that it cannot but be countered by "the grand refusal" of the general necessity of which we have already spoken. For the *absolute* nature of the right to impose itself on people's consciences, there must be certain consciences which will bear witness to this Absolute with their whole being. But the cost of such witness is precisely man's whole being; of a personality which must make a total protest. We repeat that this demands a kind of extraordinary heroism which is too great for the majority even of generous Christians, involving as it does the responsibility of implicating near relatives in the consequences of a personal rebellion.[36]

Logic when applied to the personal choices of man caught up as he is in a social and imperfect but related world, is a far cry from abstract logic. An ordinary vocation will need its own brand of heroism in trying to safeguard a sense of the absolute of spiritual values, when all are being carried away by the violence of events. Not only must we not canonize them, but we must see these things for what they are – the writhings of the Beast – knowing nevertheless that these dreadful outbursts are permitted by the Prince of Peace whose work is being mysteriously accomplished through

---

[36] Fr Lorson deals with the different cases very judiciously in his book *Un Chrétien peut-il être objecteur de conscience?* (Seuil, 1950), Chap. 9. His merit is that he admits the absolute nature of the claim of many conscientious objectors and at the same time brings out the solidarity of human beings which should – we think – restrain most of them. Priests and monks in particular have no right to act as isolated individuals.

them.[37] We must also take great care to make a clear distinction between what men are forced to *endure* and what they consent to *do*. The truth is that one is simply caught up in a war or revolution. The great majority of those who are caught up in them cannot be expected either to reject or justify them. But to the extent that men are not reduced to mere objects and that they are called upon to play a personal part, all are called to make choices often of a heroic nature. Morality in relation to war (or revolution) must be entirely re-thought in terms of this basic distinction that has to be made between inevitable consent to the uncontrollable forces of the "elements of this world", and the area of personal freedom that is still available.

There can be no question of dealing with this subject here; it would require a whole book which we are not competent to write. But let us at least state quite clearly something which really should not need saying: that every man should strive as far as possible to create a world where the spirit masters energy and uses it for peaceful ends. To recognize that man is in fact overwhelmed by the forces that are unleashed in wartime, is not to treat as quite normal what is a monstrous disorder. The greater the risk of subversion, the more people should work for love and justice. It is monstrous that men should become instruments of murders which are very likely not works of justice. Let us recall what we have already said on the sacred character of human life.[38]

Theologians have tried to reassure people's consciences by their theory of the "just war". It is not entirely academic even today and it retains a certain value. But whereas previously adversaries – who were both judges and parties involved – gave it their own interpretation to justify their case, today, on the contrary, it is against our consciences. The conditions for a "just" war are now too vague for enlightened combatants of either side to be able to regard themselves without hypocrisy as dispensers of justice in killing the enemy. A statement of these conditions seems tragically farcical in relation to the realities of total war:

(1) The cause has to be just.
(2) The right intention must be maintained throughout hostilities.

---

[37] Is 30: 29; Wisd 5: 23
[38] pp. 101 ff.

(3) The war is truly the last resort, all peaceful means having failed.

(4) The means of waging war must be fair.

(5) The good legitimately hoped for from war must be of greater benefit to mankind than the evils it involves.

(6) Victory must be certain.

(7) The ensuing peace must be just and of such a nature as to avoid a further war.

One might be able to argue about the penultimate condition, but if one examines all the others, it is difficult to see how any war could be "just" without conforming to it. Meanwhile it is clear that if ever these conditions were satisfactorily respected in the past – which will not be known with absolute certainty until Judgement Day – it is increasingly unlikely that it will happen in the future. In order to be just today warfare would have to be conducted on a very restricted basis, comparable in fact to a large-scale police operation. The single condition of a "last resort" – except in case of resistance to an attack – would be sufficient to limit the number of "just" wars, now that we have international organizations and methods of arbitration.

If these traditional conditions seem unreal, all the more reason for upholding them rigorously and taking them seriously – far from being condemned by their own unreality, they condemn the world as it is today. It is obviously with them in mind that Pius XII declared in his Easter Message for 1941 "That the belligerents have already gone beyond the bounds of what is permitted in a legitimate war", and at the time of the Suez operation he deplored "a hasty recourse to force, repeatedly and universally execrated as a means of settling conflicts and ensuring the victory of right . . . the renewal of a policy which rejects arbitration and places economic interests above human lives and moral values".[39]

But if such wars are no longer just, should not all combatants become deserters? Are they not all murderers? What excuses them – without justifying them – is not simply an erroneous conscience, whose error is in most cases practically invincible. For neither the pope nor any priest will impose an obligation of

---

[39] 10th November, 1956

254 Non-violence and the Christian Conscience

conscience *to object* upon those who have recognized the scandalous nature of the wars in which they are forced to participate. Why this apparent illogicality? If their case is considered, it will be seen that they are the victims of the overwhelming *violence* of the forces constraining them. They cannot withdraw without provoking even greater evils than those they are in danger of causing in these terrible catastrophes, and in which they are implicated rather as unwilling *instruments* than as genuinely free agents. The *sacred* character of life does not only consist in physical life itself but in human values. On the one hand these are terribly damaged in modern wars, whether a man contributes to causing death or not, but on the other hand, their destiny for better or worse is nevertheless bound up with that of the combatants. The latter regard themselves as upholding these values, and they are to a certain extent, according to circumstances and outlook, but they are above all the playthings of a sinister kind of fate. In the complex involvement of factors which make up a war, we come to recognize the predominance of fatalities which escape moral analysis, though inextricably bound up with elements of morality (like those possessions of which Pius XII spoke when he said "that they are so important for the human community that their defence against unjust aggression is without doubt fully justifiable").[40] We must face facts rather than vainly pretend to a mastery we do not possess and consequently strive to apportion responsibility, although we must repeat that certain responsibilities can be indicated. However partial these may be, they can nevertheless be decisive, like the responsibilities of Hitler and National Socialism in contributing to the last war. The cynical Clausewitz is quite right in seeing a continuity between politics and war. His remark should be given wider implications: war is not simply one form of political violence, it involves many other kinds of violence, which break out under cover of it, but which could also lead to excesses just as odious in times of so-called "peace". To equate detestable forms of violence with murder is to close our eyes to the real problems involved. The spirit of non-violence and evangelical gentleness should not just be focused on a refusal to kill, but must first of all be put into practice in tasks of peace.

---

[40] Christmas 1948

If violence unhappily breaks out in the form of a "hot war", must the moralist withdraw and leave it to the individual conscience to discriminate between what he can consent or refuse to do? We believe that it is both possible and desirable to establish some objective rules, to resolve certain typical cases, and particularly to outline some universally valid criteria where absolute refusals can be made openly and clearly and where a definite moral stand can be taken. This would apply, for example, to the pilot who was ordered to drop a nuclear bomb; this would apply also to the refusal to inflict torture or to shoot the innocent as a reprisal. There is room for a revision of the prescriptions of The Hague and Geneva Conventions by competent moralists; these rules were worked out by jurists in the hope of being acceptable to governments and military leaders; they aimed at being a complete and detailed inventory of the infringements of the "laws" of modern war. But the techniques of warfare change too rapidly and are still governed by the laws of death. Every possible means must now be used in order to infuse some humanity into the international agreements relating to war, but moralists cannot simply wait for Caesar to speak through jurists to those who are looking for God's voice. Their task is to recognize what the *human conscience in its present state of mature moral awareness* absolutely rejects in present methods of warfare; it must state this by analysing specific cases. They could not hope for exhaustive treatment or juridical precision,[41] but rather the gradual training of consciences through a completely realistic study of concrete examples.

In these perspectives, *the most radical and urgent task of our time is to prepare men for eventual refusals to obey.* "No superior authority," we are reminded by Pius XII, "is empowered to command an immoral act. There is no right, no obligation, no permission to perform an act which is immoral in itself even if it is ordered, and even if refusal to act involves the worst possible personal consequences."[42] As constraints are being multiplied, the main danger is that the principle of spiritual freedom should be stifled. Pius XII insisted on the need to cultivate freedom of judgement.

Many today look exclusively for their spiritual sustenance

---

[41] Verhaegen, art. cit, n. 14, pp. 17–20
[42] October, 1953 (referring to the shooting of hostages)

less from themselves, that is to say from their own convictions and thoughts, than in a predigested form from the press, radio, cinema or television. How can such people have a true conception of real freedom? It no longer has any place in their lives. These men are no more than mere cogs in various social organizations; they are no longer free men capable of assuming or accepting a share of responsibility in political affairs . . . It would be useless for the Church to multiply its appeals to men who have lost any awareness of true human freedom, and it would be even more useless to address such appeals to a society which had been reduced to the level of a machine. . . .[43]

FURTHER DEVELOPMENT OF CONSCIENCE

The principles governing actions in which we have seen an existential, concrete blending of supernatural faith in Christ and natural faith in man are only one stage on the path towards spiritual freedom. If one remains faithful to the light and at the same time achieves *real* understanding of the world, one goes beyond them; and we shall see how. Men make parachute drops – the army of God, the Church militant, must do no less in creating circumstances of an *economic régime on mercy and pity* diametrically opposed to the prevailing materialism. Impelled by the existence of so much misery in the world and the spirit of the beatitudes, to keep for oneself what others need is seen to be one of the most scandalous forms of violence[44] and undoubtedly one of the main causes of the worst sort of violence. The vast scale of human wretchedness demands a lowering in the standard of living among those more fortunate.

"Rise thou that sleepest and arise from the dead."[45]

What ignorance and lack of feeling to the point of cruelty are manifested by our modern so-called "civilization"! How many of its privileged members, faced with the evidence that they can be saved "only by giving up their comforts won by aggressiveness, their oppressive economic system"[46] will simply be driven into

[43] Christmas, 1951; cf. Christmas 1944 on Democracy
[44] Cf. p. 234
[45] Eph 5: 14
[46] Roger Dauphin, *Faim et Soif*, No. 20

increasing their passion for pleasure, their aggressiveness and their oppressive will to power.

Possibly some personal experience of distress might open their eyes, but it would have to be accompanied and occasioned by the demands of a concern for others and the presence of some prophetic minds who would be able to bring out the true significance of the tragedy they were experiencing. There are many today whose energies need directing to the relief of the underprivileged in the world, so many of whom are at their very doors.[47] Who is to touch the hearts of the teenagers of Stockholm who spend their evenings smashing up furniture for nothing better to do, or the so-called "happy" ones who commit suicide out of boredom, or those Americans and millions of others like them who amuse themselves in such stupid ways because they have nothing to live for? By helping those in distress they would rediscover the gospel. This is the crusade that Christians need to conduct and it alone could renew Christianity. It is of little importance that the Western world should be saved by it; what counts is the manifestation of the following values:

Any Christian, or any man worthy of the name human, should feel that he has to get rid of any wealth which is not strictly necessary to him.

As things are now, Christians are morally so insensitive that they generally find it quite normal to be enslaved to the "American way of life". There are even some Christians who are prepared to wage a holy war in its defence. An economy of waste in a world of misery is manifestly a radical negation of the gospel.

We need to have an increasingly radical view of wealth and unnecessary spending – scandalously unnecessary in view of the prevailing misery. The "American way of life" would still be abominable even if it were not condemned by the distress of so much of the world: it results in an inflation of desire, a systematic and pointless over-stimulation. Our modern pseudo "civilization" forces man, and still more a Christian, to question himself about the lawfulness of his desires, that is, desires which are not immoral of their very nature. They will eventually be seen as forms and

---

[47] Lk 16:20; the rich man in this well-known parable was wicked only in that he did not see the poor man on his own doorstep.

causes of violence to the extent that they are not in accordance with his vocation and the situation he finds himself in. This standard of behaviour will seem quite new, incredible to the majority of our contemporaries, whereas it springs from the most elementary form of wisdom. If he faces things as they are, he will recognize how much they lack this wisdom. Our present world is not only "aphrodisiac", as Bergson put it; it is ruled by a universal conspiracy to stimulate every kind of desire. How can these problems be solved without a complete reorientation? If we consider, for instance, the basic problem of world population, which is growing at such a terrifying rate, particularly in developing countries, so often all that is proposed is birth control alone. This is a complete subversion of morality, which only increases selfishness and aggressiveness and stimulates lust for pleasure. The frightening problem of world population growth can in fact only be solved through discipline of desires, whose self-imposition we are not simply recommending to the growing populations of the underprivileged, but still more to the feckless privileged. Whatever problem we consider, it is manifest that in our present situation our call to human brotherhood and the needs of the distressed demand a restraint of certain desires which might be permissible in times of well-being. One may well ask whether these desires were not themselves based on insensitivity, lack of conscience.

This may seem rather far-fetched; but we will go even further – a cry springing from the heart may suddenly awaken our consciences and guide our steps to new positions. Danilo Dolci, in the midst of the distress of a small Sicilian town, reflected on the wage-claims of the workers on the mainland: they were no doubt justifiable, he thought, but if only they realized what misery existed here on the island! "Why aren't there any strikes for those who are more miserable than oneself?" A cry of child-like simplicity? No doubt, but a cry echoing the child-like simplicity of the gospels.

We spoke previously of parachute drops. There are men who have gone forward to fresh outposts under the guidance of their faith in Christ and man; they do effective work and sometimes gain ground. But will mankind as a whole continue to shrink back or will they link up with them? They are building an economy based on respect for the needs of the human person. Consider for instance the example of certain young farm managers under the guidance of Fr Benoît Allo, who have completely reorganized their whole system of farming, by considering first of all what society may rightly ask of them rather than what will bring them the biggest profits. Furthermore, they consider the needs of their workers instead of paying a minimum wage with a view to making more money for themselves.[48] The reader may well wonder what all this has to do with non-violence. But men's actions are purified of violence to the extent that human beings are thought of as the end and that means are used which treat them as such instead of as things, or even numbers. In a world in which techniques have no purpose beyond the immediate targets which are not seriously related to the needs of the human person, these young Christians take account of the needs of men to determine what they will do. They act in such a way "in their professional and even political organizations that wheat reaches those who are hungry . . . The day when every farmer will first of all be concerned with the service he gives to society, the problem of hunger in the world will be near its solution".[49] "*Service before profit* – this motto has become for us the guiding principle of our farming and a direct application of the evangelical command 'First seek ye the Kingdom of God and its justice' . . ."[50] 'To put some love in the world of business in which we struggle . . . To cease to see a man as a mere producer of material goods . . ."[51] which is organized *violence*. To substitute an "economy of needs" for the usual "economy of profits".[52] We cannot go into detail here as to how step by step over seven or eight years these men have achieved these results.

These "experiments with truth" are achieved against the current of the chief economic, political and psychological factors of our time, but in accordance with its most seriously assessed needs. They provide an insight into the tragic nature of our society – the tragedy of man whose requirements for life, happiness and peace always seem beyond the reach of his means. Those who carry out

---

[48] These young farmers have published a bulletin, *Terre et Hommes*, since Oct., 1954.

[49] Alain Delaynoy, *Terre et Hommes*, No. 9 (Jan., 1957), p. 24

[50] *Terre et Hommes*, No. 1

[51] ibid., No. 2, pp 1, 9

[52] ibid., No. 7 (July, 1956), p. 7

such experiments need to be modest in their claims, and indeed they are. They are like weavers who weave a few inches of good solid stuff in cloth which is falling to shreds. Some day their work may no doubt be destroyed, but each man and each group of men must achieve what they can. One dreams of what the result would be if all those who have great responsibilities in the world worked in this spirit, but then "peace has never been tried".

CONVERSION AND ACTION

Whatever scope there may be left in the world for the exercise of justice, love, gentleness and peace, it requires an education of the heart. Cardinal Mercier recalls an old proverb which expresses the tone of the small community of Frenchmen in ancient times – "Unhappy times, gentle people".[53] In the second part we examined the need for and the growth of gentleness.

But is gentleness a hindrance in coping with the hard tasks that need to be done? This is a real problem that needs facing. It is quite obvious that a certain type of gentleness, which may be sanctified in its own way, lacks grip even for certain apostolic tasks and still more so in worldly fights. This is a question of vocation: the gentleness of the man of action, who fights through the power of truth, is quite different from that of the pure contemplative. It is the latter that is envisaged when it is imagined that gentleness weakens action. But there is also the "gentleness of courage", as St Francis of Sales called it. Sufficient account is not taken of the different kinds of struggles that have to be undertaken. Obviously the ruthless and cruel fighter can only conduct his battles either with unmixed and ferocious insensitiveness or frenzied hatred; both exclude any kind of gentleness. But it is precisely because these types of battle involve a surrender of all humanity that it is better to be defeated than agree to participate in them. Battles worthy of men are inspired by *parresia*,[54] this inner poise is the outcome of a well-balanced personality that has been attained through complete integrity. It presupposes an inner

---

[53] *Jesus Caritas* (Bulletin of the Association Ch. de Jésus) No. 104 (1956), p. 48.
[54] Cf. pp. 154–160 above

harmony as a result of self-mastery through gentleness. The "power of God" and "the strength from above" can even make it frightening when necessary. The loving communication between persons, which lies at the root of all truly human relationships, is in other words *gentleness*. This is the whole root of the matter. Humanity is what counts; all action, in spite of inevitable conflicts and difficulties, must be conducted in virtue of an understanding of others which is as real and complete as possible. It is through this concern for others that we must find the power to fight against all that separates, to foster everything that unites, rather than give way to the instinctive pressures of collective and personal selfishness. The choice is between an awakening of the "new man" or an abdication in favour of the "old man".

The sharpening of moral awareness and the increasing subjection of the world to the law of "death" forces man to live at a higher pitch of tension. Love and the outlook of the beatitudes need to reach a degree of intensity and persistence in his soul for which the morality, spirituality and habits of life of a comfortable age have not prepared him. Circumstances may well arise when absolute refusals may be required which will force him to temper the quality of his inner life. Dilection and the beatitudes give rise to more terrible struggles within us than the external fights they would pacify.

Whereas psychological equilibrium requires emotional relaxation, at the same time our spirit cannot ignore the conflicting demands of warring extremes; agonizing choices have to be made by those whose inspiration springs from love and hope. Thus the messianic nature of hope inclines us to look forward to human improvements often difficult to reconcile with each other, which were unknown to Christians in the past, whereas the eschatological nature of this same hope entails cutting mercilessly into everything. We must therefore ally an unswerving confidence in man's progress with an abiding awareness of his defects and shortcomings. "A tragic optimism"; Mounier's phrase applies aptly to those judgements and actions forced upon us by the realities of this age, however hard we might try to be generous and perceptive.

It takes almost unbearable tensions to spark off the kind of holy "violence" which alone can break at some points the fatal working of the laws of death.

Hence action is disproportionate in its inspiration and force. But it should therefore be all the more modest in its judgement of what is possible and its application to competently established objectives. We have already insisted upon this, but now we must outline a broader field of application for this humble activity. We may well ask ourselves[55] whether there is going to be room for achieving tangible results through non-violence in a world in which the spirit suffers increasing restraint, and in which mankind seems to be inexorably moving into a period of most dreadful violence. There is all the more reason for hoping that the spirit of gentleness and peace will salvage all that can be preserved of our Christian and human heritage through the dark and stormy period that lies ahead. Humble non-violent actions according to one's capacity, or greater ones such as those of men of the calibre of Danilo Dolci, will have their own intrinsic value. This can prepare the way for large-scale enterprises of justice and love, which could turn the course of history in a happier direction and save mankind from its terrible fate – we must admit that we hardly dare hope for this – or it can bring out spiritual resistance to the oppressive forces of evil via love and faith.

We should not wait for times of oppression to call up the spirit of heroism which non-violence demands. Even now, courage should prompt us to act in its spirit to bring freedom and love to our neighbours and brothers. It was not only in the Algerian tragedy that we saw "gentleness and friendship subjected to force", in Cardinal Mercier's striking phrase. Love and gentleness are threatened on all sides with extinction by cruelty. While there is still time, while we are still free to plan the future, at least at some points leading to a fuller life, are we going to witness a "salutary reaction against the present trend of events?"[56]

Responsible men should indicate where such action is possible. We must all of us start here and now and make friendly contacts according to the opportunities offered by our different callings. We must rebuild our lives for the service of others in fields in which we are competent to act, like the young farm managers we referred

---

[55] See Chap. 11, pp. 230 ff. where we have already debated this

[56] Danilo Dolci, in Ganachaud's *Bandits de Dieu*, p. 137

to earlier. "We must always try to extend the spirit of non-violence in actions which bear fruit and are significant."[57] We must do everything in our power to enlighten public opinion in the West, so that people can come to see that violent action is in fact an over-compensation of weakness which ultimately leads to spiritual annihilation. Whereas a policy of peace still has some chance of success today and it is, in fact, the only worthy course of action left open whatever the consequences.

Is it really necessary for men to squander so much genius and heroism on their own destruction? Is there no hope that some of this heroism and genius may be directed towards saving man's spirit and his freedom? The humblest actions are priceless if they spring from perfect love. A few are preparing themselves in this spirit for future struggles and their action bears witness to this spirit; but at present there are virtually none in high places.

Man has no aim in life; he follows will-o'-the-wisps in a series of futile activities which in the end bring him no reward, till he suddenly comes across something which brings home to him the real meaning of his life, something that cuts right across the mean-ingless pattern of his own life because it is itself related to his true end and aim. There are many well-intentioned people today who are shocked by excessive obedience and are tempted to take part in anarchical revolt. Their energies will only be mobilized fruitfully if their revolt is directed against a manifestly unjust order and leads them to enter upon ways where an obedience to the truth which is love is learnt through self-sacrifice. What was a prospect of martyrdom for Christians living in times of persecution, for us will be unnoticed resistance or downright refusals, which will meet with inglorious suppression and humiliations; but while we can still use our freedom, we should act with as much liberty as possible in order to train our spiritual judgement and free ourselves from the compulsions of our weaker nature.

What is beyond price for the world is that the dreadful chain of fate should be broken by the influence of love and the beatitudes that flow from it, even though the course of history seems to be no

---

[57] O. Lacombe, speaking at the Centre Catholique des Intellectuels Français, 5 December, 1957.

more altered by it than a stream is deflected when we plunge our hand in its waters.

> Awaken, thou who sleepest,
> Rise from among the dead,
> Christ shall enlighten thee.

INDEX